Russian Politics

Challenges of Democratization

What went wrong in Russia's decade-old post-communist transition? A group of leading young scholars answer this question by offering assessments of five crucial political arenas during the Yeltsin era: elections, executive–legislative relations, interactions between the central state and the regions, economic reforms, and civil–military relations. All of the contributors recognize that adverse historical legacies have complicated Russian democratization. They challenge structural explanations that emphasize the constraints of the preexisting system, however, and concentrate instead on the importance of elite decisions and institution building. The authors agree that elites' failure to develop robust political institutions has been a central problem of Russia's post-communist transition. The weakness of the state and its institutions has contributed to a number of serious problems threatening democratic consolidation. These include the tensions between the executive and the legislature, the frail infrastructure for successful market reform, and the absence of proper civilian control over the armed forces.

Zoltan Barany is Associate Professor of Government at the University of Texas at Austin.

Robert G. Moser is Assistant Professor of Government at the University of Texas at Austin.

T0370915

Russian Politics

Challenges of Democratization

Edited by

ZOLTAN BARANY
University of Texas, Austin

ROBERT G. MOSER
University of Texas, Austin

CAMBRIDGE
UNIVERSITY PRESS

CAMBRIDGE UNIVERSITY PRESS
Cambridge, New York, Melbourne, Madrid, Cape Town, Singapore,
São Paulo, Delhi, Dubai, Tokyo, Mexico City

Cambridge University Press
The Edinburgh Building, Cambridge CB2 8RU, UK

Published in the United States of America by Cambridge University Press, New York

www.cambridge.org
Information on this title: www.cambridge.org/9780521805124

© Cambridge University Press 2001

First published 2001

A catalogue record for this publication is available from the British Library

Library of Congress Cataloguing in Publication Data
Russian politics: challenges of democratization / edited by Zoltan Barany, Robert G.
Moser.
p. cm.
Includes bibliographical references and index.
ISBN 0-521-80119-2 – ISBN 0-521-80512-0 (pb)
1. Russia (Federation) – Politics and government – 1991– 2. Russia (Federation)
– Economic policy – 1991– 3. Democracy – Russia (Federation) 4. Post-
communism – Russia (Federation) I. Barany, Zoltan D. II. Moser, Robert G., 1966–
JN6695.R865 2001
320.947–dc21   00-049352

ISBN 978-0-521-80119-5 Hardback
ISBN 978-0-521-80512-4 Paperback

To our dissertation advisers:
Mark R. Beissinger
Timothy J. Colton
David D. Laitin
S. Neil MacFarlane
Terrence Ranger
and to the memory of Alexander Dallin

Contents

Tables and Figures

Tables

Figures

Contributors

Zoltan Barany
Associate Professor, Department of Government, University of Texas at Austin

M. Steven Fish
Associate Professor, Department of Political Science, University of California, Berkeley

Yoshiko M. Herrera
Assistant Professor, Department of Government, Harvard University

Michael McFaul
Assistant Professor, Department of Political Science, Stanford University

Robert G. Moser
Assistant Professor, Department of Government, University of Texas at Austin

Kathryn Stoner-Weiss
Assistant Professor, Department of Politics, Princeton University

Acknowledgments

This book originated in the symposium on Russian politics held at the University of Texas in November 1998. Joan Neuberger, director of the Center for Russian, East European, and Eurasian Studies, suggested the topic for the center's inaugural annual symposium and committed the requisite resources to the project. Sheldon Eklund-Olson, then dean of the College of Liberal Arts, and James S. Fishkin, chair of the Department of Government, were generous sponsors. The contributors delivered superb presentations and honored the enterprise with the timely submission of revised and updated chapters. The insightful comments of anonymous reviewers for Cambridge University Press enhanced the quality of individual chapters and the cohesion of the volume. Grants from the University Research Institute enabled us to hire Julie George and Christopher Speckhard, doctoral candidates in Russian politics, who provided valuable technical assistance in preparing the manuscript. Alex Holzman, Lewis Bateman, and Michael Holdsworth at Cambridge University Press were supportive of this project from the beginning. Thank you all. This book is dedicated to the doctoral dissertation supervisors of the contributors.

ZOLTAN BARANY
ROBERT G. MOSER

Introduction: Challenges of Russian Democratization

Robert G. Moser

It has been ten years since Russia emerged from the collapse of the Soviet Union with a leadership of self-proclaimed democrats committed to radical transformation away from communism toward democracy and a market economy. Despite, or perhaps because of, the ambitious program and high hopes of its leaders, Russia's dual transition of democratization and market reform has been a grave disappointment.

The list of failures is daunting. Although Russia now possesses the trappings of democratic governance – constitutionally guaranteed individual freedoms, an emerging multiparty system, competitive elections – consolidated democracy seems no closer now than it had been at the beginning of the process. In fact, in areas such as the freedom of the press, development of civil society, and protection of human rights, Russia has lost ground since 1991. Transformation of the command economy has been an even greater failure. More than ten years of market reform (counting the Gorbachev period) have produced periods of hyperinflation, the collapse of the currency, and chronic nonpayment of wages and pensions.

If this is not enough, Russia's post-communist development has also spawned pervasive crime and corruption, a bloody war of secession in Chechnya, and the collapse of basic social services and infrastructure. Wherever one looks, Russia seems to be facing intractable problems that threaten the ability of the elected to govern at all, making the establishment of a consolidated democracy and functional market economy seem like increasingly unrealizable goals.

Describing the problems of Russia's difficult transition and isolating a limited number of causes for Russia's troubles are challenging tasks. An exhaustive account of the major political changes of the period is virtually impossible, forcing scholars to make crucial decisions about what to highlight and what to ignore. Concentrating on a single cause or set of causes, whether they be cultural, historical, institutional, or individual, inevitably ignores other important factors that have come into play. This book approaches the task of explaining Russian democratization by offering assessments of five crucial political arenas during the Yeltsin era: national elections, executive-legislative relations, economic reform, center-periphery relations, and civil-military relations. Clearly, this is not an exhaustive list of all the important facets of political change that have taken place since the collapse of communism. Rather than presenting an exhaustive assessment of transitional politics during the Yeltsin era, this book offers an in-depth analysis of the most important developments since the collapse of the Soviet Union.

A leading specialist analyzes the developments in each of these five areas since 1991. The authors identify the opportunities and obstacles embedded in the preexisting context facing leaders as they attempted to reform, examine the institutional context in which reform took place, and assess the action and inaction of elites during the Yeltsin period. In the process, each chapter highlights the factors deemed most responsible for the typically suboptimal outcomes that came to pass. Finally, preliminary assessments of future trends in the emergent post-Yeltsin era are offered. No general theory or methodology is imposed. Thus, the interpretations are diverse. Yet, despite important differences, there are several common attributes of Russia's democratization experience that are emphasized by all the authors. The result is a nuanced picture of democratization in Russia based on a detailed analysis of the Yeltsin era and its immediate aftermath.

In this introductory chapter, I will offer three threads that tie together the chapters that follow. In the first section I examine the major theoretical approaches to the study of post-communist Russia, placing the foci of individual chapters into a broader framework of contemporary scholarship on the region. In the second section I offer a summary of the major problems impeding successful democratic reform in the five areas of investigation. While many problems were identified by the authors, problems of institutional design and insufficient attention to institution building were cited as the most important factors crippling reform efforts. Finally, in section three I review the authors' assessments of the future of democratization in Russia. I offer three interrelated but distinct perspectives regarding Russia's future that can be discerned from the contributions in this volume.

APPROACHES TO THE STUDY OF POST-SOVIET RUSSIA

The collapse of communism in the former Soviet Union and Eastern Europe has produced a corresponding shift in the methods and substantive issues of scholarship in this area. The study of Russian politics is quickly becoming integrated into mainstream political science, as area specialists adopt concepts and methods commonly used in the discipline and political scientists with expertise in other geopolitical regions turn their focus to post-communist states. This has sparked a heated debate within the field concerning the proper role of comparative analysis and the applicability of concepts and methods borrowed from other subfields.

In the most stinging critique of transitology and comparative political analysis in general, Stephen Cohen has argued that these approaches have promoted the ruin of the Russian economy through the adoption of misguided and inappropriate reforms. He also contends that current scholarship that takes a comparative perspective misreads or neglects the central realities of post-communist Russia.[1] Less extreme critics value comparative research but caution against the fallacy of assuming that post-communist transitions will resemble other transitions from authoritarian rule. Transitions from communist rule face greater challenges than transitions from other types of authoritarian regimes. These include: the simultaneous challenge of democratization and introduction of a free market economy, greater ethnic diversity and conflict, weaker civil societies, weak or absent democratic traditions, and a less hospitable international environment. These challenges have produced actors, processes, and outcomes in post-communist transitions that differ substantially from other democratic transitions.[2]

Advocates of incorporating post-communist states into broader analyses of third wave democratization argue that these differences are overstated. Philippe Schmitter and Terry Karl argue that other democratizing states also have faced radical economic restructuring while experiencing democratic transitions. Moreover, comparing democratic transitions in different contexts need not overemphasize similarities at the cost of meaningful differences. It is precisely these differences that move the study of democratization and comparative politics forward.[3] Thus,

---

[1] Stephen Cohen, "Russian Studies without Russia," *Post-Soviet Affairs*, Vol. 15, No. 1 (1999), pp. 1–37.

[2] Valerie Bunce, "Comparing East and South," *Journal of Democracy*, Vol. 6, No. 3 (1995), p. 87. See also Sarah Meiklejohn Terry, "Thinking about Post-Communist Transitions: How Different Are They?", *Slavic Review*, Vol. 52, No. 2 (1993), pp. 333–337.

[3] Phillippe C. Schmitter and Terry Lynn Karl, "The Conceptual Travels of Transitologists and Consolidologists: How Far to the East Should They Attempt to Go?", *Slavic Review*, Vol. 53, No. 1 (1994), pp. 173–185; Phillippe C. Schmitter and Terry Lynn Karl, "From an Iron Curtain to a Paper Curtain: Grounding Transitologists or Students of Postcommunism?" *Slavic Review*, Vol. 54, No. 4 (1995), pp. 965–978. For a systematic attempt to compare southern European, South American, and Eastern European democratic transitions, see Juan J. Linz and Alfred Stepan, *Problems of Democratic Transition and*

David Laitin has commended the integration of the study of Russia into mainstream political science as beneficial for both parties. He claims that concepts and hypotheses gleaned from the experience of other countries provide valuable lessons and frameworks for the study of the post-communist experience. Moreover, the different socioeconomic and cultural contexts of Russia and other post-communist states provide a new test of the generalizability of hypotheses developed in other contexts, improving theories of democratization by establishing how well these hypotheses travel.[4]

This book is predicated on the latter approach to the study of Russian democratization. Certainly, Russia possesses characteristics that make it very different from consolidated democracies and other democratizing states. However, such differences enhance the utility of comparative analysis rather than hindering it. It is only through comparison and the use of concepts and criteria from comparative politics that one can discern what is unique and what is common about Russia's transition. Moreover, the Russian case has much to contribute to our broader understanding of democratization, but only if it is placed in comparative perspective. All contributors apply concepts and hypotheses from the broader comparative politics literature in their assessments of Russian democratization and compare Russia to other cases. For example, Michael McFaul utilizes the concept of the mode of transition to account for electoral outcomes. M. Steven Fish and I borrow extensively from the debate over presidentialism in new democracies. Yoshiko Herrera, Kathryn Stoner-Weiss, and Zoltan Barany concentrate on the effects of a weak state. The authors do not contend that Russia always conforms to the expectations of political science theorists or to the experience of other countries. Indeed, this volume shows that Russia defies expectations as often as it follows them. But a comparative perspective is indispensable in identifying precisely how and to what extent unique features of Russian development have affected the trajectory of regime change.

Of course, a common commitment to a comparative approach toward Russian democratization can still produce diverse explanations of outcomes. While any categorization of perspectives toward regime change in Russia is a gross oversimplification, I argue that explanations of the trajectory of Russia's transition can be grouped into three general categories: structural, institutional, and elite-driven.

Consolidation: Southern Europe, South America and Post-Communist Europe (Baltimore: Johns Hopkins University Press, 1996).
[4] David D. Laitin, "Post-Soviet Politics," *Annual Reviews of Political Science*, Vol. 3 (2000), pp. 117–148.

Structural explanations tend to emphasize the effects of long-term realities arising out of political culture, class configurations, and other historical legacies. Structural explanations emphasize the constraints that Russian history has placed on the potential for successful democratic development. Ken Jowitt argues that the experience of Communist Party rule has left a lasting imprint on societies in Eastern Europe and the former Soviet Union that has made democratic development exceedingly difficult. He claims that scholars fixated on the "transition to democracy" in this region mistakenly see post-communism as a blank slate on which any ideological and political system can be founded. Jowitt claims that communist rule reinforced a traditional political culture that promotes an exclusive and oligarchic elite and a mass population that is distrustful of politics and thus poorly equipped for democratic participation.[5] Moreover, the inevitable chaos and fragmentation that Jowitt sees following the breakdown of communist regimes "offers a firmer foundation for transiting to some form of authoritarian oligarchy (in response to perceptions of anarchy) than to democracy."[6]

Stephen Hanson has offered a couple of refinements to Jowitt's arguments to account for variations in the experience of post-communist states, particularly the relative success of some East European countries in introducing democratic institutions. First, Hanson argues that external factors, namely access to Western markets and investment, have allowed some countries in Eastern Europe and the Baltics to overcome their Leninist legacies and establish democratic and market institutions much more successfully than have the countries of southeastern Europe and the former Soviet Union. Second, Hanson argues that the Leninist legacy is multifaceted and must be disaggregated into its ideological, political, economic, and cultural elements. These elements have affected regime change in varying degrees. While the ideological legacy of communism has been relatively easy to eliminate, political and economic legacies have been much more difficult to overcome. Cultural legacies have been the most persistent and continue to hinder evolution toward consolidated democracy even in the most successful post-communist transitions.[7]

Other scholars have focused on more specific effects of historical legacies. For example, Charles Fairbanks argues that Russia is plagued by the chronic problem of a weak state, which is also emphasized in

[5] Ken Jowitt, *New World Disorder: The Leninist Extinction* (Berkeley: University of California Press, 1992), pp. 286–300.
[6] Jowitt, *New World Disorder*, p. 300.
[7] Stephen Hanson, "The Leninist Legacy and Institutional Change," *Comparative Political Studies*, Vol. 28, No. 2 (1995), pp. 306–314.

the chapter by Stoner-Weiss in this volume. Fairbanks claims Russia's weak state has its roots in the "feudalization" of the state during Soviet times, in which the state turned over its own resources and powers to private forces in exchange for support or a valuable service.[8] Herbert Kitschelt argues that the nature of emergent party systems in post-communist states is influenced by the type of communist rule and by pre-communist experience with industrialization and democratization. He argues that longer and harsher communist rule and later industrialization have made Russia and other former Soviet republics less likely than Eastern European states to have programmatic, cleavage-based parties that are conducive to democratic development.[9] Kathryn Hendley focuses on how the vagaries of "socialist law" have undermined the establishment of a democratic rule of law.[10] The penetration of the Communist Party into all realms of social activity decimated civil society, and socialist economic development precluded the establishment of an entrepreneurial class, both of which are deemed essential to democratic development.[11] In its most extreme form, an emphasis on historical legacies denies that Russia has experienced any form of democratization at all. Rather, the new post-communist system is seen as an authoritarian system combining the ideology and elite behavior of Soviet communism and Russian tsarism. Boris Yeltsin, although twice popularly elected as president, is perceived to have been an autocrat cut from the same mold as former Communist Party general secretaries or Russian tsars.[12]

However, the evidence of some sort of cultural deficit of democratic norms has not gone unchallenged. Much of the early survey research has

---

[8] Charles H. Fairbanks, Jr., "The Feudalization of the State," *Journal of Democracy*, Vol. 10, No. 2 (1999), pp. 47–53.

[9] Herbert Kitschelt, "Formation of Party Cleavages in Post-Communist Democracies," *Party Politics*, Vol. 1, No. 4 (1995), pp. 447–458.

[10] For discussions of historical legacies impinging upon the development of a multiparty system, see M. Steven Fish, *Democracy from Scratch* (Princeton: Princeton University Press, 1995) and Herbert Kitschelt, "Formation of Party Cleavages in Post-Communist Democracies: Theoretical Propositions," *Party Politics*, Vol. 1, No. 4 (1995), pp. 447–472. It must be noted that Fish also places much emphasis on elite actions taken after the collapse of communism to explain Russian party development. For the development of the rule of law, see Kathryn Hendley, *Trying to Make Law Matter* (Ann Arbor: University of Michigan Press, 1996).

[11] Even scholars who emphasize more elite decisions in explaining post-communist transitions have noted this detrimental precondition in Russia and other post-communist states. See Linz and Stepan, *Problems of Democratic Transition and Consolidation*, pp. 376–378.

[12] Vladimir Brovkin, "The Emperor's New Clothes: Continuity of Soviet Political Culture in Contemporary Russia," *Problems of Post-Communism*, Vol. 43, No. 2 (1996), pp. 21–28.

shown a reasonably high level of commitment to democratic values.[13] Moreover, Nicolai Petro has claimed that an alternative democratic tradition has existed throughout the course of Russian history.[14] Clearly, the centuries-long history of autocracy in Russia and the legacies of seventy years of communist rule have produced constraints on democratization in Russia. These constraints were much greater for Russia and the other states emerging out of the Soviet Union than for those in Eastern Europe. Even so, the character and extent of those constraints on Russian democratization remain contested.[15] The question is not whether the Soviet past produced difficult legacies for Russia's post-communist transition, but rather how determinative the weight of history has been as opposed to the impact of institutions or contemporary elite actions. Martin Malia captured the structuralist perspective well when, describing Russia's turmoil at the end of the 1990s, he stated, "It is this [communist] heritage, not the mistakes of the past decade, real though those were, that is the major source of the present impasse."[16]

Institutional analysis occupies an intermediary position in the study of political outcomes. Institutions are both outcomes and causes of political action. Institutions are created by elites to best serve the interests of those in power, but once in place they also have an important influence over elite actions. Furthermore, institutional effects are conditioned by the environment in which they operate. Thus, constitutional frameworks or electoral systems that have relatively uniform effects in most democracies around the world have been shown to have wildly different effects in the Russian context, increasing the uncertainty of constitutional engineering.[17]

Institutions have been seen as an important element in Russian democratization. For example, the introduction of an element of proportional representation in the mixed electoral system has promoted the

---

[13] See, for example, Jeffrey W. Hahn, "Continuity and Change in Russian Political Culture," *British Journal of Political Science*, Vol. 21, No. 4 (1991), pp. 393–421; Ada Finifter and Ellen Mickiewicz, "Redefining the Political System of the USSR: Mass Support for Political Change," *American Political Science Review*, Vol. 86, No. 4 (1992), pp. 857–874; James L. Gibson, "A Mile Wide but An Inch Deep (?): The Structure of Democratic Commitments in the Former USSR," *American Journal of Political Science*, Vol. 40, No. 2 (1996), pp. 396–420.

[14] Nicolai Petro, *The Rebirth of Russian Democracy* (Cambridge, Mass.: Harvard University Press, 1995).

[15] Frederic Fleron, "Post-Soviet Culture in Russia: An Assessment of Recent Empirical Investigations," *Europe-Asia Studies*, Vol. 48, No. 2 (1996), pp. 225–260.

[16] Martin Malia, "The Haunting Presence of Marxism-Leninism," *Journal of Democracy*, Vol. 10, No. 2 (1999), p. 43.

[17] Robert G. Moser, *Unexpected Outcomes: Electoral Systems, Political Parties, and Representation in Russia* (Pittsburgh: University of Pittsburgh Press, 2000).

establishment of national political parties in Russia despite cultural and social impediments to party formation.[18] Rules governing the internal organization of the State Duma have made a crucial difference in the greater centrality of parties in the State Duma compared to its predecessor, the Congress of People's Deputies.[19] Russia's strong presidency, a central concern for Fish and me in this volume, has become a crucial case study in the continuing debate over whether presidentialism has a positive or a negative impact on the survival and quality of new democracies.[20]

Emphasis on elite decisions often takes the form of historical counterfactuals, hypothesizing what might have occurred had some particular action been taken that was not. For example, President Yeltsin has been criticized for prioritizing economic reform over political reform at the beginning of Russia's dual transition, failing to call early elections after the collapse of the Soviet Union, and refusing to create a presidential party.[21] From this perspective, faulty institutional design, elite mistakes, and missed opportunities for decisive elite action, all rooted in the politics of the transitional period rather than in any long-term conditions, are viewed as the culprits for the poor results of Russia's democratic experiment.

The effects of elite decisions are most emphasized in debates over economic reform. Critics of Russia's economic reforms have contended that these policy decisions have led directly to the chronic problems crippling the Russian economy, while defenders of shock therapy argue that the fault lies with poor implementation of an otherwise correct policy.[22] Due to the path-dependent nature of political and economic development, such faulty decisions or implementation create interests and political equilibria that influence the future trajectory of democratization. Thus, Joel Hellman argues that, once established, the dysfunctional market system produced by Russia's reforms may be perpetuated by power-

---

[18] Robert G. Moser, "Electoral Systems and the Number of Parties in Post-Communist States," *World Politics*, Vol. 51, No. 3 (1999), pp. 359–384.

[19] Thomas F. Remington and Steven S. Smith, "The Development of Parliamentary Parties in Russia," *Legislative Studies Quarterly*, Vol. 20, No. 4 (1995), pp. 457–489.

[20] Eugene Huskey, *Presidential Power in Russia* (Armonk, N.Y.: M. E. Sharpe, 1999).

[21] Fish makes all of these claims in his conclusion. See also Linz and Stepan, *Problems of Democratic Transition and Consolidation*, pp. 390–397.

[22] The extensive literature on this question is covered by Herrera in Chapter 4 of this volume. The most rigorous defense of shock therapy comes from Anders Aslund. See Anders Aslund, *How Russia Became a Market Economy* (Washington, D.C.: Brookings Institution Press, 1995). For a critique of shock therapy see Chapter 5 of this volume and Josef C. Brada, "The Transformation from Communism to Capitalism: How Far? How Fast?", *Post-Soviet Affairs*, Vol. 9, No. 2 (1993), pp. 87–111.

ful economic interests who benefit from its corrupt, rent-seeking environment.[23]

Of course, structural, institutional, and individual explanations of Russia's transition are not mutually exclusive. Indeed, much of the literature centers around attempts to integrate structural, institutional, and elite-based explanations of political outcomes. The study of the origins of new institutions demonstrates this trend. Institutions are constructs created by elites to further their interests. Thus, one way that legacies from the preexisting system can influence post-communist institutions is by affecting the interests of the individuals who are creating these institutions.[24] Barbara Geddes argues that the communist experience affected the nature of the party system, namely through the emergence of new parties rather than the persistence of historical parties, which in turn had an impact on the electoral and constitutional institutions introduced by elites.[25] Gerald Easter argues that strong presidential systems, which are often cited as a primary source of delegative democracy in Russia and other post-communist states, can be traced to historical legacies embodied in the elite configurations emerging from the collapse of the Soviet system. Thus, the debate over the merits of presidential and parliamentary systems should be recast, since the "choice" of a constitutional framework for post-communist states may be significantly constrained by prior elite configurations.[26]

At the other end of the spectrum, it has been argued that the origins of post-communist institutions have been contingent upon elite decisions made during the transitional period. From this perspective, new institutions emerged in a context of great uncertainty in which powerful elites were not able to easily design institutions that would further their interests. Institutional design was instead marked by miscalculation and a relatively conservative approach taken by those in power. Once in place, these institutions have had profound effects on democratization that often contradicted the interests of the original designers.[27]

---

[23] Joel S. Hellman, "Winners Take All: The Politics of Partial Reform in Postcommunist Transitions," *World Politics*, Vol. 50, No. 2 (1998), pp. 203–235.

[24] Barbara Geddes, "A Comparative Perspective on the Leninist Legacy in Eastern Europe," *Comparative Political Studies*, Vol. 28, No. 2 (1995), p. 239.

[25] Ibid., pp. 239–274.

[26] Gerald M. Easter, "Preference for Presidentialism: Postcommunist Regime Change in Russia and the NIS," *World Politics*, Vol. 49, No. 2 (1997), pp. 184–212.

[27] For analyses emphasizing political context and contingency surrounding decisions of institutional design, see Michael McFaul, "Institutional Design, Uncertainty, and Path Dependency during Transitions: Cases from Russia," *Constitutional Political Economy*, Vol. 10, No. 1 (1999), pp. 27–52.

The following chapters acknowledge the influence of structure, institutions, and elite decisions in their analyses. But clear emphases exist. This volume tends to concentrate on institutional and elite actions and deemphasizes structural constraints. When structural constraints from the preexisting system do come into play, they are not interpreted as so constraining that they somehow determined elite action or shut off alternative routes of development. Moreover, legacies are generally not viewed as insurmountable. For example, Hererra emphasizes the importance of starting conditions for explaining the failure of shock therapy in Russia but its apparent success in Poland. Yet, she stresses the inappropriate set of policies enacted in this atmosphere rather than the constraining effects of the structural conditions themselves.

OBSTACLES TO RUSSIAN DEMOCRATIZATION

What went wrong in Russia? Clearly, a process as complex as the transformation undertaken in Russia after the collapse of the Soviet Union is historically overdetermined. What is striking when evaluating change across the five political arenas examined here is the myriad of problems facing reformers as they pursued revolutionary change. Building a new democratic and capitalist order to replace the dismantled Soviet system was truly a colossal endeavor. Democratic reform not only entailed introducing competitive elections at the national and local levels but also required crafting a new constitution, establishing new legal codes, constructing a new judicial system, and promoting the formation of new political organizations like political parties and interest groups. Market reform required a similarly daunting set of interrelated tasks that included painful policy decisions and institution building. While tackling these two pillars of the dual transition, the center was faced with increasing pressures from subnational entities to devolve power, which in turn undermined the center's authority and its capacity to implement its ambitious program of social transformation. In the midst of all this change, basic social institutions deteriorated because of a lack of resources and neglect.

Given the circumstances, it is not surprising that Russia's transition was full of complications, obstacles, and potential setbacks. The question is whether these problems were a consequence of preexisting conditions – be they long-term historical continuities or more proximate consequences of the Soviet collapse – and thus largely unavoidable, or whether problems arose primarily from poor elite decisions and institutional design. Not only does this volume reflect a consensus surrounding the latter approach, but a general consensus also emerges here that institutions or their absence played an extremely important role in shaping political outcomes. Of course, there are also some discrepancies between authors over the institutions and elite decisions emphasized and their implications for political outcomes. A closer look at each chapter will highlight the areas of consensus and disagreement.

In Chapter 1, McFaul challenges the conventional wisdom that volatility has been the hallmark of Russian elections. McFaul argues that Russian voter behavior has been remarkably stable since the introduction of relatively competitive elections under Gorbachev. Rather than volatility, McFaul sees a stable bifurcated polarization within the electorate between those in favor of change, movement away from the communist system, and those opposed to change. There has been great volatility in support for individual parties, but McFaul discounts this volatility as change within these two ideological camps.

McFaul claims that the root cause of this stable polarization of the electorate is a protracted and conflictual transition from communism, which was due to a lack of elite consensus over basic issues surrounding the borders of the state, organization of the economy, and the form of the political system.[28] As opposed to more successful Eastern European transitions with more unified elites, two rival elite camps with diametrically opposed views of the future battled one another for ascendancy. This polarization was also manifested in voters' preferences. Electoral institutions – namely, the contrasting incentives produced by parliamentary and presidential elections – and campaign tactics account for the significant discrepancies in outcomes between elections.

Two important implications follow from McFaul's analysis. First, while a polarized political spectrum has produced attractive outcomes in the most important elections – namely, reformist victories in binary elections such as the constitutional referendum and presidential election – these victories have come at a cost to democratic consolidation. Such polarization has hindered the development of partisan affiliation among voters. The weakness of parties has in turn undermined coherent policy making as well as cordial executive-legislative relations. Moreover, because of a lack of retrospective voting, Russian voters have failed to vote out of office incumbents with poor records. This kept an unpopular, unhealthy, and incompetent leader like Yeltsin in power.

Second, by concentrating on the side effects of elite discord McFaul brings together structural and individual factors to explain the outcomes

[28] For an overview of elite-centered analyses in post-communist states, see John Higley, Jan Pakulski, and Wlodzimierz Wesolowski, "Introduction: Elite Change and Democratic Regimes in Eastern Europe," in John Higley, Jan Pakulski, and Wlodzimierz Wesolowski (eds.), *Postcommunist Elites and Democracy in Eastern Europe* (Houndmills, Basingstoke: Macmillan, 1998), pp. 1–33.

of Russian elections and their implications for democratization. The contrast with Eastern Europe suggests that elite dissension in Russia emerged out of a uniquely Russian context, in which there was bound to be less elite support for democratic and market change than in countries with a shorter history of foreign-imposed communist rule. However, McFaul argues that this historical legacy is already beginning to wane. He sees a less polarized elite emerging in the post-Yeltsin era due to the consolidation of a market economy, which removes any realistic hope of the radical left to return to the old system.

In his conclusion, Fish offers an explanation of electoral dynamics of the Yeltsin era that places even more emphasis on the ability of elites to influence the mode of transition highlighted by McFaul. Fish argues that Yeltsin could have dissolved the Congress of People's Deputies at the height of his popularity after the failed August coup and called early elections. In the euphoria of 1991, Fish claims that early elections would have produced a new legislature dominated by Yeltsin supporters, breaking the deadlock of polarized elite conflict that plagued Russia's transition and producing a much more propitious mode of transition.

In Chapter 2, I analyze the problems of executive-legislative relations during the Yeltsin era. I challenge the conventional wisdom that Russia's constitutional system approximates an electoral autocracy with an overweening executive. Clearly, the concentration of power in the presidency produced some very detrimental side effects due to Yeltsin's capricious use of the powers of the office. Yet, the executive-legislative relationship has become significantly more stable since the adoption of the 1993 Constitution, which provided a much clearer division of powers between the executive and legislative branches. Moreover, while the current constitutional arrangements surely are biased toward the executive, interbranch relations have been marked by instances of conciliatory behavior from both branches. An overview of the whole Yeltsin period shows that the rise and fall of executive-legislative conflict is best explained by a combination of factors, including institutional design, strength of ideological conflict, and public opinion. The largest obstacle to long-term cooperation between the two branches of government was the low level of party institutionalization in the system. The lack of well-developed parties denied the system the necessary intermediary institution that could link politicians in the executive and legislative branches.

In Chapter 3, Stoner-Weiss contends that a major obstacle to successful development has been a weak central state. Implosion of the Russian Federation is not deemed to be a serious threat, at least in the short term, especially now that President Putin has made the recentralization of federal power a top priority. However, the dramatic devolution of power away from the center that took place under Yeltsin posed serious problems for policy coherence and consistency as well as provision of basic services and legal protections. The ambitious transformative goals of the Yeltsin regime faltered in large part due to the inability of the central state to implement its policies in the regions. Despite efforts to remedy the situation, the same fate may await President Putin.

According to Stoner-Weiss, the decline of central governing capacity has been pushed by pressure from the regions. Under Yeltsin, the center's reaction to this pressure was to accommodate most regional demands for greater autonomy, either through negotiation in a series of bilateral treaties with individual regions or by default. In the latter case, the center simply did not fulfill its constitutional duties or fund the federal mandates passed down, leaving the regions to fend for themselves. Contrary to other observers, Stoner-Weiss does not see much of a coherent strategy by which the center maintained as much central authority as it could through strategic negotiation with the most restive regions.[29] If this was the strategy, Stoner-Weiss argues, it backfired, setting dangerous precedents of increased autonomy that other regions sought to emulate.

Stoner-Weiss attributes central state weakness in large part to the absence of national institutions that could serve an integrative role, uniting the center and regions. This was partially a result of the natural devolution of power following the collapse of the overly centralized Soviet state. The Soviet institutions that kept regions in line, such as the Communist Party and central ministries, were destroyed. The problem is that no corresponding national institutions were created to replace them. The absence of well-developed political parties undermined center-periphery relations, because parties serve a crucial integrative role by tying national and local politicians together in a single national organization. A weak Constitutional Court failed to adjudicate conflicts between the center and regions, because its rulings were often ignored. Institutional innovations specifically intended to improve center-periphery relations – the Federation Council, which provides a voice for regional leaders in national policy making, and the presidential representative, which provides the president an advocate in the regions – were generally ineffective.

In Chapter 4, Herrera examines the results of economic reform. Reforms that were intended to increase efficiency and prosperity instead produced economic collapse, endemic corruption, and poverty. These

---

[29] She contrasts her argument with the work of Treisman and Solnick. See Daniel Treisman, "Russia's Ethnic Revival: The Separatist Activism of Regional Leaders in a Postcommunist Order," *World Politics*, Vol. 49, No. 2 (1997), pp. 212–249 and Steven Solnick, "Federal Bargaining in Russia," *East European Constitutional Review*, Vol. 4, No. 4 (1995), pp. 52–58.

outcomes are not attributed to the inevitable hardships of economic transformation, nor to the failure to implement the tough but necessary policies of shock therapy. Rather, Herrera attributes this failure to an inappropriate reform program constructed by officials who misread the initial conditions in Russia and misunderstood the central relationship between the state and the market.

Herrera argues that neoliberal ideas of reform were particularly neglectful of institution building due to their faith in markets and disdain for state interference in economic activity. Influenced by neoliberal ideas, Russian reformers concentrated on stabilization, liberalization, and privatization, expecting the necessary legal and state institutions to spontaneously emerge from the demands of the new market economy. This approach was not a problem for post-communist economies like Poland, Hungary, and the Czech Republic that possessed stronger states with better developed legal and financial systems. But it was a devastating course of action in the context of Russia's weak legal and institutional arrangements.

For Hererra, the failure to build institutions was not predetermined by historical legacies, nor were alternative reform programs that emphasize institution building somehow unavailable because of previous developments that forced the hand of reformers. In the interrelationship between structure, institutions, and elite decisions, elite decisions again take precedence. Russia's economic collapse was a policy failure that could have been avoided had elites followed a different path of economic reform, one that emphasized institutional development.

In Chapter 5, Barany graphically shows the consequences of the denigration of state power and declining financial resources for the Russian military. The decline of the military could be seen as part of a broader decay of social infrastructure due to the lack of resources. But, while noting the dramatic shortfall of funds available for the military in these extraordinarily tight times, Barany sees the root of the problem of the military as political. The major problem has been the predominant control over the military by the executive.

The result has been a military that has suffered from a combination of neglect and politicization. Economic hardship meant a shortage of resources that impoverished and frustrated the military, producing a perception of irresponsible neglect by the state. At the same time, intraelite conflict provided opportunities, even invitations, for intervention in political conflicts between ruling elites. Given these conditions, it is surprising how little the military intervened in domestic politics.

Barany attributes the lack of military intervention in politics to a lack of institutional cohesion that makes the military a less effective political actor. While the stimuli for intervention were present (economic and political crises, poor material conditions within the military) internal cleavages undermined collective action. Moreover, survey research suggests that the Russian officer corps possessed democratic values and attitudes that were not conducive to military intervention. Finally, there was a historical legacy of professionalism and noninterference in politics within the military.

As in other realms, a poor situation following the collapse of the Soviet Union was made worse by inaction (the failure to restructure the military) and poorly designed institutions (the development of over-weening and capricious executive control over the military). While a military coup may not be the end result of such disastrous decisions, democratic consolidation surely will not be promoted either.

In his conclusion, Fish argues forcefully for emphasizing institutions and elite decisions over structural factors such as culture and historical continuity. Fish claims that Russia's "low-caliber democracy" can be explained by the single institutional factor of an overly strong executive and three related policy decisions: the failure to call early elections, the loans-for-shares plan of privatization, and the weakening of state law enforcement bodies. For Fish, these four factors, all products of elite decisions rather than preexisting structural forces, account for the major deficiencies of post-communist Russian politics such as ideological polarization, executive-legislative confrontation, widespread corruption, and a weak state.

The analyses found in this book offer a series of interrelated institutional and elite decisions as the primary explanations for the destructive outcomes of the Russian transition. The most commonly cited problems are elite inattention and hostility to institution building. Weak political parties lie at the heart of continual executive-legislative tension and are also a key source of weak central state capacity. The weak state has established neither the necessary infrastructure for successful market reform nor the proper civilian controls over the military. All of these developments are seen as primarily the product of contingent elite decisions taken at the time of the transition, decisions that were not necessarily imposed by confining preexisting conditions.

CONCLUSIONS

It is always hazardous and problematic to engage in prediction, especially when analyzing a country as unstable as Russia. Yet, part of the task presented to the contributors to this volume was to speculate on future trends within their areas of political development. The study of elite decisions and institutions is attractive because these factors seem more susceptible to change than structural conditions. Leaders and their policies come and go, particularly if they face competitive elections and term limits. Institutions tend to have greater staying power than particular policies but are usually deemed more malleable than culture or social class configurations. Given the emphasis placed on elite decisions and institutions in this book, one may expect more optimism, relatively speaking, concerning the future as long as certain corrective actions are taken. If democratization, even in a place like Russia, is a matter of getting the institutions and policies right, then there is hope.

But the assessments of the future provided in the following chapters, while not uniformly pessimistic, are far from optimistic. This is primarily because policies and institutions established during the initial transition have produced their own legacies, most notably powerful political and economic actors who benefit from the status quo and will use their immense resources to keep it intact. To the extent that development in Russia is path-dependent, poorly designed institutions and wrongheaded reforms have further complicated a situation that was already an unlikely candidate for successful democratic consolidation.

No contributor could be called optimistic about future prospects for democratic reform. All see more difficulties than auspicious trends in the future. But there is a range of opinion about future trends that can be gleaned from the following chapters. Of course, the perspective on the future is greatly influenced by the facet of political life that one is examining. Some problems appear to be more intractable than others. With this in mind, I offer three general perspectives that emerge from the various analyses.

First, there is a reformist perspective that emphasizes the steps that need to be taken if Russia is to escape its syndrome of low-caliber democracy. Fish offers the clearest example of this perspective. In his conclusion, Fish argues that Russia can escape the dysfunctions of the emerging system that were created by poorly designed institutions and wrongheaded policies. Fish calls for substantially curbing the powers of the presidency, introducing economic policies that reduce disparities in wealth, and reestablishing the state's monopoly over legitimate coercion. According to Fish, implementation of these measures will meet significant but not necessarily insurmountable resistance. Fish notes that other former Soviet republics and Eastern European states have been able to enact similar policies and consequently have experienced much more successful democratic transitions.

Second, there is a (relatively) optimistic perspective that acknowledges certain promising developments for future democratization that already have begun to take shape in Russia. McFaul's analysis of elections and my examination of executive-legislative relations fit this perspective. For McFaul, polarized politics has come to an end in Russia, which means the extreme ends of the ideological spectrum stand to lose ground to more centrist forces. Russian voters may begin to vote according to interests rather than ideology, and patterns of electoral support similar to more successful transitions in Eastern Europe may emerge. I also see room for hope in the end of the Yeltsin era. The growing consensus among major political forces surrounding the need for some type of market economy with significant state intervention should mitigate interbranch conflict. Finally, despite being Yeltsin's chosen successor, President Putin has had opportunities for cooperative relations with the legislature because his personal popularity helped to elect a less confrontational legislature. There is a threat not of interbranch conflict, but of the State Duma becoming overly docile and subservient to presidential influence under Putin.

Unlike Fish, I do not believe that reducing presidential powers would improve executive-legislative relations. I am more wary than Fish of the possibility that such changes would inadvertently promote the kind of institutional conflict witnessed in the First Russian Republic, when the two branches had more equal powers. If there is to be constitutional reform, one must remember that contention over the composition of the government has been the major source of interbranch conflict. Thus, the most productive reform may be to further separate the powers of the two branches in order to reduce conflict. Such separation of powers not only would lessen the likelihood of interbranch conflict, but also would reduce the power of the president by removing his ability to dissolve the legislature.

Finally, there is a (relatively) pessimistic perspective that neither sees promising developments nor forsees the implementation of a reformist agenda that could remedy the deteriorating situation in Russia. The analyses of economic reform, center-periphery relations, and civil-military relations fit this perspective. While Herrera has called for greater attention to institution building in economic reform, there is little hope that the failed shock therapy program will be replaced by a vigorous attempt to build the institutional infrastructure necessary for successful reform in the context of a weak state. Indeed, shock therapy is perhaps the best example of the path dependence of Russia's post-communist reforms. This policy has produced powerful forces that will struggle to maintain the dysfunctional market dynamics of the status quo.[30] Stoner-Weiss argues that Putin's attempts to arrest the devolution of power from the center to the regions will face many of the same problems of similar attempts at recentralization under Yeltsin. Likewise, while Barany calls

---

[30] Hellman, "Winners Take All."

for depoliticization of the military and more balanced civilian control, there is no indication that either of these reforms are likely to occur in the near future. In fact, the military campaign in Chechnya suggests that the problems in the Russian military may yet pose a serious threat to the existence of democracy itself.

Of course, a myriad of different scenarios are also possible. Rather than producing moderate election outcomes and better executive-legislative relations, an increasingly unified elite under President Putin could centralize power, ending the limited pluralism and political freedoms that had been allowed to exist under Yeltsin. Such a scenario associates greater elite consensus with authoritarian moves to end the last vestiges of democratic rule. This possibility and countless others, both good and bad, demonstrate how perilous speculation on the future under such fluid conditions can be. The range of possibilities also shows how contingent the fate of Russian democracy is on elite decisions and institutions, which is the major premise of this book.

1

Russian Electoral Trends

Michael McFaul

Conventional explanations of Russian electoral outcomes paint a very volatile picture. The conventional story is roughly the following. The popularity of the "democrats" – the catchall label assigned to those political leaders and parties loosely associated with Boris Yeltsin – grew rapidly from the first national elections in 1989 until Boris Yeltsin's first presidential victory in June 1991. After the introduction of shock therapy in January 1991, popular support for the democrats rapidly declined, as demonstrated by their abysmal showing in the 1993 parliamentary elections and their even worse performance in the 1995 parliamentary elections. As support for the "democrats" declined, a new force – nationalism – began to fill the vacuum, as demonstrated most dramatically by Vladimir Zhirinovsky's surprising electoral performance in 1993. Between 1993 and 1995, however, Zhirinovsky discredited himself with silly theatrics, thereby providing a political opportunity for a communist comeback in the 1995 parliamentary elections. The combination of nationalist and communist resurgence convinced many by the winter of 1996 that the "democrats," and Boris Yeltsin in particular, had little chance of winning the summer presidential vote.[1] Had Yeltsin lost, Russia would have followed a pattern similar to that of other post-communist countries in which those that started economic reforms after the collapse of communism were voted out of office in the second election.[2]

---

[1] See, for instance, Jerry Hough, Evelyn Davidheiser, and Susan Goodrich Lehman, *The 1996 Russian Presidential Election*, Brookings Occasional Papers (Washington, D.C.: Brookings Institution, 1996) and Peter Reddaway, "Red Alert," *The New Republic*, January 29, 1996.

[2] This pattern, which occurred in much of the post-communist world, was first predicted in Adam Przeworski, *Democracy and the Market: Political and Economic Reforms in Eastern Europe and Latin America* (Cambridge: Cambridge University Press, 1991).

Table 1.1. Outcomes in binary elections

Ideological Camp	1991[a]	April 1993[b]	December 1993[c]	July 1996
"Reform"	59.7%	58.7%	58.4%	53.8%
"Opposition"	36.7%	37.7%	41.6%	40.3%

[a] For 1991, these labels of reform and opposition should be reversed.
[b] Here we are reporting the results of the first question.
[c] This is the result of the constitutional referendum.

But Yeltsin did win, in defiance of the trend in the region. Moreover, he won with an incredible record of underachievement, including negative growth rates for every year of rule, a disastrous war in Chechnya, and an explosion of crime and corruption. For many analysts, Yeltsin's victory could only be explained as the consequence of fraud, television control, and a "brilliant" campaign, as the trajectory of electoral support for the "democrats" was in the opposite direction.

This chapter offers a different explanation for Russia's seemingly volatile electoral history. First and foremost, Russian voters have not been as volatile in their voting patterns as the conventional account implies.[3] If a Russian voter cast her ballot for a communist candidate in 1991, she probably voted against Yeltsin in the April 1993 referendum, probably voted for an opposition party (that is, either the LDPR, the CPRF, or the Agrarian Party of Russia, the APR) in the December parliamentary vote in 1993 and probably voted against the constitution in the referendum held at the same time, probably voted for an opposition party again in 1995 and 1999, and probably voted for Gennady Zyuganov in the 1996 presidential election. The converse is true for anticommunist, pro-reform supporters. A very small number of voters cast their ballots for a communist candidate in one election and then for a "democrat" in the next vote. Voters did migrate to other parties with great frequency in the 1993 and 1995 parliamentary votes, but they did not cross the boundary between "reformist" and "antireformist" camps.[4]

In elections in which voters had only two essential choices, however, voter preferences look rather stable through this entire period.[5]

[3] Michael McFaul, *Russia's 1996 Presidential Elections: The End of Polarized Politics* (Stanford: Hoover Institution Press, 1997) and Mikhail Myagkov, Peter Ordeshook, and Alexander Sobyanin, "The Russian Electorate from 1991 to 1996," *Post-Soviet Affairs*, Vol. 13, No. 2 (1997), pp. 134–166.

[4] On these migrations, see Timothy Colton, *Transitional Citizenship: Voting in Post-Soviet Russia* (Cambridge, Mass.: Harvard University Press, 2000), Chapter 3.

[5] This aggregate data in no way proves that *individual* voter preferences remained stable. On this problem, see Gerald Kramer, "The Ecological Fallacy Revisited: Aggregate-versus Individual-Level Findings on Economics and Elections and Sociotropic Voting," *American Political Science Review*, Vol. 77, No. 1 (March 1983), pp. 92–111.

Given all that happened in Russia during this period, this apparent electoral stability is especially striking. Despite economic depression, a violent standoff between parliament and president in October 1993, the Chechen war, and explosive social ills, the balance of support between opponents and proponents of reform remained stable and polarized from 1991 until 1996. Voters did not behave in these elections in accordance with retrospective voting models.[6] On the contrary, only 29 percent of the voting electorate were satisfied with Yeltsin's performance when asked in an opinion poll in June 1996.[7] When asked in November 1996, "When did you family live the best?", 10 percent responded that the period since the beginning of market reforms was the best, 13 percent named the Gorbachev period, and an amazing 61 percent cited the "stagnation" period before 1985.[8] Nor could voters have been motivated solely by economic considerations. If Russian voters had made electoral decisions based on either the depth of their own pocketbooks or their evaluations of the health of the national economy, then the incumbent Yeltsin most surely would have been tossed out of office in 1996.[9]

A different kind of cleavage issue divided the Russian electorate from 1991 to 1996 – those for "reform," however defined, and those against. This issue overrode concerns about individual interests or specific issues. Jerry Hough's summation of the 1990 Russian elections could be applied to all of the binary votes in this period, including the 1996 presidential election: "In 1990 the basic issues of the election were clear. Did the voter want to vote against the party apparatus and the system it oversaw? Were the radicals demanding too much change too rapidly or representing alien values, or both? Voters were not likely to be greatly influenced by biased press coverage or the quantity of leaflets distributed in choosing between a radical candidate and a conservative."[10] During a period of change in the fundamental organization of the political and economic system in Russia, we should expect Russian voters to have been less concerned with evaluating the incumbent's past performance and more interested in choosing the candidate who most closely represented their

---

[6] Morris Fiorina, *Retrospective Voting in American National Elections* (New Haven: Yale University Press, 1981).

[7] This poll was conducted by All-Russia Opinion Research Center and reported by the Associated Press, November 13, 1996.

[8] VTsIOM, "Pyat' Let Reforma," ms., 1996.

[9] On "pocketbook" versus "sociotropic" effects on voting behavior, see Roderick Kiewit, *Macroeconomics and Micropolitics: The Electoral Effects of Economic Issues* (Chicago: University of Chicago Press, 1983).

[10] Jerry Hough, *Democratization and Revolution in the USSR, 1985–1991* (Washington, D.C.: Brookings Institution, 1997), p. 291.

conception of Russia's future economic and political system.[11] The relative weakness of other cleavage issues, such as ethnic or religious divides, further accentuated the importance of this single factor in organizing electoral preferences.[12]

The perception of volatility in electoral outcomes is produced when the results of binary votes (presidential elections and referenda) and multiple-candidate votes (parliamentary elections) are compared. This one cleavage issue did not shape Russia's parliamentary elections. Other factors contributed to a more complicated electoral outcome. First, the institutional effects of parliamentary elections with proportional representation (PR) are different than in presidential elections. Presidential elections with run-offs produce a winner-take-all outcome between two candidates, while PR electoral laws allows many to win, and thereby tend to stimulate multiparty systems.[13] As expected, Russia's mixed system, in which half of the seats (225) were allocated according to PR and the other half in single-mandate districts, encouraged the proliferation of political parties and provided few incentives for party consolidation.[14] In 1993, thirteen parties participated in the Duma elections; in 1995, forty-three parties made the ballot.[15] These elections obviously offered voters a wider range of choices than two. Second, these parliamentary elections were not as critical to the fate of the system, as Russia's 1993 constitution relegated the legislative body to a secondary status in national policy making. Russians could vote with their hearts in 1995

[11] During periods of revolutionary change, national politics also impact on the daily lives of individuals in a more direct way than during periods of stability or evolutionary change. For instance, when Nikolai Ryzhkov outlined his "stabilization" plan in the spring of 1990, millions of Soviet citizens rushed to stores to buy anything and everything available. By contrast, few decisions in Washington have such a direct and immediate impact on millions of citizens. Under these conditions, we should expect voters to be much more in tune with national politics than during more stable periods, making them less susceptible to media manipulation.

[12] On the weakness of these other cleavage issues in the Russian case, see Stephen Whitefield and Geoffrey Evans, "The Emerging Structure of Partisan Divisions in Russian Politics," in Matthew Wyman, Stephen White, and Sarah Oates (eds.), *Elections and Voters in Post-Communist Russia* (Glasgow: Edward Elgar, 1998), pp. 68–99.

[13] Maurice Duverger, *Political Parties: Their Organization and Activity in the Modern State* (New York: Wiley, 1954); Giovanni Sartori, *Comparative Constitutional Engineering* (New York: New York University Press, 1994).

[14] Thomas Remington and Steven Smith, "Political Goals, Institutional Context, and the Choice of an Electoral System: The Russian Parliamentary Election Law," *American Journal of Political Science*, Vol. 40, No. 4 (1996), pp. 1253–1279.

[15] The number of "effective parties" to emerge from these elections also increased. See Robert Moser, "Electoral Systems and the Number of Parties in Postcommunist States," *World Politics*, Vol. 51, No. 3 (1999), pp. 359–384.

and then vote with their heads in 1996. Third, the sequence of the parliamentary and presidential votes served to give them a different logic. When parliamentary and presidential elections occur concurrently, they can influence each other. The converse is equally true. In the 1993 and 1995 parliamentary elections, Yeltsin did not participate, and actually had incentives, especially in 1995, to encourage fragmentation.

These factors combined to shape the outcomes of the 1993 and 1995 parliamentary elections in a more nuanced way than the other binary votes during this period. Centrist, nationalist, special-interest, and corporatist parties had room to wiggle in these kinds of elections. These votes also stimulated the partial emergence of a multi-party system in Russia rather than one dominated by only two groups – pro-reform and antireform, or anticommunist and pro-communist.[16]

In the aggregate, however, core support for reformist parties and core support for opposition parties did not change. Within these two broad camps, the balance of support between parties changed considerably.[17] Within the opposition camp, the Communists improved dramatically over 1993, while the Agrarian Party and Zhirinovsky won less than half of their 1993 support in 1995. Within the reformist camp, the newly created Our Home Is Russia electoral bloc gained at the expense of the former "party of power," Yegor Gaidar's Democratic Choice of Russia. In 1995, the centrist vote – voters who had tended to support the reformist side in binary votes – also was spread across several parties, adding to the impression that support for reformists was decreasing over time. In retrospect, however, the 1993 and 1995 votes look very similar. Reformists won a minority share of the vote in 1995, but they also were in the minority in 1993. Likewise, the opposition performed well in 1995, but they also did well in 1993.

Although different from the outcomes in binary votes during this period, even the outcomes in these parliamentary elections suggest stability and polarization in Russian electoral politics between 1991 and 1996. More than any single factor, attitudes about the general course of Russia's political and economic revolution shaped electoral politics during this transitional period. The balance between those for and those against revolutionary change remained fairly constant.

In 1996, Russia's protracted transition from communism ended.[18] The specter of a return to communism receded after the 1996 vote. When

---

[16] M. Steven Fish, "The Advent of Multipartism in Russia," *Post-Soviet Affairs*, Vol. 11, No. 4 (1995), pp. 340–383.

[17] Colton, *Transitional Citizenship*, Chapter 3.

[18] On the definition of "end of transition," see Juan Linz and Alfred Stepan, *Problems of Democratic Transition and Consolidation: Southern Europe, South America, and*

given the choice between the communist past and an anticommunist future, Russians overwhelmingly voted for the latter. After the 1996 vote, the communist/anticommunist divide faded in importance. The Communist Party of the Russian Federation (CPRF) continued to dominate the antigovernment segment of the electorate, but the CPRF evolved to become a within-system party. By the 1999 parliamentary election, a vote for the CPRF no longer meant a vote for going back to the old communist system. Anticommunism also died as a rallying cause after the 1996 vote. With the collapse of communism now complete, the anticommunist bloc lost its raison d'être, allowing new political formations to enter the fray and new issues to dominate the electoral process. The polarization between communist and anticommunist forces that helped to produce Yeltsin's reelection victory in 1996 played only a marginal role in Vladimir Putin's victory in Russia's March 2000 presidential election.

To develop this set of arguments about electoral outcomes in Russia in the last decade, this chapter proceeds as follows. The first section sketches the general patterns of electoral outcomes observed in transitions. This section underscores how Russia's protracted and confrontational transition from communist rule accorded elections a different dynamic. Section two discusses how the rules of the game can shape the outcome and the perception of the outcome of an election. This section focuses in particular on why presidential and parliamentary elections follow a different dynamic. Armed with the analytic framework outlined in the first two sections, the next several sections discuss in brief each national election in Russia since 1989. In addition to accounting for the influence of the structural and institutional variables described in sections two and three, these analyses of individual elections also consider the role of the campaigns and the actions of candidates. Section nine, the final section, discusses how electoral dynamics in the 1999–2000 electoral cycle differed from previous polarized votes earlier in the decade.

1. THE CAUSES AND CONSEQUENCES OF RUSSIA'S POLARIZED ELECTORATE

In most transitions to democracy, the successful completion of a series of elections produces the following results. First, electoral support for the democratic challengers wanes. In first or founding elections,

Post-Communist Europe (Baltimore: Johns Hopkins University Press, 1996), p. 3. On the Russian case specifically, see Michael McFaul, "Lessons from Russia's Protracted Transition from Communist Rule," *Political Science Quarterly*, Vol. 114, No. 1 (1999), pp. 103–130.

"founding father" figures and their coalitions tend to score dramatic electoral victories. In second-round elections, the romantic era of transition usually ends, as expectations of voters formed during transition are almost never met.[19] This reaction against the new leaders has proven especially acute in transitions from communist rule, in which political transition usually has been accompanied by painful economic transformation.[20] Throughout Eastern Europe, anticommunist leaders who won electoral victories in first elections lost to former communist leaders in second elections.[21] Militantly anticommunist Poland voted out Lech Walesa. Even in the Czech Republic, Vaclav Klaus and his allies failed to win enough seats to reconstitute their old right-of-center coalition government.[22] Sali Berisha, president of Albania, managed to "win" a second election only through massive fraud.[23]

This electoral reaction against those political leaders who initiated economic reform is predicted by retrospective theories of voting behavior.[24] This approach to explaining elections posits that voters look retrospectively back on the tenure of the incumbent and decide if they are better or worse off during the candidate's time (or candidate's party's time) in office. If the voter feels better off, then he will likely vote for the incumbent or the incumbent's party. If the voter feels worse off, then he will likely vote for the challenger. This assessment about the past is

---

[19] O'Donnell and Schmitter have called this electoral phenomenon the "pendulum effect" in transitions. See Guillermo O'Donnell and Philippe Schmitter, *Transitions from Authoritarian Rule: Tentative Conclusions about Uncertain Democracies* (Baltimore: Johns Hopkins University Press, 1986), p. 62.

[20] Przeworski, *Democracy and the Market*. Although Przeworski's basic predictions about electoral backlash have proven correct, the relationship between economic reform and voting has proven to be much more complicated. Most strikingly, voters may have voted against reformers in second-round elections, but not against reform itself. Rollback did not occur. Moreover, there may be other reasons besides economics that the reformers lost second-round elections, including, for instance, the lack of unity among reformist forces. This argument is made in Anders Aslund, Peter Boone, and Simon Johnson, "How to Stabilize: Lessons from Post-Communist Countries," *Brookings Papers on Economic Activity*, No. 1 (1996), p. 227.

[21] Marcin Krol, "Poland's Longing for Paternalism," *Journal of Democracy*, Vol. 5, No. 1 (1994), pp. 85–94; Wiktor Osiatynski, "After Walesa: The Causes and Consequences of Walesa's defeat," *East European Constitutional Review*, Vol. 4, No. 4 (1995), pp. 35–44.

[22] Christine Spolar, "Czech Elections Leave PM, Once Dominant, Position Weakened," *The Washington Post*, June 3, 1996, p. A16.

[23] Christine Spolar, "Albania Reverts to a One-Party Government," *The Washington Post*, June 22, 1996, p. A19.

[24] Fiorina, *Retrospective Voting in American National Elections*.

usually undertaken with respect to individual utility and is most concerned with economic issues.[25]

This theory offers much guidance in analyzing electoral trends in post-communist Eastern Europe. Anticommunist leaders and parties won landslide victories in most first electoral contests. Upon assuming office, these new leaders then implemented painful market reforms, which in the short run made the majorities in their countries worse off. By the time of the second round of elections, most post-communist countries were still experiencing declines in growth rates. Not surprisingly, therefore, most of the first post-communist leaders were voted out of office in the next election.

Through the 1996 presidential elections, Russia did not appear to be following this general trend. First, electoral support for opposition parties and candidates – be they communists, national patriots, or opposition "democrats" – has not grown dramatically. Instead, those who won big during Russia's first elections continued to stay in power. This sustained support for Russia's original challengers to the Soviet ancien régime was demonstrated most dramatically in the 1996 presidential election, when Boris Yeltsin became the first incumbent in the post-communist world to win reelection in a relatively free and fair election.[26] This election result was especially surprising considering all that Russians had endured under Yeltsin's reign. After all, Yeltsin's five-year tenure included a sustained and deep economic depression, civil war briefly in Moscow in 1993 and then the prolonged war in Chechnya, and significant increases in crime.[27] In 1996, opinion polls demonstrated

---

[25] Much of the literature on voting in the United States focuses on the role of economic variables, at the level of both the individual and the national economy. See, for instance, Fiorina, *Retrospective Voting in American National Elections*; Michael MacKuen, Robert Erikson, and James Stimson, "Peasants or Bankers? The American Electorate and the U.S. Economy," *American Political Science Review*, Vol. 86, No. 3 (1992), pp. 597–611; Roderick Kiewet, *Macreconomics and Micropolitics* (Chicago: University of Chicago Press, 1983); and Donald Kinder and Roderick Kiewiet, "Sociotropic Politics: The American Case," *British Journal of Political Science*, Vol. 11 (1981), pp. 129–162.

[26] International Republican Institute, *Russia Presidential Observation Report* (Washington, D.C.: International Republican Institute, 1996).

[27] For a comparison of Russia's economic decline relative to Eastern European countries, see *Transition Report 1995: Investment and Enterprise Development* (London: European Bank for Reconstruction and Development, 1996). For comparisons between Russia's current depression and the American Great Depression, see Branko Milanovic, *Income, Inequality and Poverty during the Transition from Planned to Market Economy* (Washington, D.C.: World Bank, 1998).

definitely that most people thought they were better off under communism than under the current system.[28]

Explaining why Russia did not follow the same electoral patterns as those witnessed in other post-communist transitions requires a comparative understanding of the nature of Russia's transition from communist rule. In contrast to more speedy and successful transitions in Eastern Europe, Russia's transition has been protracted and confrontational. If the starting point of Russia's transition from communist rule can be located in the mid-Gorbachev years, then Russia's transition to democracy is one of the longest in recent history. Linz and Stepan define a successful democratic transition as the moment when "[s]ufficient agreement has been reached about political procedures to produce an elected government, when a government comes to power that is the direct result of a free and popular vote, when this government de facto has the authority to generate new policies, and when the executive, legislative, and judicial power generated by the new democracy does not have to share power with the other bodies *de jure*."[29] Russia most certainly did not meet these conditions until December 1993, when Russian voters ratified a new constitution and elected a new national parliament. The transition may well have ended only after the 1996 presidential election. Before then, the head of state had not been elected under the new constitution. Some argue that the transition will only have been completed when a change of executive power takes place through an electoral process.[30] Whether the end of transition is 1993, 1996, 2000, or 2004, the process has been a long one, especially when compared to the more successful transitions from communist rule in Eastern Europe.

Russia's transition has been not only long, but also confrontational and at times violent. Negotiation between the ancien régime leaders and democratic challengers never produced pacts or interim institutional arrangements.[31] Rather, imposition has been the only mode of transition. In 1991, opposing sides failed to negotiate a new set of political rules,

---

[28] See Richard Dobson, "Is Russia Turning the Corner? Changing Russia Public Opinion, 1991–1996," R-7-96 (Washington, D.C.: United States Information Agency, September 1996) and All-Russian Center for Public Opinion (VTsIOM), "Pyat' Let Reforma" (Moscow: VTsIOM, November 1996).

[29] Linz and Stepan, *Problems of Democratic Transition and Consolidation*, p. 3.

[30] Still others, of course, argue that Russia is not in transition to democracy at all, but rather is an authoritarian state. See Vladimir Brovkin, "The Emperor's New Clothes: Continuities of Soviet Political Culture in Contemporary Russia," *Problems of Post-Communism*, Vol. 43, No. 2 (1996), p. 21.

[31] On the importance of pacts for successful transitions, see O'Donnell and Schmitter, *Transitions from Authoritarian Rule*.

but instead did battle with each other until one side won. This drama of dual sovereignty was replayed again in October 1993, when two opposing governments each claimed to be the legitimate government in Russia. Like the one in 1991, this confrontation ended only after one side prevailed over the other by using military force. The expanded, contested agenda of change helps to explain why Russia's transition to electoral democracy has been so long and conflictual. In transitions from authoritarian rule in Latin American and southern Europe, only the political institutions of the state were up for negotiation. Questions concerning the organization of the economy were explicitly off limits. In comparison to democratization efforts in capitalist countries, transitions from communist rule expanded the agenda of change by placing economic questions on the table, complicating the transition process. Multiethnic states such as the Soviet Union and Yugoslavia had to face a critical issue – defining the borders of the state(s).

In terms of complexity, then, Soviet and Russian leaders faced a greater challenge in negotiating this triple transition than did their counterparts in Poland, let alone in Spain. Yet, it was the intensity of opposing preferences about this agenda that really prolonged the transition process and fueled confrontation. The extent to which plans for reform become *contested* agendas is a function of the degree of homogeneity of preferences among political actors. The greater the degree of homogeneity, the smaller the contested agenda of change. The greater the degree of heterogeneity of preferences, the wider the contested agenda of change. At the beginning of the Soviet/Russian transition, no consensus existed among political elites about the borders of the state, the nature of the economy, or the kind of political system. Conflicting ideas about the borders of the state precipitated the first armed conflict between Soviet and Russian political actors in August 1991. After one side – Yeltsin's side – won this military confrontation, the victors dictated a resolution to this hotly debated issue by dissolving the Soviet Union. In other words, the state border issue was resolved through unilateral action, not negotiation.

Antithetical ideological positions also crystallized in Russia regarding the organization of the economy. Throughout the Gorbachev period and the first years of the Russian republic, communist leaders maintained real opposition to market reforms, promoting instead a brand of state-led socialism. After Yeltsin achieved a new political advantage after the failed August 1991 putsch, he and his new team of young economic reformers initiated a radical economic reform package that began with price liberalization followed by macroeconomic stabilization and privatization. However, only months into the reform process, conservative opposition – this time located in the Russian Congress of People's Deputies – mobilized to amend, impede, and eventually halt market reforms. If many post-communist countries debated what kind of market reforms to pursue after the fall of communism, Russia debated whether to pursue market reforms at all. Only after Yeltsin defeated his opponents through violence in October 1993 did his government have the capacity to pursue unilaterally policies that they considered necessary for ensuring capitalism's irreversibility. Over time and out of weakness, most opponents of capitalism eventually recognized the legitimacy of private property and the necessity of markets. In comparative perspective, this recognition came very late in Russia's transition, and the parameters of the debate about the relationship between the state and the market is still much wider in Russia than in the post-communist countries of Eastern Europe.

The third issue on the agenda of change – debates about the kind of political system – took the longest to resolve. Until the fall of 1993, communists persisted in pushing for the system of soviets as the basic organization of the Soviet and Russian governments. Some nationalists argued for a return of the monarchy. Even the anticommunist movement was divided as to whether democracy was appropriate for Russia during its transition from communist rule. Many prominent advisors to Yeltsin maintained that Russia needed an authoritarian regime to manage the transformation to capitalism. At a minimum, these "democrats" urged that Yeltsin erect a strong executive system that could pursue economic reform autonomous from societal pressures. Only after the October 1993 tragedy did Yeltsin turn his attention to creating new political institutions. He dictated a solution to resolve previous debates about the form of government and then offered his opponents a binary choice of either acceptance or rejection of this order. Out of weakness and the lack of a better alternative, Yeltsin's opponents acquiesced to the new rules and began to participate in the new constitutional order after the December 1993 elections. Whether Yeltsin would agree to abide by the new rules, however, remained uncertain. Most ominously, no one knew if Yeltsin would accept the results of the 1996 presidential election if he lost. Well into the presidential campaign, Yeltsin's advisors repeatedly hinted that he would not.

Resolving Russia's contested agenda of change took so long also because of the relatively equal balance of power between those for and against revolution. In transitional periods, stalemate created through a relatively equal balance of power between forces for democracy and forces for preservation of the ancien régime can create propitious conditions for democratic transition.[32] However, stalemate also can have

---

[32] Dankwart Rustow, "Transitions to Democracy: Toward a Dynamic Model," *Comparative Politics*, Vol. 2, No. 3 (1970), pp. 337–363.

precisely the opposite effect. If opponents believe that their enemies cannot defeat them, they may be tempted to fight either to preserve or to overthrow the status quo. In the Soviet/Russian transition, stalemate played such a negative role. Rather than compelling opposing sides to compromise, the relatively equal balance of power between opponents fostered conflict. In the first transition period during the Gorbachev era, the balance of power between conservatives and democrats was not tilted in favor of one side or the other. Given this condition, conservatives eventually decided in August 1991 to exercise military power to preserve the Soviet Union and squelch the opposition. They miscalculated.

In contrast to democratic movements in Poland, Hungary, and Czechoslovakia, the Russian "democrats" who enjoyed a temporary advantage in the wake of their August 1991 victory did not have over-whelming support within either the elite or the population as a whole.[33] Importantly, and again in contrast to most East European transitions, communist groups refused to recognize the democratic victory of August 1991 and considered illegitimate and undemocratic the policies pursued by the democrats soon thereafter. In particular, Yeltsin's decisions to dissolve the USSR and to begin radical economic reform did not enjoy wide-spread support and did not result from negotiations with his political opponents. Had Yeltsin enjoyed a preponderance of power over his political opponents, he might have been able to ignore the opinion of his enemies regarding these consequential decisions. However, because the balance of power between those "for the revolution" and those "against the revolution" was relatively equal, Yeltsin's opponents recovered from their August 1991 setback and remobilized to challenge Yeltsin's reforms and eventually Yeltsin's regime. Tempted (again) by the perceived ability to achieve political objectives through military force, the two sides eventually did battle again in October 1993. Even after 1993, the electoral victories of opposition forces in the 1993 and 1995 parliamentary elections kept alive the belief that rollback of the revolution might still be possible. In sharp contrast to their social-democratic comrades in Eastern Europe, Russian communists openly rejected social democracy and remained committed to reconstructing communism well beyond the collapse of the communist regime in the Soviet Union. As late as the spring of 1996, the deputy chairman of the Russian Communist Party declared that "the death of communism never happened . . . the Soviet Union never collapsed, [and] people still think of themselves as Soviets."[34]

---

[33] For this comparison, see Michael McFaul, *Post-Communist Politics: Democratic Prospects in Russia and Eastern Europe* (Washington, D.C.: Center for Strategic and International Studies, 1993).

[34] Aleksandr Shabanov, Deputy Chairman of the CPRF, speech at the Moscow Carnegie Center, March 28, 1996. See also *III S'ezd Kommunisticheskoi partii Rossiiskoi Feder-*

Electoral Consequences of Protracted Transition

This protracted and confrontational mode of transition had real consequences for elections in Russia. While second elections in Eastern Europe occurred after the transition from communist rule was over, Russia held several elections, including most importantly the 1996 presidential election, during the transition process. Even throughout the 1996 campaign, the specter of communist restoration loomed, at least in the minds of Russian voters. From 1990 to 1996, voters in Russia remained polarized between those who supported and those who lamented the transition from communism. Under these circumstances, interest cleavages were fashioned more by general attitudes about the revolutionary project than by particular economic, social, or ethnic concerns. More conventional cleavages – cleavages that demarcate the contours of stable party systems – have developed slowly as a result of Russia's protracted transition from communism to a market economy and democratic polity.[35]

The numerous labels assigned to these two camps have produced confusion and misinterpretation of Russian electoral outcomes, in both Russia and the West. In part, this confusion originates from the fact that those once defending the ancien régime became challengers to the new status quo after 1991, and vice versa. In other words, the communists were the "conservatives" before 1991, seeking to preserve the established order, while anticommunist leaders and groups – called in Russia the "democrats" – constituted the "liberals" or "progressives" seeking to change the old order. By 1993, these terms became even more confused as the "democrats" were now in power seeking to preserve the new order, while the communists became the opposition seeking to alter the status quo.[36] However confusing to outsiders, the basic contours of the bipolar ideological divide seem to have been understood by Russian voters. While opinion polls have demonstrated that centrist and nationalist

atsii (21–22 Yanvarya 1995 goda) (Moscow: Informpechat', 1995) and *Rossiya, Rodina, Narod! Predvybornaya platforma kandidata na post prezidenta rossiiskoi federatsii G.A. Zyuganova*, mimeo, 1996.

[35] S. W. Rivera, "Historical Cleavage or Transition Mode? Influences on the Emerging Party Systems in Poland, Hungary and Czechoslovakia," *Party Politics*, Vol. 2, No. 2 (1996), pp. 177–208 and Evans and Whitefield, "Identifying the Bases of Party Competition in Eastern Europe."

[36] Observers also get bogged down in defining "reform," assuming that greater precision in characterizing Yeltsin's policies will produce a better explanation of electoral outcomes. Those in search of political party formation also (mis)apply categories such as left and right or labels such liberal, social democrat, and conservative to a political landscape in which these terms have lost their meanings.

labels produce confusion in the electorate, the basic divide between these two camps is easily recognized.[37]

In highlighting the high degree of elite and societal polarization from the first elections in Russia in 1989 until the 1996 presidential election, this approach suggests that Russian voter preferences are best understood as falling within two broad categories – those in support of "reform" (however defined) and those against it. Survey data about voter attitudes may provide a more complex picture about preferences regarding specific issues, but the framework outlined in this chapter suggests that attitudes about the system, and not positions on specific issues, motivated voters throughout this period. When confronted with a choice between candidates representing alternative political and socioeconomic systems, voters are less likely to make decisions based strictly on personal, egocentric preferences.[38] Rather, during such periods of revolutionary change, when national politics impact directly on individual lives, we should expect voter concerns about systemic issues to be more salient than "pocketbook" issues.

This framework for understanding Russian politics suggests that Russian voters should be inclined to make choices based more on expectations about the future than on merely short-term calculations about past events, economic or otherwise.[39] During static periods, studies of American voting behavior have demonstrated that voters are most likely to make electoral decisions based on evaluations of past outcomes rather than future policies.[40] At the same time, advocates of the retrospective voting hypothesis have recognized specific conditions in which such behavior is less likely. As Morris Fiorina writes, "traditional retrospective voting should be most evident on issues that are not bound up in strongly held ideologies and/or among citizens who not conceptualize political affairs in ideological terms. Conversely, I doubt that the traditional theory of retrospective voting will shed much light on the behav-

[37] Author's interview with Aleksandr Oslon, president of the Foundation of Public Opinion and chief pollster for the Yeltsin campaign in 1996 (December 13, 1996). See also William Zimmerman, "Foreign Policy, Political System Preference, and the Russian Presidential Election of 1996," AAASS paper, November 16, 1996.

[38] On the differences between the "personal experiences" hypothesis and the "national assessments" hypothesis, see Roderick Kiewiet, *Macro-economics and Micro-politics*, pp. 15–20.

[39] For arguments that treat voters as prospective, concerned more with the national economy than with personal economic circumstances, see MacKuen, Erikson, and Stimson, "Peasants or Bankers?"; Kiewet, *Macro-economics and Micro-politics*; and Kinder and Kiewiet, "Sociotropic Politics: The American Case," pp. 129–162.

[40] Fiorina, *Retrospective Voting in American National Elections*; V. O. Key, *The Responsible Electorate* (New York: Vintage, 1966); and Anthony Downs, *An Economic Theory of Democracy* (New York: Harper and Row, 1957).

ior of the highly ideological or the disposition of issues considered touch-stones of particular ideologies."[41] The political context in Russia after the collapse of the Soviet Union constituted one of these rare, highly ide-ological electoral settings identified by Fiorina. The assumption of prospective voting does not mean that the past is not important, since voters do not make prospective calculations in a historical void. On the contrary, a voter's best information about the future is based on past experiences. In the Russian case, most voters (except the youngest) had lived in both the communist and post-communist systems. In making cal-culations about the expected utility of these systems in the future, there-fore, they were able to compare systems and did not have to believe necessarily in campaign promises about future policies.

This argument about Russia's revolutionary transition also suggests why party identification should not be an important determinant of voter behavior during this period, especially in binary voting situations.[42] The crystallized divide between those for and against the "revolution" impeded interest-based party development and the emergence of third candidates. When politics are polarized, all ideological differences, class divisions, religious affiliations, and ethnic identities are subsumed by two broad categories – reform or antireform, status quo or status quo ante.

The general profiles of the two electoral camps – "communists" and "democrats" – are distinct. Younger voters have tended to vote for reformist candidates, while older voters have tended to vote for com-munist candidates.[43] Urban voters have been more likely to vote for reformist candidates, while rural voters have been more likely to vote for communist candidates. Richer voters have tended to support reform-ers, while poorer voters have tended to back communist candidates.[44]

---

[41] Fiorina, *Retrospective Voting in American National Elections*, p. 15.

[42] Colton, in *Transitional Citizenship*, identifies the early effects of partisanship on voting. These effects are still infant, however, as the party system is still weak and candidates often run without identifying with a party (e.g., Yeltsin in 1996). Moreover, the litera-ture on American elections suggests that a generation must pass before party identifi-cation plays a salient role, as the party label is usually passed through families. See Part 3 of Warren Miller and Merrill Shanks, *The New American Voter* (Cambridge, Mass.: Harvard University Press, 1996).

[43] This is a generalization. Upon closer inspection, one can identify a good deal of support for Yeltsin from older voters. For an incisive dissection of the Yeltsin coalition, see Jerry Hough and Susan Goodrich Lehmann, "The Mystery of Opponents of Economic Reform among the Yeltsin Voters," in Mathew Wyman, Stephen White, and Sarah Oates (eds.), *Elections and Voters in Post-Communist Russia* (Northhampton, Mass.: Edward Elgar Publishers: 1998), pp. 190–227.

[44] For analysis of these socioeconomic factors, see Colton, *Transitional Citizenship*, Chapter 4, and Stephen White, Richard Rose, and Ian McAllister, *How Russia Votes* (Chatham, N.J.: Chatham House Publishers, 1997).

2. PRESIDENTIAL VERSUS PARLIAMENTARY ELECTIONS

Polarization in Russian politics has not always appeared to produce polarized electoral outcomes. For instance, the bipolar logic of Russian electoral politics was not readily apparent in the three parliamentary elections during the 1990s. The alleged dissipation of polarized politics in these elections compelled some analysts to suggest that the 1996 presidential election would also be shaped by multiparty politics.

Such analyses, however, failed to account for how institutions shape choices and outcomes. In particular, Russia's presidential electoral law structured the vote in 1996 differently than the rules that guided parliamentary elections in 1995 and 1993.[45] Most importantly, Russia's parliamentary elections stimulated fragmentation and proto-party development, while the presidential election reinforced the polarizing tendencies in society already identified.[46] The same was true in the 1999–2000 electoral cycle.

While half of Russia's parliamentary seats were allocated in single-mandate districts, the other half were determined by a national system of proportional representation (PR) in 1993, 1995, and 1999 parliamentary votes. As in other countries, Russia's PR system encouraged the proliferation of political parties and provided few incentives for party consolidation.[47] By contrast, presidential elections tend to produce two-party systems, majoritarianism, and polarization.[48] This is because the electoral district magnitude for electing a president is usually one – that is, the entire country chooses one person for president. Elections in which only one candidate can win create strong incentives to consolidate alliances and narrow the field before the vote, pushing political systems toward bipolarity and majoritarianism.[49] Because the winner takes all for

---

[45] See especially Robert Moser, "The Electoral Effects of Presidentialism in Post-Soviet Russia," *The Journal of Communist Studies and Transition Politics*, Vol. 14, No. 1/2 (1998), pp. 54–75.

[46] Juan Linz, "Presidential or Parliamentary Democracy: Does It Make a Difference?", and Arend Lijphart, "Presidentialism and Majoritarian Democracy," in Juan Linz and Arturo Valenzuela (eds.), *The Failure of Presidential Democracy: Comparative Perspectives, Vol. I* (Baltimore: Johns Hopkins University Press, 1994).

[47] This tendency is often called Duverger's law or Duverger's rule. See Maurice Duverger, *Political Parties: Their Organization and Activity in the Modern State* (New York: Wiley, 1954).

[48] See Linz, "Presidential or Parliamentary Democracy"; Matthew Shugart and John Carey, *Presidents and Assemblies* (Cambridge: Cambridge University Press, 1992), Chapter 2; and Giovanni Sartori, *Comparative Constitutional Engineering* (New York: New York University Press, 1994), Chapter 5.

[49] Lijphart, "Presidentialism and Majoritarian Democracy," especially pp. 97–99. See also Gary Cox, *Making Votes Count: Strategic Coordination in the World's Electoral Systems* (Cambridge: Cambridge University Press, 1997), Chapter 6.

a fixed term, presidential elections become more important and confrontational than other kinds of elections. As Juan Linz notes, "The zero-sum game raises the stakes in a presidential election for winners and losers, and inevitably increases the tension and the polarization."[50] The combination of the extreme ideological divide between Yeltsin and Zyuganov and Russia's super-presidential system that grants extraordinary powers to the president magnified the stakes of this presidential election even more.

Within the universe of presidential systems, some electoral laws are more narrowing than others.[51] Plurality systems in which the winner is the candidate with the most votes after one round of voting generate the strongest incentives for two-party systems. Electoral laws that include a run-off between the top two candidates in the first round tend to be more fragmentary, as they offer incentives for candidates to stay in the race. For instance, in elections with a run-off, underdog candidates can hope to squeeze into the second round and then unite all forces that lost in the first round to produce a winning coalition in the second.[52] Between rounds, defeated candidates from the first round can attempt to trade their endorsement of one of the top two finishers in exchange for individual, ideological, or organizational gain.

Russia's presidential electoral law requires a run-off if no one receives more than fifty percent in the first round. Consequently, consolidation into large blocs need not take place before the first round. As no one expects any candidate to win more than fifty percent in the first round, this two-ballot system encourages "third-party" or "spoiler" candidates to remain in the race until the end.[53] In 1996, this two-ballot majoritarian system even raised the specter of surprise outcomes, whereby a newcomer such as General Lebed might sneak past Yeltsin in the first round and then defeat Zyuganov in a run-off.[54] Nonetheless, the more general polarizing effects of a presidential race, as opposed to a parliamentary party-list election, shaped the contours of this election.

---

[50] Linz, "Presidential or Parliamentary Democracy," p. 19.

[51] Shugart and Carey, *Presidents and Assemblies*, Chapter 8.

[52] Cox, *Making Votes Count*, pp. 231–233.

[53] The financial rules of the campaign further encouraged these candidates, as presidential hopefuls who pulled out before the first round were required to pay for the "free" television and radio time they had received as presidential candidates.

[54] This is how Alberto Fujimori emerged from nowhere to be elected president in Peru. The same pattern was repeated in Belarus when the relatively unknown Aleksandr Lukashenko won in a majority run-off system. On Fujimori, see Gregory Schmidt, "Fujimori's 1990 Upset Victory in Peru," *Comparative Politics*, Vol. 28, No. 3 (1996), pp. 321–354 and Shugart and Carey, *Presidents and Assemblies*, pp. 214–215.

The electoral cycle constitutes another institutional factor that influences electoral outcomes.[55] When parliamentary and presidential elections occur concurrently, they can influence each other. The converse is equally true. That Russia's presidential and parliamentary elections have not occurred at the same time helps to explain why the outcomes could vary so widely. In June 1991, during the referenda of April 1993 and December 1993, and again in the 1996 presidential votes, Yeltsin's participation and the binary nature of these votes helped to polarize the Russian electorate into two camps. When divided in such a way, majorities have coalesced consistently for Yeltsin and his policies. Conversely, in the 1993 and 1995 parliamentary elections, when Yeltsin did not participate and the number of choices on the ballot was greater than two, the outcome appeared to be less positive for liberal parties and candidates.[56] A similar effect occurred during the 1999–2000 electoral cycle. Even in the first round, the 2000 presidential vote was dominated by two candidates – Putin and Zyuganov.

Taken together, two factors – the polarizing effects of Russia's protracted transition and the different institutional effects of parliamentary versus presidential elections – combine to provide a basic explanation for Russian electoral outcomes over the last decade. However, a third factor – the candidates and their campaign strategies – also must be brought into the analysis to explain particular electoral outcomes. To illustrate how these three factors interact, the next sections discuss individual electoral outcomes over the first decade of competitive electoral politics in Russia.

3. THE 1989 ELECTIONS TO THE SOVIET CONGRESS OF PEOPLE'S DEPUTIES[57]

Elections to the USSR Congress of People's Deputies in 1989 were the first semicompetitive elections in Soviet history. Communist Party General Secretary Mikhail Gorbachev initiated these elections as a way

---

[55] Shugart and Carey, *Presidents and Assemblies*, Chapter 9.
[56] In the one election in which voters cast separate ballots in a binary, "presidential" way (the referendum on the constitution) and in a multiparty election (the parliamentary elections), the results varied. While over 50 percent of participating voters ratified the president's constitution in the referendum, only a third of these same voters supported pro-reformist political parties on the multiparty ballot.
[57] Complete results and discussion of this election and all others can be found in Michael McFaul and Nikolai Petrov (eds.), *Politicheskii Almanakh Rossii 1997* (Moscow: Moscow Carnegie Center, 1998). Other overviews of electoral behavior and electoral outcomes during this period include White, Rose, and McAllister, *How Russia Votes*; Colton, *Transitional Citizenship*; and Wyman, White, and Oates (eds.), *Elections and Voters in Post-Communist Russia*.

to stimulate support for his reform program, perestroika.[58] Unable to garner support for his reform ideas within the Party as a whole, Gorbachev hoped to resurrect the soviets as a set of state institutions that could assume governing power away from the Communist Party.[59]

These elections were only partially democratic. One-third of the 2,250 seats in the Congress were allocated to "social organizations," which included everything from the Communist Party of the Soviet Union to the Soviet Academy of Sciences.[60] All of the remaining seats, divided equally between districts determined by territorial divisions and districts carved according to population, were in principle open for contestation. In practice, however, the cumbersome electoral procedures, padded with several veto gates for the Communist Party, made the nomination of "democratic" challengers – that is, candidates outside of the *nomenklatura* system – nearly impossible.[61] To be nominated, candidates had to receive the endorsement of either a worker's collective or a public meeting of at least 500 people. After nomination, district electoral committees had the power to disqualify any candidate, a power exercised against almost half of all candidates.[62]

Nonetheless, these elections constituted a direct threat to CPSU elites, as only the Party's top 100 officials were "elected" through the social organization list.[63] The vast majority of local CPSU secretaries had to compete in contested elections, and the results were disastrous. Only nine out of thirty-two CPSU first secretaries won in contested races. Out of seventy-five secretaries running unopposed, six still lost because they

---

[58] On Gorbachev's political strategy, see Mikhail Gorbachev, *Memoirs* (New York: Doubleday, 1996) and Archie Brown, *The Gorbachev Factor* (Oxford: Oxford University Press, 1996).

[59] Anatolii Sobchak, *Khozhdenie vo Vlast'* (Moskva: Novosti, 1991).

[60] Some of these social organizations' seats were contested internally, including the famous battle for Andrei Sakharov's election within the Soviet Academy of Sciences. The CPSU list, however, was not competitive. After considering competitive elections within the Party, Gorbachev opted for the nomination of exactly 100 candidates to insure that the Party leadership received seats in the Congress. See Giorgii Shakhnazarov, *Tsena Svobody: Reformatsiya Gorbacheva Glazami ego Pomoshchnika* (Moscow: Rossika Zevs, 1993), pp. 74–75.

[61] For a chronicle of the electoral reform process leading up to the 1989 elections, see Peter Lentini, "Reforming the Electoral System: The 1989 Elections to the USSR Congress of People's Deputies," *The Journal of Communist Studies*, Vol. 7, No. 1 (1991), pp. 69–94. For a personal memoir of the election process, see Sobchak, *Khozhdenie vo Vlast'*, Chapter 2.

[62] See V. A. Kolosov, N. V. Petrov, and L. V. Smirnyagin (eds.), *Vesna 89: Geografiya i Anatomiya Parlamentskikh Vyborov* (Moskva: Progress, 1990).

[63] The Komosomol and official Soviet trade unions also were accorded seats, giving CPSU officials additional routes for securing a place in the new Congress without facing the electorate.

failed to receive the required 50 percent threshold of support.[64] The
failure of CPSU *nomenklatura* was most impressive in Leningrad, where
both the first and second secretaries as well as the majority of other
lower-level Party officials failed to win seats. More generally, these
elections brought new people into the Russian political process, as an
estimated 88 percent of successful candidates had been elected for the
first time.[65]

Although local CPSU leaders were humiliated, their losses did not
translate directly into gains for new political actors, or "democrats," as
they were then labeled.[66] Eighty-five percent of the new Soviet legislature
were members of the CPSU, while none at the time of elections was a
member of any alternative political party. The most successful candidates
in 1989 were CPSU officials such as Boris Yeltsin and Telman Gdlyan,
who had pushed for campaigns against corruption or advocated radical
reform from within the existing system. More moderate candidates dis-
tinguished themselves from other CPSU candidates by their degree of
enthusiasm for perestroika. At this early stage in the Soviet/Russian transition, polarization between "democrats" and "communists" did not
play an important role.

4. THE 1990 ELECTIONS TO THE RSFSR CONGRESS OF PEOPLE'S DEPUTIES

The 1990 elections for the Russian Congress of People's Deputies were
more democratic and more competitive than elections to the Soviet Congress the previous year.[67] Most importantly, the Russian electoral law did
not set aside any seats for "public organizations." Instead, all seats were
filled in first-past-the-post elections in two kinds of electoral districts –
one defined by the status of region (168 seats) and the other by number
of voters (900 seats). If no candidate won 50 percent approval in the
first round, a run-off between the top two finishers in the first round
occurred two weeks later.

Formally, parties did not compete in this election, as noncommunist
parties were just forming. Article 6 of the Soviet Constitution, which

[64] For details, see McFaul and Petrov (eds.), *Politicheskii Almanakh Rossii 1997*.
[65] White, Rose, and McAllister, *How Russia Votes*, p. 29.
[66] On the role of genuine outsiders in these elections, see Boris Kagarlitsky, *Farewell Per-estroika* (London: Verso, 1990).
[67] Surprisingly little has been written in either Russia or the West on these pivotal elec-tions. See Timothy Colton, "The Politics of Democratization: The Moscow Election of 1990," *Soviet Economy*, Vol. 6, No. 4 (1990), pp. 285–344. On the regional elections that occurred simultaneously with the national vote, important contributions include Gavin Helf and Jeffrey Hahn, "Old Dogs and New Tricks: Party Elites in the Russian Regional Elections of 1990," *Slavic Review*, Vol. 51, No. 3 (1992), pp. 511–530.

guaranteed the Communist Party of the Soviet Union the leading role in Soviet society, was reformulated in February 1990, only weeks before the vote, not giving new political parties enough time to organize. Nor did the printed ballot identify the party affiliations of candidates. Nonetheless, these elections stimulated an explosion of grassroots political activity throughout Russia.[68] The mere number of seats open for contestation meant that a large segment of the Russian population was involved in the nomination and campaign process. The nature of single-mandate elections, coupled with the absence of real political parties and a growing divide within the CPSU, meant that each district contest had its unique characteristics. At the same time, polarization first appeared in this vote. Two main camps formed – the "democrats" and the "communists."

The "democrats" – the label that both their enemies and friends adopted – had begun to organize as a united political force well before the spring of 1990.[69] In January 1990, these leaders met to plot campaign strategy for the upcoming spring elections. They founded a new organization, Democratic Russia, which assumed primary responsibility for coordinating candidate recruitment and campaign activity for Russia's nascent democratic movement. Anti-communist, anti–status quo, and even anti-Gorbachev sentiments were the common themes of Democratic Russia's "ideology of opposition," nothing more, nothing less.[70] The articulation of concrete alternative programs or appeals to special ethnic or class interests did not occur.

The Communist Party of the Soviet Union (CPSU) constituted the second main player in the 1990 elections. However, the CPSU did not participate as an electoral party, but as the representative of the ancien régime, or the incumbent "party of power" in contemporary Russian parlance. Moreover, because the CPSU leadership was split at the time between reformists and conservatives, the Party did not orchestrate a national electoral campaign. Gorbachev and his immediate circle devoted little attention to these elections, incorrectly assuming that

---

[68] For accounts, see M. Steven Fish, *Democracy from Scratch* (Princeton: Princeton University Press, 1993); Geoffrey Hosking, *The Awakening of the Soviet Union* (Cambridge, Mass.: Harvard University Press, 1991); and Michael Urban with Vyacheslav Igrunov and Sergei Mitrokhin, *The Rebirth of Politics in Russia* (Cambridge: Cambridge University Press, 1997).

[69] For details, see Michael McFaul and Sergei Markov, *The Troubled Birth of Russian Democracy: Political Parties, Programs, and Profiles* (Stanford: Hoover Institution Press, 1993).

[70] See Sergei Stankevich and Mikhail Schneider, *Rekomendatsii po Taktike Kandidatov Democraticheskogo Bloka i Ikh Kompanii, 1989–90 g.g.* (Moscow: Informtsentr Moskovskogo Narodnogo Fronta, 1990).

republican-level soviets were not as important as the USSR Congress of Peoples Deputies.[71] Under the banner of the Democratic Platform, many CPSU officials actually competed in these elections as challengers and opponents of the "party of power."[72]

Several nationalist individuals and organizations who did not identify with either Democratic Russia or the "party of power" competed in these elections. For instance, Alexander Rutskoi, the future vice president, ran as a leader of the patriotic group *Otechestvo*. On the whole, though, these groups played only a marginal role in these elections.[73]

Compared to the 1989 elections, the 1990 elections was regarded as a tremendous victory for Russia's "democrats." Though difficult to count, given Democratic Russia's decentralized organizational structure and the defection of many Democratic Russia candidates soon after the elections, democrats won roughly one-third of the 1,061 seats in the Russian Congress.[74] Communists won roughly 40 percent of Congress seats, while "centrists" occupied the *boloto* (the swamp) in the middle. Eighty-six percent of peoples' deputies were members of the CPSU – the same high percentage as a year before – but CPSU membership was no longer an accurate indicator of political affiliation. As in 1989, the geographic cleavages between "democrats" and "communists" were striking; Democratic Russia fared best in large urban areas, performing especially well in Moscow, Leningrad, and the Ural cities, while the communists dominated rural electoral districts.

The 1990 vote was a referendum on the status quo. In urban areas where people wanted more change, "democrats" won decisively. In rural areas where people feared change, communist candidates won. More sophisticated or more nuanced issues of political cleavage were not salient in this vote. This dichotomous spectrum also served to marginalize candidates or political groups that attempted to carve third posi-

---

[71] Many "democrats" also underestimated the importance of this Russian-level election and did not participate. At the time, the Russian Federation had almost no autonomy from the Soviet state.

[72] The history of the Democratic platform is chronicled in Chapter 5 of McFaul and Markov, *The Troubled Birth of Russian Democracy.*

[73] See U.S. Commission on Security and Cooperation, *Report on the Congress of People's Deputies Elections in the Russian Republic* (Washington, D.C.: March 28, 1990), p. 18.

[74] Authors' interview with Vladimir Bokser, one of the campaign organizers for Democratic Russia in this election (February 1997). The number of deputies who identified with Democratic Russia changed over time, depending on the nature of the crisis. See Thomas Remington, Steven Smith, Roderick Kiewiet, and Moshe Haspel, "Transitional Institutions and Parliamentary Alignments in Russia, 1990–1993" and Alexander Sobyanin, "Political Cleavages among the Russian Deputies," both in Thomas Remington (ed.), *Parliaments in Transition: The New Legislative Politics in the Former USSR and Eastern Europe* (Boulder, Colo.: Westview Press, 1994).

tions or different political issues, such as nationalists and social democrats. Proportional representation, which may have helped third parties develop, did not exist as part of the electoral system in 1990.

5. THE JUNE 1991 PRESIDENTIAL ELECTION

The Russian presidential campaign began immediately after the March 1991 referendum, in which 71 percent of voters supported the idea of the introduction of the office of the presidency.[75] Throughout this pivotal year, politics in Russia remained polarized, pitting Boris Yeltsin and Russia's "democrats" against the increasingly isolated Soviet president, Mikhail Gorbachev.[76] Beginning in January 1991, the Democratic Russia movement organized a series of mass actions in response to Gorbachev's increasingly conservative actions. This period of street mobilization culminated on March 28, 1991, when hundreds of thousands of Democratic Russia activists throughout Russia defied Gorbachev's ban on demonstrations to show their support for Boris Yeltsin. A month later, strikes by coal miners recharged the polarized context of all politics in Russia. Battle lines were drawn between the "democrats" created by popular support within society, and the "communists" entrenched in the state. This polarized context shaped the presidential campaign, pitting Yeltsin against everyone else.

Assuming that he could rely on the liberal, urban electorate, Yeltsin selected a moderate communist and nationalist – Colonel Alexander Rutskoi – as his running mate. Yeltsin campaign organizers believed that Rutskoi, as the head of the new parliamentary faction Communists for Democracy, would bring in votes from the moderate wing of the CPSU. As a decorated Afghan veteran, Rutskoi also was expected to help win Yeltsin votes from nationalists and military men.

Nikolai Ryzhkov, the former CPSU Politburo member and Soviet prime minister, represented the ancien régime in this vote. By this time, however, Ryzhkov was considered to be more conservative than his former ally and colleague Gorbachev. He hoped to win votes from those disenchanted with perestroika in general. Four other candidates qualified for the ballot – Vladimir Zhirinovsky, Aman Tuleev, Albert Makashov, and Vadim Bakatin. At the time, Yeltsin's campaign team believed that all of these candidates were being supported by the Soviet regime in order to appeal to different parts of Yeltsin's electorate.

---

[75] For a detailed account of the 1991 campaign, see Michael Urban, "Boris El'tsin, Democratic Russia and the Campaign for the Russia Presidency," *Soviet Studies*, Vol. 44, No. 2 (1992), pp. 187–207.

[76] The best chronology of this period is John Dunlop, *The Rise of Russia and the Fall of the Soviet Empire* (Princeton, N.J.: Princeton University Press, 1993).

Zhirinovsky was chosen to pull populist voters away from Yeltsin. Tuleev was to deliver the ethnic vote, Makashov the military vote, and Bakatin the "reformist" vote within the CPSU. Together, so the strategy went, this disparate group of candidates could cut deeply enough into Yeltsin's support to deny him a first-round victory.

Yeltsin, however, did win a first-round victory, capturing 59.7 percent of the popular vote, compared to 17.6 percent for Ryzhkov, a surprising 8.1 percent for Zhirinovsky, followed by Tuleev (7.1%), Makashov (3.9%), and Bakatin (3.6%). The vote reflected the crescendo of popular support for a change in the status quo. Voters wanted neither to return to the old communist order, nor to continue with Gorbachev's confused and muddled ideas euphemistically referred to as perestroika. Like the elections in 1989 and 1990, Communist Party elites saw this vote as a threat to their interests, while challengers to the Soviet communist system saw the vote as an opportunity to consolidate their new political power.

6. 1993 PARLIAMENTARY ELECTIONS AND CONSTITUTIONAL REFERENDUM

Between June 1991, the time of the last competitive national election in Russia of the Soviet era, and December 1993, when the first set of competitive elections in the post-Soviet era were held, monumental changes unfolded in Russia. After rebuffing an attempted coup in August 1991, Boris Yeltsin collaborated with his counterparts in Ukraine and Belarus to dissolve the USSR in December 1991. The following month, Yeltsin's new government in a now-independent Russia launched a radical economic reform designed to transform the Soviet command economy into a Russian market economy. Consumed by these two revolutionary tasks, Yeltsin did not pursue fundamental political transformation at the same time. He did not push to adopt a new constitution, he did not call for new elections, he did not create a new political party, and he left in place many political institutions and political leaders from the old order. Most saliently, Yeltsin did not threaten deputies in the Russian Congress or local CPSU elites with a new round of elections. The Congress assumed the role of parliament, while Yeltsin appointed several former CPSU first secretaries to the new position of head of administration in their regions.

Not surprisingly, Yeltsin's attempt to transform the economy and reconfigure the boundaries of the state stimulated resistance from elites and organizations that had benefited from the old order. The lack of change regarding the political system aided the conservatives' cause, as the Congress of People's Deputies soon became the leading institution opposing Yeltsin's revolutionary agenda. With no formal or even informal institutions to structure relations between the president and the Congress, polarization crystallized yet again, with both Yeltsin and the Congress claiming sovereign authority over Russian territory. This condition of dual sovereignty ended in bloodshed in October 1993, when Yeltsin defeated his Congress opponents by military force. No longer was Russia's revolution completely peaceful.

In his decree dissolving the Congress of People's Deputies, Yeltsin also called for immediate elections for a new bicameral parliament and a referendum to adopt a new constitution. These elections were held on December 12, 1993.[77] Different actors assigned different priorities to the four national ballots in December. For Yeltsin, the most important vote was for his new constitution, as this new basic law granted extraordinary powers to the president's office. Ratification of a new constitution also was seen as way to legitimate de jure the de facto shift in the balance of power that occurred in October between Yeltsin and his challengers. Unlike the votes in 1989, 1990, and 1991, Yeltsin used this election to reinforce (rather than challenge) the existing order. Strikingly, Yeltsin did nothing to influence the electoral campaigns for either house of parliament.

For regional elites, the upper house poll mattered most. Like Yeltsin's constitutional vote, this election offered these elites a mechanism to fortify their existing political power. The electoral regulations and the short campaign period aided incumbents tremendously. Rather than two single-mandate districts, each oblast, republic, and *krai* constituted one electoral district with two mandates. This electoral system helped incumbents avoid defeat, as name recognition alone virtually assured a sitting head of administration at least a second-place finish. The combination of a minimal registration period and a high signature requirement (2 percent of the region's total population) meant that with few exceptions only candidates supported by the local administration could get on the ballot.[78] In dozens of regions, three candidates made the ballot – two from the local administration and a third, unknown candidate allowed to register simply to insure that the electoral results were legitimate.

---

[77] The most comprehensive analysis of this election is Timothy Colton and Jerry Hough (eds.), *Growing Pains: Russian Democracy and the Election in 1993* (Washington, D.C.: Brookings Institution Press, 1998).

[78] At the same time that Yeltsin dissolved the Russian Congress of People's Deputies, dozens of local soviets were also disbanded. As the chair of these local legislatures was usually the leading opposition figure as well, these dissolutions robbed these potential challengers to local executive authorities of organizational and institutional resources to conduct a campaign only weeks before the 1993 vote.

For the Moscow political elite, and especially for Russia's "democratic" forces, the lower house or Duma vote was most important, as the new electoral system offered them a way to maintain or obtain a job within the state without winning a direct election.[79] Yeltsin's decree on elections stated that the lower house would be elected according to mixed system: half the seats (225) were to be determined by a majoritarian system in newly drawn electoral districts, while the other half (225) were to be allocated according to a system of proportional representation (PR). Parties had to win at least 5 percent of the vote to win seats on the PR ballot.[80]

The mixed electoral system, especially the PR ballot, created a new set for incentives for participants, as the imperative for unity in both the reformist and opposition camps appeared to wane. From the reformist side of the ledger, four electoral blocs once united in Democratic Russia qualified for the ballot: Russia's Choice, Yabloko, the Party of Russian Unity and Accord, and the Movement for Democratic Reform.[81] Generally, these party leaders believed that reformists would win more seats running as separate blocs rather than as one party or organization.

The communists, now considered the "opposition," also ran as two parties, the Communist Party of the Russian Federation (CPRF) and the Agrarian Party of Russia (APR). This split, however, had little to do with ambition, and more with survival. In October 1993, Yeltsin temporarily banned the CPRF for the second time in as many years, raising uncertainty about whether they would be allowed to compete in the December elections. In case the CPRF were to be disqualified, communist leaders organized the APR as a alternative party. Several communist leaders from the Congress of People's Deputies, including Vladimir Isakov and Ivan Rybkin, ran on the APR ticket, even though neither had any special interest in agrarian affairs. Like their opponents, communist leaders also reasoned that the sum of these two class-focused parties would be greater than one united party. Russia's most militant communist groups, such as Viktor Anpilov's Working Russia, boycotted these elections, as they did not want to legitimate Yeltsin's unconstitutional act of disbanding the Russian Congress of People's Deputies.

---

[79] Roughly 40 percent of all those deputies elected to the Duma through the PR system were from Moscow.

[80] For elaboration, see Robert Moser, "The Impact of the Electoral System on Post-Communist Party Development: The Case of the 1993 Russian Parliamentary Elections," *Electoral Studies*, Vol. 14, No. 4 (1995), pp. 377–398.

[81] Nikolai Travkin's Democratic Party of Russia was also a member of Democratic Russia, though the relationship between the two organizations had been difficult from the beginning.

Russia's political space also expanded in 1993 to include several centrist groups, such as the Civic Union, Women of Russia, and the Democratic Party of Russia, as well as several smaller electoral blocs devoted to specific issues. In the wake of the tragic October events, these organizations asserted that Russia needed a third, moderate political force to temper the polarized politics of "democrat" versus "communist." Several nationalist parties also tried to register on the PR ballot, but only Vladimir Zhirinovsky's LDPR succeeded. For the first time in Russia's electoral history, parties dominated the menu of electoral choices.

The results of the first two ballots went according to plan. In the referendum, 58.4 percent supported Yeltsin's constitution, while 41.2 percent opposed. Turnout was reported at 54.8 percent, insuring that the referendum was valid, although several observers, including party representatives to the Central Electoral Commission, asserted that the turnout was egregiously inflated by the Yeltsin Administration.[82] Claims of falsification tarnished the validity of the referendum vote, prompting some to assert that these elections were less free and fair than previous votes.[83]

Elections to the upper house, the Federation Council, also produced few surprises. Of the sixty-six heads of administration who competed in these elections, only eight lost. Strikingly, only a handful of winning candidates were not affiliated with either the old or new regional elite, both of which came from the former CPSU *nomenklatura*. With few exceptions, successful candidates were not members of new parties; they were members of either the Russian Communist Party (a successor organization to the seventy-year-old CPSU) or the ruling "party of power." The unique (for Russia) two-mandate ballot also created opportunities for falsification. Unaccustomed to voting for more than one candidate, many voters marked only one name, giving local electoral commissions an easy opportunity to mark a second name during ballot counting.[84]

The one extraordinary electoral outcome in 1993 occurred on the PR ballot for the Duma, in which Vladimir Zhirinovsky's extreme nationalist LDPR won almost a quarter of the popular vote. At the same time, Russia's Choice secured a paltry 15 percent, less than half of what was expected, and all of the other "democratic" parties combined won less

---

[82] A. A. Sobyanin and V. G. Sukhovolskii, *Demokratiya, Ogranichennaya Falsifikatsiyami: vybory i referendumy v Rossii v 1991–1993 gg.* (Moscow: Planning Group on Human Rights, 1995).

[83] Ibid.

[84] See Michael McFaul and Nikolai Petrov (eds.), *Politicheskii Al'manakh Rossii 1996* (Moscow: Moscow Carnegie Center, 1997).

than 10 percent of the popular vote. The Russian Communist Party and their rural comrades, the agrarians, combined for less than 20 percent of the vote, while new "centrist" groups combined for nearly a quarter of the vote.

This vote, more than any previous vote in Russia, was dominated by new political forces, as leaders of several of the successful electoral blocs from the "reformist," "centrist," and "nationalist" camps were not closely affiliated with the former Soviet *nomenklatura*.[85] As expected, the PR vote had stimulated the formation of a party system at the national level in Russia. Quite unexpectedly, however, an extreme nationalist party initially dominated the belated arrival of multiparty politics in Russia.

Elections for Duma single-mandate seats did not parallel the PR ballot at all. Instead, successful candidates were predominantly from the old Soviet *nomenklatura*, though at a significantly lower level than their counterparts in the Federal Council. In rural areas, Agrarian candidates won, in the "red belt" (Russia's poor rust-belt region), communists dominated, and in major urban areas, candidates supported by the local party of power prevailed. "Outsiders" – be they democrats, nationalists, neocommunists, or centrists – fared rather poorly. As party affiliation was not allowed on the ballot, parties did not play a significant role in determining single-mandate races.

Most interpretations of the 1993 elections focused on Zhirinovsky's phenomenal performance on the party list ballot.[86] Although he placed third in the 1991 presidential vote, Zhirinovsky and his party were not considered serious contenders in the 1993 vote. As late as mid-November, public opinion surveys assigned Zhirinovsky's Liberal Democratic Party less than 2 percent of popular support.[87] His sudden, dramatic surge in the final days of the campaign shocked everyone. Because he spouted venomous nationalist and racist rhetoric and criticized in equal measure the communists and the democrats, Zhirinovsky appeared to represent a new, third force in Russian electoral politics – militant nationalism.

---

[85] On the national party campaigns, see Michael McFaul, "Russia's Choice: The Perils of Revolutionary Democracy," Daniel Treisman, "Between the Extremes: The Moderate Reformist Blocs," and Evelyn Davidheiser, "Right and Left in Hard Opposition," in Colton and Hough (eds.), *Growing Pains*. On party development as a partial consequence of the election, see M. Steven Fish, "The Advent of Multipartism in Russia, 1993–1995," *Post-Soviet Affairs*, Vol. 11, No. 4 (1995), pp. 340–383 and Moser, "The Impact of the Electoral System on Post-Communist Party Development," pp. 377–398.

[86] For an excellent analysis of Zhirinovsky's surprising showing, see Davidheiser, "Right and Left in the Hard Opposition," pp. 177–210.

[87] VTsIOM, "Predvybornaya Situatsiya v Rossii," (Moscow: VTsIOM, 1993).

With the advantage of hindsight, however, Zhirinovsky's 1993 victory does not appear (yet) to mark the beginning of fascism's ascendance in Russia.[88] Rather, Zhirinovsky was able to capture a large portion of Russia's opposition vote in 1993 because Russia's communists were still regrouping after their October 1993 defeat. Everyone expected that the opposition or protest vote in 1993 would be large. After two and a half years of falling production, double-digit inflation, and general economic uncertainty, Russian voters should have been expected to follow their counterparts throughout Eastern Europe and vote against those affiliated with the incumbent government. Unlike the standard East European experience, however, Russia's communists had not reorganized as social democratic parties after their fall from power. Rather, they continued to advocate a return to the past, a position that helped to precipitate the October 1993 standoff between Yeltsin and the Congress of People's Deputies. In the immediate aftermath of this mini–civil war in downtown Moscow, the communists were in disarray. Weeks before the December vote, it was uncertain whether members of the Russian Communist Party would even be allowed to participate. By contrast, Zhirinovsky offered voters opposed to the Yeltsin government a new choice, beyond the tired and disappointing communists. Zhirinovsky's brilliant television campaign, the first real mass media campaign in Russian electoral history, established his party as the most aggressive and abrasive enemy of the status quo.[89] Finally, the importance of the PR electoral system cannot be underestimated in accounting for Zhirinovsky's surprising victory. Capturing almost a quarter of the popular vote on the party list, the LDPR won fifty-seven seats in the Duma through the PR system.[90] In single-mandate races, however, LDPR candidates won only five seats in the Duma and no seats in the Federal Council. In a pure majoritarian electoral system, the Liberal Democratic Party would have won fewer than ten seats in the parliament.

Zhirinovsky's stellar campaign performance accentuated the abysmal effort of Russia's democrats. Their greatest mistake was to run as four blocs instead of one. These divisions had several deleterious

---

[88] It is still too early to tell whether fascism in Russia has faded forever. After all, Weimar Germany completed several rounds of elections before Hitler took over. On the comparison, see Stephen Hanson and Jeffrey Kopstein, "The Weimar/Russia Comparison," *Post-Soviet Affairs*, Vol. 13, No. 3 (1997), pp. 252–283 and Stephen Shenfeld, "The Weimar/Russia Comparison: Reflections on Hanson and Kopstein," *Post-Soviet Affairs*, Vol. 14, No. 4 (1998), pp. 355–368.
[89] Zhirinovsky appeared more often on television than any other electoral bloc leader. See *Russian Media Coverage of the Campaign* (Moscow: Russian-American Press and Information Center, December 15, 1993).
[90] *Rossiiskaya Gazeta*, December 28, 1993, pp. 2–3.

consequences. Symbolically, the vote for democratic parties on the PR ballot was split, making the democratic defeat look worse than it really was. An electoral outcome in which a democratic coalition won 34 percent of the popular vote – the total won when adding Russia's Choice, Yabloko, PRES, and RDDR together – would have looked very different from the December outcome, in which the leading democratic party won only 15 percent.[91] Additionally, in dozens of single-mandate races, multiple candidates from democratic parties split the vote, allowing both communists and nationalists to win the seat with sometimes as little as 15 percent of the popular vote. Finally, running as opponents, democratic leaders Gaidar and Yavlinsky spent most of their campaign time quarreling with each other rather than criticizing more serious opponents, such as Zhirinovsky.

Additionally, the campaign performance of the leading democratic bloc, Russia's Choice, must fully be appreciated to explain their poor showing.[92] The biggest setback to Russia's Choice was Yeltsin's nonparticipation. As mentioned earlier, Yeltsin's only concern in these elections was the ratification of his constitution; he showed little interest in the Duma election. Without Yeltsin, Russia's Choice was forced to run the uncharismatic, unpopular Yegor Gaidar as their bloc's leader. Russia's Choice also lacked organization. Founded only two months before the election, the bloc tried to fuse together government elites (both federal and regional) with grassroots activists from the Democratic Russia movement. The alliance had limited success, resulting in a disorganized and divided campaign effort.

Finally, Russia's Choice had no campaign strategy. As devised by the bloc's chief strategist, Gennadii Burbulis, the strategy of Russia's Choice was to create the image of a party already in power that was destined to win in December. As a result, leaders of Russia's Choice promised nothing to voters, and instead insolently asserted that there was no alternative to their course of reform but a return to the old communist system. To the extent that they did explain the government's plan of action, Gaidar and others delivered long, monotonous, academic discussions about the macroeconomics of financial stabilization – a stark contrast to the pithy, pointed ads run by Zhirinovsky.

Zhirinovsky's shocking victory on the PR ballot dominated news reports and analyses of the December 1993 vote, overshadowing the

---

[91] Regarding parliamentary seats, the democrats would have acquired an additional ten or eleven seats had RDDR and its 4 percent of the popular vote been part of one of the pro-reform parties that did exceed the 5 percent threshold.

[92] For elaboration, see McFaul, "Russia's Choice: The Perils of Revolutionary Democracy," pp. 115–140.

results of the other three national votes that also took place. When the other three votes are taken into account, the results look rather different. Most strikingly, in the one vote that was binary, a solid majority supported the new constitution. As there was little time for voters to become acquainted with the details of this basic law, this vote has to be considered yet another referendum on Yeltsin's reform or on the revolution more broadly understood. The results showed that Russian society was still divided between those supporting and those opposing "reform," but that a slight majority favored moving forward rather than turning back. Second, elections in single-mandate districts for the Duma and for seats in the Federal Council were dominated by elites, from either the new party of power – those affiliated with Yeltsin – or the old party of power – the CPSU. New or outside challengers, including those from the LDPR, won only a handful of seats, and party affiliation played little role in deciding these races. When taken together, the 1993 vote was not as different from other Russian votes as it first seemed.

7. 1995 PARLIAMENTARY ELECTIONS

Yeltsin's decree triggering the 1993 vote stipulated that the first elected parliament was only an interim body whose term expired after two years. Almost immediately after the 1993 vote, therefore, preparations were under way for the next election. As this next parliamentary vote came only six months before the next scheduled presidential election, many thought of the 1995 ballot as a primary for the bigger electoral prize in 1996.[93]

The political context of the 1995 vote was less polarized than that of previous Russian elections. For the first time in Russia's tumultuous democratic transition, a legitimate constitution was in place. Although communists criticized the document for giving too much power to the president, they neither challenged the basic law's legitimacy nor practiced extra-constitutional politics. Yeltsin's willingness to abide by the new rules of the game was more equivocal, as dramatized most tragically by his decision to invade Chechnya in December 1994. Throughout the 1995 campaign, however, he and his administration abided by the electoral law passed by the Duma.

---

[93] For detailed accounts of the 1995 vote, see Michael McFaul, *Russia between Elections: What the 1995 Parliamentary Elections Really Mean* (Washington, D.C.: Carnegie Endowment for International Peace, 1996); Nikolai Petrov (ed.), *Parliamentskie vybory 1995 goda v Rossii* (Moscow: Moscow Carnegie Center, 1996); Laura Belin and Robert Orttung, *The Russian Parliamentary Elections of 1995* (New York: M. E. Sharpe, 1997); and Stephen White, Mathew Wyman, and Sarah Oates, "Parties and Voters in the 1995 Russian Duma Election," *Europe-Asia Studies*, Vol. 49, No. 5 (1997), pp. 767–798.

The new electoral system differed from Yeltsin's 1993 decree in several important ways.[94] Most importantly, the new law stipulated that the Federal Council would be composed of two officials from each subnational territory – the chairman of the legislature and the head of administration. Both of these officers had to be elected locally, unleashing a slew of gubernatorial elections throughout the country in the fall of 1996. This new formulation meant that Duma elections occurred independent of votes for Federal Council members. This cardinal change represented a major victory for regional elites, as it offered them a legal way to retain both local power and a legislative voice in national affairs. This new electoral law also insured that parties would continue to play only a marginal role in the affairs of the upper house, as few oblast and *krai* governors or republican presidents publicly identified with a political party.

The new election law on the formation of the Duma did not change fundamentally, despite numerous attempts by Yeltsin's supporters to increase the number of single-mandate seats and decrease the numbers of seats allocated according to proportional representation. Yeltsin's team proposed these amendments as a way to impede party development and thereby to increase disorganization within the Duma. Based on the 1993 experience, Yeltsin's aides also reasoned that deputies from single-mandate districts were both more likely to be controlled by regional elites and more prone toward cooperation with the Kremlin. Conversely, half of the Duma deputies who voted on this new electoral law made it to the parliament on the PR list, and thus had no incentive to decrease the number of PR seats available in the next round of elections. In this legislative battle, the Duma prevailed.

Two other electoral rules had major consequences. First, the new law stipulated that candidates running in single-mandate districts could specify their party affiliations on the ballot. Second, it was decided that parliamentary elections and presidential elections would not occur simultaneously. This meant that Yeltsin did not have to associate with any one electoral bloc competing in the parliamentary vote.

The number of electoral blocs that registered for the ballot rose dramatically, from thirteen in 1993 to forty-three in 1995. Party proliferation was greatest within the reformist and centrist blocs. Eight of the

---

[94] On the politics behind these changes, see Michael McFaul, "Institutional Design, Uncertainty, and Path Dependency during Transitions: Cases from Russia," *Constitutional Political Economy*, Vol. 10, No. 1 (1999), pp. 27–52 and Thomas Remington and Steven Smith, "Political Goals, Institutional Context, and the Choice of an Electoral System: The Russian Parliamentary Election Law," *American Journal of Political Science*, Vol. 40, No. 4 (1996), pp. 1253–1279.

new electoral blocs in 1995 were direct descendants of Russia's Choice from 1993, while an amazing twenty electoral blocs emerged from the Democratic Russia of 1991. Early in the campaign period, the Yeltsin Administration openly promoted the formation of two new electoral blocs, led by Viktor Chernomyrdin and Ivan Rybkin, that would be loyal to the Yeltsin regime. Chernomyrdin's Our Home Is Russia was supposed to represent the right-of-center, while Rybkin was ordered to form a left-of-center bloc. Both of these blocs were dominated by former CPSU apparatchiks who had switched allegiance to Yeltsin's consolidating "party of power." Leaders and parties that had emerged from the grass-roots movement Democratic Russia were not invited to join these new blocs. The gap between Yeltsin and the "democrats" was becoming increasingly wide.

Months before the 1995 vote, it became clear that the two parties initiated by the Yeltsin Administration were not capable of winning a majority between them. Subsequently, the Kremlin's strategy changed. Instead of seeking to organize a two-party system in which both parties would be loyal to the president, Yeltsin's team began to stimulate party proliferation. Yeltsin had institutional and political incentives to encourage fragmentation among his party supporters, as these divisions (1) weakened the Duma's effectiveness, (2) impeded the development of strong liberal political parties that could counter or constrain Yeltsin's own personal power, (3) discredited potential presidential candidates, including Viktor Chernomyrdin and Grigorii Yavlinsky, and (4) helped fuel support for Yeltsin own candidacy as the only person capable of uniting reformist forces and defeating the communists.[95] Yeltsin's team deemed fragmentation within Russia's reformist forces in the December 1995 elections to be especially important to Yeltsin's electoral prospects in the following year.[96] If Chernomyrdin, Yavlinsky, or Lebed had

---

[95] Institutionally, presidential systems in general encourage weak parties and fragmented party systems. See Lijphart, "Presidentialism and Majoritarian Democracy," p. 98.

[96] Author's interview with presidential advisor Giorgii Satarov, November 1995. According to some Kremlin officials, Yeltsin pressured Chernomyrdin to form a new bloc and run in the parliamentary elections as an act of self-destruction. Strikingly, Yeltsin neither endorsed the bloc during the parliamentary campaign nor associated with Our Home is Russia during his presidential bid. Officials in the Congress of Russian Communities (KRO) tell a similar story about presidential manipulation regarding General Lebed. While obviously the most popular and charismatic leader with KRO, Lebed was not allowed to campaign freely or to appear in major roles in KRO television advertisements. Instead, Yurii Skokov, Yeltsin's former head of the Security Council, dominated the campaign and overshadowed Lebed, resulting in a disappointing electoral result for KRO. Several original KRO officials were convinced that Skokov was sent by the Kremlin to deliberately sabotage Lebed and the bloc's electoral prospects.

emerged from the December 1995 elections as a viable competitor with a chance to defeat Zyuganov, reformist forces and voters quickly would have gravitated to one of them and not Yeltsin. In 1995, it must remembered, Yeltsin polled even with or sometimes behind these potential challengers from the reformist or anticommunist side of Russia's political ledger.

Competition for the nationalist vote also increased when several new nationalist and patriotic groups appeared on the ballot in 1995, including, most importantly, the Congress of Russian Communities headed by Yurii Skokov and General Alexander Lebed, *Derzhava* led by former vice president Aleksandr Rutskoi, and Power to the People headed by former Soviet premier Nikolai Ryzhkov and Sergei Baburin.

Comparatively, the communists maintained their unity between elections. Viktor Anpilov's radical Working Russia was the only major new electoral bloc to compete in 1995 for the communist vote. Moreover, the Russian Communist Party had devoted tremendous energy and resources between 1993 and 1995 to rebuilding their party organization throughout Russia.[97] Building upon networks and structures that remained from several decades of Communist Party rule in Russia, the CPRF used the resources accorded to the party by the Duma to strengthen regional party organizations during the two-year interval between parliamentary votes. Entering the 1995 campaign season, the CPRF boasted the largest and most efficient organization in Russia.

This organizational work paid off, as the CPRF made impressive gains over its 1993 showing by winning almost a quarter of the popular vote and thereby reclaiming its role as the leader of the opposition. Buoyed by party identification on the ballot, CPRF candidates also dominated single-mandate races, winning an astonishing fifty-eight seats. Zhirinovsky won less than half his 1993 total, but still placed second with 11 percent of the popular vote. On the other side of the ledger, Viktor Chernomyrdin's Our Home Is Russia was the only "reformist" party to break into the double digits. Grigorii Yavlinsky's Yabloko, the self-proclaimed leader of Russia's democratic opposition, won 7 percent, well below expectations and almost a full percentage point below Yabloko's 1993 showing. However, former acting prime minister Yegor Gaidar and his Democratic Choice of Russia (DVR) suffered the greatest setback in 1995, winning only 3.9 percent of the popular vote, less than one third of their 1993 total.

Most analysts interpreted these results as a victory for hard-line forces, a major setback for democratic parties, and a firm rebuff to both Yeltsin

---

[97] See Joan Barth Urban and Valerii Solovei, *Russia's Communists at the Crossroads* (Boulder, Colo.: Westview Press, 1997), Chapter 6.

and Prime Minister Chernomyrdin.[98] When framed through a bipolar lens, however, the 1995 vote looked very similar to previous elections. The Communist Party doubled its share of the popular vote, but their victory came at the expense of their rural comrades, the Agrarian Party, and Vladimir Zhirinovsky's Liberal Democratic Party. The Agrarians performed so poorly that they failed to cross the 5 percent threshold needed to win PR seats. The combination of a communist surge, an agrarian collapse, and Zhirinovsky's comparatively poorer showing meant that the total votes cast for opposition parties had changed only marginally in two years.

The same stability of voter attitudes is found when comparing results from 1993 and 1995 on the other side of the ledger. In 1993, Gaidar's Russia's Choice, Yavlinsky's Yabloko, and the now-defunct Russian Movement for Democratic Reforms combined to win 28 percent of the popular vote. In 1995, Chernomyrdin's Our Home Is Russia, Yabloko, and Russia's Choice together collected 21 percent of the vote. An additional 7 percent of the vote was divided among small reformist parties, meaning that roughly 30 percent of the vote in 1995 went to reformist parties.

Two significant changes, however, did occur in 1995. First, the balance of support within these two broad camps of voters changed considerably. Within the opposition camp, the communists improved dramatically over 1993, while the Agrarian Party and Zhirinovsky won less than half of their 1993 support in 1995. Within the reformist camp, the newly created Our Home Is Russia electoral bloc gained at the expense of Yegor Gaidar's Democratic Choice of Russia. Leaders and parties from the old Soviet *nomenklatura* now dominated both the "reformist" and "opposition" wings of Russia's polarized political spectrum. On both sides new political actors with weak ties to the old Soviet elite – be it Zhirinovsky, Yavlinsky, or Gaidar – had been pushed even further toward the margins.

A second shift since 1993 was the collapse of electoral support for apolitical, ideologically vague "centrist" parties and blocs. Whereas these kinds of parties and personalities won almost a quarter of the popular vote on the party list ballot and roughly a third of the single-mandate seats in 1993, they were obliterated in 1995 on both ballots.[99] Once again, Russian politics looked increasingly bipolar, not multipolar.

---

[98] Reddaway, "Red Alert"; Hough, Davidheiser, and Lehman, *The 1996 Russian Presidential Election*; Peter Stavrakis, "Russia after the Elections: Democracy or Parliamentary Byzantium?", *Problems of Post-Communism*, Vol. 43, No. 2 (1996), pp. 13–20; Andrei Zhukov, "Yeltsin's Three Blows," *Prism*, Vol. II, No. 6, part 2 (March 22, 1996); and Dmitri Glinski, "Yeltsin's Reelection Campaign: A Big Boost to the Communist Cause," *Prism*, Vol. II, No. 7, part 3 (April 4, 1996).

[99] For elaboration, see Michael McFaul, "Russia between Elections: The Vanishing Center," *Journal of Democracy*, Vol. 7, No. 2 (1996), pp. 90–104. For evidence sug-

8. 1996 PRESIDENTIAL ELECTION

For those who participated, the 1995 election served as a primary for the 1996 presidential election.[100] The parliamentary vote established Communist Party leader Gennadii Zyuganov as the leading candidate of the opposition, eclipsing the presidential aspirations of Vladimir Zhirinovsky as well as other potential opposition candidates from within the CPRF. On the reformist side, the results were much less conclusive, as neither Chernomyrdin, Yavlinsky, nor even Lebed emerged from the parliamentary vote as the undisputed leader. This flat showing by reformist candidates in 1995 created propitious conditions for Yeltsin to reassert his electoral image as the only candidate capable of defeating Gennadii Zyuganov.

Given the polarization among Russia's voters, only one candidate from the reform side of the ledger stood a chance of advancing past the first round of Russia's two-round presidential electoral system, as the other finalist was sure to be Gennady Zyuganov. By March 1996, polls unambiguously showed that Boris Yeltsin had captured that core reformist vote. To win in the second round, then, both Yeltsin and Zyuganov had to reach beyond their core supporters to the amorphous centrist voters who had not voted for either top contender in the first round. Yeltsin's strategy was successful; Zyuganov's strategy was not.

Yeltsin's strategy for capturing the center was simple – convince these voters that Yeltsin was the lesser of two evils and scare them into thinking that revolutionary turmoil would ensue should Zyuganov win. To make it easier for voters to support Yeltsin, his campaign first worked to eliminate or mute the president's negatives. First, Yeltsin's image had to be changed. The president lost twenty pounds, stopped drinking, and began to appear frequently in public again. Second, negative policies had to be changed. Public opinion polls demonstrated that two were most salient – unpaid wages and the war in Chechnya.[101] To create a sense of urgency around the issue, Yeltsin created a special government commission tasked with paying all salaries by April 1. In the process of fulfill-

gesting that the centrist vote did not dissipate, see Mikhail Myagkov, Peter Ordeshook, and Alexander Sobyanin, "The Russian Electorate, 1991–1996," *Post-Soviet Affairs*, Vol. 13, No. 2 (1997), pp. 134–167.

[100] For more elaboration see Michael McFaul, *Russia's 1996 Presidential Election: The End of Polarized Politics* (Stanford: Hoover Institution Press, 1997).

[101] Fond, "Obshchestvennoe mnenie," "Klyuchevye problemy predvybornoi kampanii v zerkale obshchestvennogo mneniya," *Rezultaty sotsiologicheskikh issledovannii*, No. 29 (May 10, 1996), pp. 4–5.

ing this goal, Yeltsin fired numerous regional government heads as well as several of his own cabinet officials, including deputy prime minister Anatolii Chubais.[102]

Yeltsin also raised pensions, increased salaries of government employees (including military personnel), and began doling out government transfers on the campaign trail. Yeltsin addressed his other big negative at the end of March, when he pledged to end the war in Chechnya. In May, the first Russian troops began to leave.

Parallel to this positive campaign to remake Yeltsin's image, policies, and government, Yeltsin's team also unleashed a hard-hitting negative media blitz against communism. The Yeltsin campaign successfully defined the election as a referendum on seventy years of Soviet communism, and deftly avoided letting the vote be about Yeltsin's record.[103] As defined by the mass media (virtually monopolized by Yeltsin), this election was not between two individuals, but between two ways of life. When defined in these terms, the majority of Russia's centrist voters opted for the current course of reform, rather than a return to the past. To communicate this message, the Yeltsin campaign spent millions of dollars on television time, radio programs, and printed material.

The last component of Yeltsin's campaign strategy was a pact with General Alexander Lebed, which was consummated in March. Lebed agreed to join Yeltsin's government between the first and second rounds of the presidential election. In return, Yeltsin's campaign gave their financial allies the green light to support Lebed's presidential campaign and also allowed Lebed to appear in mass media outlets loyal to (if not outright controlled by) Yeltsin. The Lebed deal not only helped Yeltsin to win additional votes between rounds, but also effectively squelched a possible "third force" alliance between presidential hopefuls Lebed, Yavlinsky, and Svyatoslav Fyodorov.

Zyuganov started his presidential campaign in a much stronger position than Yeltsin. In the wake of his party's 1995 electoral victory, Zyuganov began the 1996 campaign with 25 percent of the population already pledged to vote for him in June; Yeltsin's popular support in January was in the single digits. To win a majority of votes in the second round, however, Zyuganov and his campaign understood that they had

---

[102] In later March, Chubais nonetheless returned to the Yeltsin team to run the campaign.

[103] This account of Yeltsin's campaign strategy comes from dozens of interviews with Yeltsin campaign officials, including Igor Charities, Aleksandr Oslon, Georgii Satarov, and Vyacheslav Nikon (fall 1996). See also Alexia Machine, Andrei Zapeklyi, and Nikita Tyukov, *Rossiya: Presidenskaya Kampaniya – 1996* (Moscow: SPIK-Tsentr, 1996).

to move beyond their traditional opposition electoral base and capture a segment of the so-called centrist vote.[104] In plotting their strategy, they misread this part of the electorate. Zyuganov's strategists erroneously believed that Russia's political spectrum consisted of three parts – "democrats," "communists," and "nationalists." To reach beyond his core communist supporters, therefore, Zyuganov championed national- ist and patriotic themes rather than economic issues or social- democratic slogans.[105] This strategy partially succeeded, in the sense that Zyuganov did receive more support in the second round than commu- nist parties had won in previous elections. Ultimately, however, Zyuganov's nationalist rhetoric frightened away centrist voters tired of confrontational politics and longing for stability.

Zyuganov's campaign also lacked the means to communicate to these centrist voters. Unlike any other party in Russia, the CPRF had the or- ganizational capacity to run a grassroots, door-to-door campaign. As demonstrated by the high voter turnout in rural areas, these methods proved extremely effective in mobilizing loyal communist supporters. However, these tactics were ineffective at reaching new, undecided voters, who generally obtained their political information from television. Because the Communist Party had limited financial resources, no expe- rience in using television for campaign purposes, and limited access to Russia's pro-Yeltsin television networks, Zyuganov failed to communi- cate to these centrist voters. In the second round, this segment of Russia's electorate voted overwhelmingly for Boris Yeltsin. Yeltsin captured 54 percent of the popular vote, compared to 40 percent for Zyuganov.

Compared to the 1995 parliamentary vote, this election was marred by several irregularities. Most dramatically, Yeltsin enjoyed total control of the national television airwaves. Every nightly news program reported favorably, and often, on the Yeltsin campaign, while either ignoring or airing negative news about other candidates. Second, Yeltsin's campaign grossly violated the campaign spending limit of three million dollars. Backed by every major financial and industrial group in the country, the Yeltsin campaign enjoyed a limitless budget, spending by some estimates $500 million on the reelection effort.[106] Third, there were scattered

[104] See the interview with Valentin Kuptsov, Zyuganov's campaign manager, in *Vek*, June 14, 1996, p. 5.
[105] See especially Gennady Zyuganov, speech before the fourth Party conference, February 15, 1996, reprinted in *Informatsionnyi byulleten'* (CPRF), No. 2 (35) (February 20, 1996) and Zyuganov's campaign platform, *Rossiya, Rodina, Narod! Predvybornaya platforma kandidata na post prezidenta rossiiskoi federatsii G.A. Zyuganova*, reprinted in *Zavtra*, No. 12 (120), p. 3.
[106] Lee Hockstader and David Hoffman, "Yeltsin Campaign Rose from Tears to Triumph," *The Washington Post*, July 7, 1996, p. A1.

reports of falsification throughout Russia, but especially in the national republics, where vote swings away from Zyuganov between rounds were dramatic. In Tatarstan, for instance, Zyuganov won fewer votes in the second round than he had in the first.

Finally, throughout the entire campaign period, Yeltsin government officials openly advocated the postponement of the vote altogether. Observers began to insist that Yeltsin planned to remain in power no matter what the electoral outcome.[107] While Yeltsin ultimately abided by the electoral process and fired from his administration the advocates of postponement, this specter of postponement cast a long, undemocratic shadow over the electoral process. Retrospectively, some communist campaign officials asserted that Zyuganov essentially gave up toward the end of the race, believing that he had no chance of taking power.[108]

The 1996 presidential vote reaffirmed Russia's divided and polarized electorate. When offered only two choices, a majority once again opted for reform over regress. The balance of support for both positions had not changed appreciably over previous binary votes. In contrast to the electoral history of most of post-communist Europe, Russian voters opted to retain their first democratically elected leader for a second term.

9. THE END OF POLARIZATION: THE 1999–2000 ELECTORAL CYCLE

For the first seven years of competitive elections in Russia, candidates and voters were divided between those who defended the old Soviet order and those who opposed it. This observation is extraordinary in two respects. The first is the length of time that this cleavage issue dominated Russian electoral politics. In most successful transitions to democracy from communist rule, the communist/anticommunist cleavage no longer remained significant after the first election. In Russia, this divide continued to shape electoral contests several years after the collapse of Soviet communism in 1991. The second extraordinary aspect of Russia's polarized electorate has been how stable the balance of support between the two camps has remained. Again, in other successful transitions to democracy from communist rule, electoral preferences have changed considerably in a short period of time, moving from overwhelming support for anticommunists in the first round, to support for incumbent challengers in the second vote, and then swinging back to those originally affiliated

---

[107] Lilia Shevtsova, "Yeltsin ostanetsya, dazhe esli proigraet," *Nezavisimaya gazeta*, April 26, 1996, p. 3.

[108] Author's interviews with three CPRF campaign officials who asked not to be identified (July 1996).

with the "democratic revolution" in the third round. In Russia, however, voter preferences have been frozen into two camps, with only marginal changes in the level of support for each over the past several years. This stability in electoral preferences is especially striking when contrasted with the tremendous socioeconomic and political changes that unfolded during this period.

This stable polarization was prolonged principally by the lack of agreement regarding the new political and economic rules of the game in the post-Soviet period. Whereas successful democratic transitions in the former communist world reached a minimum level of consensus regarding the basic contours of the new political and economic system during, or quickly after, the communist collapse, Russian elites were slower to agree. Yeltsin's victory over his opponents in the fall of 1993 – his second such victory in as many years – shifted the balance of power in favor of the new order. The ratification of a new constitution soon thereafter further helped to consolidate a new political order. Nonetheless, Zyuganov's Communist Party still looked like an antisystemic organization throughout the 1996 presidential campaign.[109] Only after Zyuganov's electoral defeat in 1996 did the communist/anticommunist divide begin to subside.

The 1999 Parliamentary Vote

The withering of this divide changed Russian electoral politics thereafter. In the 1999 parliamentary vote, the waning of polarization allowed new centrist coalitions – Fatherland and Unity – to emerge and capture a much greater proportion of the popular vote than in 1995 or 1993. More generally, all of Russia's parties appeared to gravitate toward the center in this election. Cleavage issues were much harder to identify. In comparing party platforms written for the 1995 parliamentary elections to those written for the upcoming election in December, the growing convergence among party position on virtually every major issue was striking.[110] In 1995, fundamental debates could be discerned regarding the nature of the economy, the war in Chechnya (the first war), and foreign policy. In the 1999 campaign, only the real specialist could identify different positions regarding these issues. To be sure, Yabloko eventually

---

[109] By contrast, former communists in Eastern Europe abandoned their commitment to the *ancien régime* and became social democratic parties almost immediately after the first election. See Michael Waller, "Party Inheritances and Party Identities," in Geoffrey Pridham and Paul Lewis (eds.), *Stabilising Fragile Democracies: Comparing New Party Systems in Southern and Eastern Europe* (London: Routledge, 1996), pp. 23–43.

[110] See Tatyana Krasnopevtseva, "Comparing Party Platforms," Russia's 1999 Duma Elections: Pre-election Bulletin No. 1 (Moscow: Moscow Carnegie Center, December 2, 1999).

did adopt a unique position in opposition to the war in Chechnya (though Yavlinsky originally supported the Russian military response), and the Communist Party of the Russian Federation (CPRF) still advocated a greater role for the state in the economy than did the Union of Right Forces. Likewise, the Liberal Democratic Party of Russia (LDPR) and the CPRF promoted a much more ethnic-based version of nationalism than did Yabloko or the Union of Right Forces. But in comparison to 1995, the similarities between programs were much more striking than the differences.

At the same time, the 1999 parliamentary vote demonstrated that the levels of electoral identification for Russia's "old" parties remained similar to those in earlier parliamentary votes. The CPRF won almost exactly the same percentage, improving just slightly over its 1995 showing. Yabloko lost a percentage point – a big blow to the party, but a small variation when compared to the Yabloko totals in 1995 or even in 1993. The Union of Right Forces performed surprisingly well in 1999, though the total electoral support in 1995 (when adding together the small blocs that divided their vote in 1995) is not that different than in 1999. Zhirinovsky's LDPR suffered a sharp decline and lost nearly half its electoral support, suggesting that the LDPR may be the weakest of these four "old" parliamentary parties. As a whole, though, what is most striking about these results is the stability, not volatility, of aggregate support.[111] Three of these parties won plus or minus five percentage points of what they won in 1995. Given all that had happened in Russia over the previous fours years – the 1996 presidential election, the August 1998 financial crash, rotating prime ministers, and the wars in Kosovo and Chechnya – these numbers represent stability on a par with other European PR parliamentary democracies.

The 2000 Presidential Vote

In the summer of 1999, Russian electoral politics looked like they might catch up with the faster East European transitions from communism. With the battle over communism finally over, electoral politics were no longer polarized between advocates of two antithetical systems. This end of polarization appeared to create a window of opportunity for those opposed to the Yeltsin regime, as electoral analysts expected the Russian voters to behave more retrospectively in the 2000 election. And the record for Yeltsin and his allies did not look good. In August 1998, Russia had endured a major financial meltdown that punctuated one of

---

[111] Of course, aggregate stability does not mean that individuals are consistently supporting the same parties. Measurement of individual voters' preferences must be discerned from national surveys.

Table 1.2. Results of party-list voting in Russian Duma elections (as percentage of national PR vote), 1995 and 1999

Political Party/Bloc	1999	1995
Communist Party of the Russian Federation (CPRF)	24.29%	22.7%
Yabloko	5.93%	7.0%
Union of Right Forces	8.52%	3.9% (Democratic Choice of Russia)
		8.1% (all right-wing parties)[a]
Liberal Democratic Party of Russia/Zhirinovsky Bloc	5.98%	11.4%
Unity (Medved')	23.32%	N/A
Fatherland-All Russia	13.33%	N/A
Our Home Is Russia	1.2%	10.3%
"None of the above" and parties below 5%	18.63%	49.6%

[a] "All right-wing parties" includes: Democratic Choice of Russia (3.86%), Forward Russia! (1.94%), Pamfilova-Gurov-Lysenko (1.6%), and Common Cause (0.7%).

the longest and steepest economic declines in history. Most voters were dissatisfied with the status quo, disliked Yeltsin, and wanted change. While Zyuganov's negative ratings were too high for him to take advantage of this anti–status quo sentiment, former prime minister Yevgeny Primakov looked to be in a prime position to capture the protest vote.

Several factors converged in the summer and fall of 1999, however, to allow Yeltsin's choice as his successor, Vladimir Putin, to be elected president in March of the following year. These factors helped to turn the 2000 election into another vote about the future instead of an evaluation of the past. The first important new factor was the Chechen military incursion into Dagestan in the summer of 1999 and the Russian response. The invasion, followed shortly thereafter by terrorist attacks on apartment buildings in Moscow and elsewhere, made the Russian people feel like a nation under siege.[112] Society demanded a response from its leaders, and Prime Minister Putin responded. The relatively more successful campaign and the limited media scrutiny of the war helped to make this second Chechen war more popular than the first and

[112] We still do not know who actually is responsible for these terrorist bombings, but we do know how society reacted to these actions.

to deliver a very positive approval rating to Putin. By the end of 1999, he enjoyed an astonishing 72 percent approval rating.[113]

Putin's decisive response to the sense of insecurity that prevailed in Russia in the fall of 1999 is the reason why he initially rose in the polls. Yet his Chechnya policy is not the only factor that enabled Putin to maintain a positive approval rating throughout the spring of 2000. Other factors – more psychological than material or issue-based – also came into play. Putin symbolized for voters the end of revolution. For the first several years of the 1990s, Russian politics was polarized by the struggle between communists and anticommunists. In contrast with the more successful transitions from communist rule in Poland or Hungary, in Russia the debate about communism as a political and economic system continued for many years after the Soviet collapse. A period of volatile and unpredictable politics resulted. In his last years of power, Yeltsin further fueled political instability by constantly changing prime ministers. Putin's coming to power signaled for many an end to this volatile period and the advent of the "Thermidor" of Russia's current revolution. Putin's youth and energy also provided a striking contrast to his old and sick predecessor. Voters welcomed this generational change. In focus groups commissioned by the author in December 1999 and March 2000, Russian voters uniformly stated that Putin's youth was a positive attribute.

Putin's lack of a record as a public leader also helped, allowing voters to project onto him their wishes and desires for the future. With the exception of his policy toward Chechnya, he was a tabula rasa on which voters could write what they wanted. In focus groups commissioned on the eve of the presidential election, participants had a long and diverse list of expectations about Russia's future under Putin's leadership, which included everything from order in Chechnya, respect for Russia on the international stage, and a crackdown on crime, to higher pensions, a better educational system, and more job opportunities for young people. In other words, his supporters were casting their votes for Putin as a future leader, not supporting him for his past achievements, ideological beliefs, or policy positions. Understanding this mood in the Russian electorate, Putin and his campaign managers deliberately refrained from articulating a program or set of policies before the election.[114]

This motivation on the part of Putin voters was radically different from what we witnessed among Yeltsin supporters in 1996. In that

---

[113] Agentstvo regional'nykh politcheskikh issledovanii (ARPI), *Regional'nyi Sotsiologicheskii Monitoring*, No. 49 (December 10–12, 1999), p. 39. Sample size: 3,000 respondents in 52 Federation subjects.

[114] Author's interview with Putin campaign manager, Mikhail Margelov (February 2000).

election, voters knew exactly what they were getting with Yeltsin and had no illusions about a more promising future. In 1996, people were voting against communism, supporting the lesser of two evils. In the spring of 2000, Putin supporters had a much more positive assessment of their leader and were much more optimistic about the future. They were motivated more by this emotional feeling about the future than by individual material interests, ideological beliefs, or party identification. For instance, when asked in a January 2000 poll about their attitudes concerning Russia's political future, 41 percent of respondents believed that the new year would be an improvement over the previous year, while only 9 percent believed that the political situation would worsen. Similarly, 39 percent of respondents believed that the economy would improve in 2000, while only 12 percent believed that it would worsen.[115] The last time that Russians had been so optimistic about the future was the fall of 1991.

Another important reason why Putin won was the weak competition he faced. The Communist Party of the Russian Federation (CPRF) continued to dominate the space of opposition parties in Russian electoral politics in this electoral cycle, yet it had not generated new leaders or a new image. To be sure, the CPRF's economic platform in the 1999 parliamentary election and 2000 presidential election was considerably more market-friendly than the communist ideas the party had advocated in 1995 and 1996. Zyuganov tried to look and sound more modern, and even appeared on a campaign poster with young people. Yet, Zyuganov failed to reach beyond his loyal electorate in the March 2000 vote. And strikingly, no new outside challenger to the Kremlin moved in to fill the void. Grigory Yavlinsky also competed again in the 2000 presidential election, but only managed to capture his core electorate. The one challenger who had a chance of mobilizing the opposition vote was former prime minister Yevgeny Primakov. When Yeltsin fired him as prime minister, Primakov's popularity soared, and many regional leaders and part of the Moscow elite rallied to his cause. But during the 1999 parliamentary elections, the Kremlin's media empire launched a full-scale negative campaign against Primakov and his electoral bloc, Fatherland–All Russia. With varying degrees of truth and evidence, the Kremlin's media accused the former prime minister of being a feeble invalid, a lackey of NATO, a Chechen sympathiser, a closet communist, and a destabilizing force in international affairs who had ordered the assassination attempt against Georgian president Eduard Shevardnadze. This smear campaign, in combination with Putin's spectacular rise in popularity, helped to

---

[115] FOM, *Soobshcheniya fonda "Obshchestvennoe mnenie,"* 001 (536) (12 January 2000), p. 30.

undermine popular support for Fatherland–All Russia, which won only 12 percent of the popular vote. Subsequently, Primakov opted not to compete in the presidential election, leaving Zyuganov as the strongest challenger to Putin in the race. This is exactly the kind of competition that Putin wanted to face.

A final factor facilitating Putin's election was Yeltsin's decision to resign as president on December 31, 1999, a move that made Putin acting president and moved the electoral calendar forward three months. Putin benefited enormously from the shortened campaign period and his new presidential status. On election day – March 26, 2000 – he captured 52.9 percent of the vote in the first round, compared to Zyuganov's 29.2 percent. No other candidate broke into the double digits.

10. CONCLUSION

The end of polarized politics after the 1996 presidential election represented a positive development for electoral politics in Russia. Votes structured as simply a choice "for the revolution" or "against the revolution" offered voters limited opportunities to express their preferences through the ballot box. It is a healthy sign that Russian political parties with identities and positions on policy issues have begun to consolidate. In the 1999 parliamentary vote, the contours of a multiparty system appeared to be emerging.[116]

At the same time, the continued domination of the state's candidate in the 2000 presidential election suggests that the bipolar thaw may not necessarily produce better choices for the highest elected office in Russia. Yeltsin appeared to win in 1996 because the choice was framed as a choice for or against the revolution, and the majority opted to proceed with change rather than to restore the old regime. Putin appeared to win in 2000 because he also managed to convince a majority of voters that those in power were better at moving Russian forward than those challenging from the outside. If the next several presidential elections produce the same result, however, then we will need to seriously reevaluate the meaning of elections in the Russian political system.

[116] For elaboration, see Michael McFaul, *Party Formation and Non-Formation in Russia*, Working Paper No. 12 (Washington: Carnegie Endowment for International Peace, May 2000), pp. 1–31.

2

Executive–Legislative Relations in Russia, 1991–1999

Robert G. Moser

During the initial years of Russian statehood, the tumultuous relationship between the executive and legislature in Russia seemed to be the major impediment to democratic consolidation. In the First Russian Republic the power struggle that developed between President Boris Yeltsin and the Congress of People's Deputies led to a constitutional crisis that was ultimately decided by the use of force in the streets of Moscow. In the wake of this constitutional crisis, President Yeltsin, unfettered by the need for approval from the disbanded legislature or a constitutional assembly, constructed a political system that concentrated most formal powers in the executive branch. However, contrary to the initial expectations of the Yeltsin team, new parliamentary elections did not produce a more reform-minded legislature.

Instead, throughout the Yeltsin years the Russian state continued to be divided between a "reformist" president and an "antireformist" legislature. Opposition parties solidified control over the State Duma in 1995, and the Communist Party of the Russian Federation (CPRF) emerged as the largest political party in the country and the center of an opposition that controlled a working legislative majority. Six months later President Yeltsin managed to win reelection despite initially anemic approval ratings. Thus, conflict remained a constant feature of Russian executive-legislative relations, waxing and waning depending on the domestic political environment and leaders' strategic decisions. Institutional design was also a crucial factor, as the ambiguous division of powers of the First Russian Republic was replaced by a constitutional structure that gave most powers and advantages to the president in hopes of mitigating conflict by firmly establishing one branch, the presidency, at the top of the system.

The conventional wisdom has been that in adopting a system with an extremely strong executive, Russia increasingly showed tendencies toward authoritarianism or at least dysfunctional democracy.[1] Russia seemed to fit Guillermo O'Donnell's definition of a delegative democracy "that rest[s] on the premise that whoever wins election to the presidency is thereby entitled to govern as he or she sees fit constrained only by the hard facts of existing power relations and by a constitutionally limited term in office."[2] In delegative democracies, other political institutions such as parliaments and constitutional courts are viewed "as unnecessary encumbrances" that are ignored or intentionally undermined.[3]

The behavior of the Yeltsin government seemed to fit this depiction in certain key respects. Yeltsin issued executive decrees on several important matters rather than build the coalitions necessary to gain majority support for parliamentary legislation.[4] More importantly, Yeltsin was able to effectively dominate the other half of Russia's dual executive branch, frequently changing the line-up of the government at will in fitful attempts to jump-start or throttle economic reform. As Yeltsin became more frail and politically isolated in the latter years of his rule, his interest in and control over policy waned. But he continued to manipulate government appointments in a cynical attempt to maintain his grip on power by ridding himself of potential rivals.

This depiction of executive-legislative relations in Russia captures a significant part of the truth about Russia's emergent political system during the Yeltsin years, rightly placing much of the blame for Russia's tortuous evolution away from communism on the arbitrary rule of an unpopular president who was out of touch with the needs of the citizenry. But this depiction also tends to exaggerate the power of the president and the marginality of the State Duma and the Federation Council, the upper house of the legislature made up of powerful regional leaders. Both placed significant checks on presidential power. Emphasis on conflict and formal constitutional powers neglects the elements of compromise that can also be found in the system. From the beginning of his presidency, Yeltsin showed some vulnerability to the will of the legislature and the overall balance of political forces. In composing the government, Yeltsin was as apt to remove reformists in favor of more conservative politicians as the other way around (especially after

[1] See Paul Kubicek, "Delegative Democracy in Russia and Ukraine," *Communist and Post-Communist Studies*, Vol. 27, No. 4 (1994), pp. 423–441.
[2] Guillermo O'Donnell, "Delegative Democracy," in Larry Diamond and Marc F. Plattner (eds.), *The Global Resurgence of Democracy*, 2nd ed. (Baltimore: Johns Hopkins University Press, 1996), p. 98.
[3] O'Donnell, "Delegative Democracy," p. 99.
[4] Eugene Huskey, "Democracy and Institutional Design in Russia," *Demokratizatsiya: The Journal of Post-Soviet Democratization*, Vol. 4, No. 4 (1996), p. 462.

electoral defeats of reformists in parliamentary elections). For its part, the State Duma also dropped the penchant for confrontation of its predecessor and developed mechanisms for more cordial relationships with the executive branch. When healthy, Yeltsin managed to develop a working relationship with the Duma on key issues through the use of cooptation of the Duma leadership, patronage, and personal relations.[5] His successor, Vladimir Putin, although much more popular and powerful than Yeltsin in his final years, has continued to chart a relationship with the legislature based on a combination of coercion and cooptation.

The oscillations in the relative power of the executive and the legislature during the first decade of post-communist Russian statehood suggest that the constitutional framework remains a work in progress. But the care taken by both the president and the legislature to avoid a constitutional breakdown similar to what occurred in the fall of 1993 also suggests that a modicum of political stability has been established.

This chapter will examine the peaks and valleys of executive-legislative relations, pointing out the sources of conflict and conciliation in Russia's emergent constitutional system. The Russian political system will be depicted as one with a dual personality, one that has shown signs of a destructive concentration of power in the chief executive but also an unwillingness and inability of the president to use the full force of his constitutional powers to enforce his will and rule around and over the head of parliament. Two interrelated variables are deemed crucial in determining the fluctuation between cooperation and conflict in executive-legislative relations.

First, the broader political context in which both institutions are embedded has determined the relative power and legitimacy of the two branches among the mass public and other important political actors. Actors in both branches have made their strategic decisions about whether to confront or compromise with the other side depending on their perceptions of their own popular legitimacy and that of their opponents. Thus, it was not an accident that Yeltsin moved on the Congress of People's Deputies in the wake of his successful showing in the national referendum held in April 1993. Nor was it a coincidence that he compromised on his prime ministerial candidate in 1998 in the midst of a devastating economic crisis, when his popularity and the legitimacy of his reform program were in tatters.

Second, the institutions structuring politics have made a crucial difference in the level and character of conflict and compromise between

[5] Huskey, "Democracy and Institutional Design in Russia."

the two branches of power. Formal constitutional divisions of power have been important in resolving or escalating executive-legislative conflict but have not been the only institutions affecting the relationship. The electoral system, internal policy-making processes in the State Duma, and formal and informal levers over patronage wielded by the president have also channeled behavior and regulated conflict.

I argue that Russia's constitutional structure has produced a strong *presidency* but not always a strong *president*. This argument does not deny the concentration of power in the hands of the president or its often deleterious effects on democratic processes and consolidation in Russia. But it does compromise aspects of a characterization of Russia as some type of electoral autocracy.[6] First, despite his formidable constitutional powers, President Yeltsin was not always able to rule without regard for the State Duma and public sentiment. He had to compromise with the Duma and other political forces (e.g., regional leaders and the military) on numerous crucial issues. His failure to construct a presidential party or stable majority coalition in parliament seriously undermined his ability to govern. He did not use his decree-making powers to fully compensate for this. Second, popular sentiment and social interests played an important role in the relative influence of the two competing branches of power, despite the insulation from societal pressures that the president enjoys due to his fixed term in office. Yeltsin was severely weakened and occasionally marginalized as a political force due to his illegitimacy (along with his physical infirmity), despite the fact that his constitutional powers were never diminished. The Russian experience shows that even in "super-presidential" systems, leaders need to be build consensus and coalitions to wield power over an extended period.

The resignation of Yeltsin and the rise of a healthy and popular president in Vladimir Putin further strengthen this argument. During his first months in office, President Putin quickly established himself as the most powerful actor in the political system. His broad popular and elite support has thus far enabled Putin to use the substantial powers of the presidency to much greater effect than Yeltsin had, particularly in the latter years of his rule. In particular, Putin's strong standing with the public has virtually remade executive-legislative relations. The 1999 parliamentary elections produced a sea change in the composition of the State Duma that has provided Putin with a supportive legislative majority. This was brought about in large part by Putin's coattails, which carried Unity, the newest party of power formed only months before the parliamentary election, to its position as the second largest party in

---

[6] For this characterization see Peter Rutland, "A Flawed Democracy," *Current History*, Vol. 97, No. 621 (October 1997), p. 318.

the Duma. While the waning years of the Yeltsin presidency showed how limited strong constitutional powers could be in the hands of an unpopular, embattled president, the Putin years may show how powerful such powers can be in the hands of a healthy and popular chief executive.

This chapter is divided into four sections. The first section defines and compares the institutional design of presidential, parliamentary, and semi-presidential regimes. The second section is a discussion of the debate surrounding institutional design of executive-legislative arrangements and its purported effects on democratization. The third section outlines the major contours of executive-legislative relations, from the First Russian Republic through the resignation of President Yeltsin at the end of 1999 and the initial months of the presidency of Vladimir Putin. In the fourth and concluding section, I argue that the greatest obstacle to more stable and cooperative executive-legislative relations is a lack of party institutionalization. Whatever the constitutional structure, effective political parties are needed to aggregate social interests, construct majority coalitions, and serve as a bridge between the executive and legislative branches of power. I conclude with some speculations on the future of executive-legislative relations in the post-Yeltsin era.

PARLIAMENTARY, PRESIDENTIAL, AND SEMI-PRESIDENTIAL SYSTEMS

One of the basic differences among democratic polities is the constitutional division of powers between the executive and legislative branches. Democracies have been divided into three major constitutional types: presidential, parliamentary, and semi-presidential. These types are often further differentiated by the type and degree of political power held by each competing branch of government. Thus, presidential systems can be "strong" or "weak" depending on the amount of decree-making powers, for example. Semi-presidential systems, which divide executive power between a president and a prime minister, can provide either the president or parliament with the upper hand in initiating and maintaining executive authority.

Presidential and parliamentary systems are differentiated by the origination and maintenance of executive power.[7] In terms of origination, in

---

[7] These defining characteristics are based on Arend Lijphart, "Presidentialism and Majoritarian Democracy: Theoretical Observations," in Juan Linz and Arturo Valenzuela (eds.), *The Failure of Presidential Democracy: Comparative Perspectives* (Baltimore: Johns Hopkins University Press, 1994), pp. 91–105 and Matthew Soberg Shugart and John M. Carey, *Presidents and Assemblies: Constitutional Design and Electoral Dynamics* (Cambridge: Cambridge University Press, 1992), Chapter 2.

presidential systems the chief executive is elected directly by the people (or indirectly through an electoral college), while in parliamentary systems the chief executive is chosen by the legislature. The maintenance of executive power is also quite different in presidential and parliamentary systems. In presidential systems, the executive is elected to a fixed term in office and can be removed only through the arduous and infrequently used process of impeachment. In parliamentary systems, the executive, chosen by the legislature, maintains his or her power only through maintenance of majority support in parliament. Prime ministers can be removed by a no-confidence vote.

While other characteristics may distinguish presidential and parliamentary systems, these two criteria capture their essential differences. In parliamentary systems, legislative and executive power are fused. The chief executive is not separately elected; rather, he or she is the head of the majority party or coalition in parliament. Not only does the chief executive emanate from the legislature, he or she is maintained in office through majority confidence in parliament. Executive authority is dependent upon legislative support. Not so in presidential systems. The chief executive is independent of the legislature. The president has his or her own electoral mandate directly from the people and maintains power with or without legislative support. A separation of powers and system of checks and balances govern relations between independent executive and legislative bodies.

As the definition suggests, semi-presidential systems combine elements of both parliamentary and presidential systems. Like presidential systems, there is a president who is elected directly by the people for a fixed term and is not easily removed from office before that term is completed. But, like parliamentary systems, semi-presidentialism also includes a prime minister and a government that requires the support (or at least the tolerance) of a majority in the legislature. Under semi-presidential systems, the president is also frequently given the power to dissolve the legislature and call new elections, which is denied to presidents in pure presidential systems. The key question for semi-presidentialism is how well the two executives (president and prime minister) coexist. When the president and a majority in the legislature are from the same party, there should be relative consensus in the system. But when the presidency and the legislature are controlled by rival parties, "cohabitation" becomes a potential problem. In this situation there is a potential crisis over who should be the predominant executive power – the president, who was elected directly by the people, or the prime minister, who enjoys majority confidence of the legislature.

Scholars basically agree that semi-presidential systems work best when they alternate between presidential and parliamentary characteristics.[8] In the paradigmatic case of the French Fifth Republic, the dilemma of cohabitation was resolved through the development of a norm according to which the French president ceded predominant executive authority to the prime minister if his party did not have a majority in the assembly. Thus, the French model of semi-presidentialism "contains a safety valve that avoids the clash and crises of two popularly elected legitimacies by permitting the political system to function now as a presidential system, now as a parliamentary system."[9] Shugart and Carey conceptualize this distinction by distinguishing between semi-presidential systems that alternate between parliamentary and presidential tendencies, like the French Fifth Republic, which they call "premier-presidential" systems, and semi-presidential systems that provide more powers to the president to form and dismiss the government in the face of parliamentary opposition, calling these regimes "presidential-parliamentary." Premier-presidential systems are deemed more conducive to stability and democratic consolidation than presidential-parliamentary systems, because the former give the legislative branch priority over the maintenance of the government. Presidential-parliamentary systems raise the likelihood of interbranch conflict, because the government is dependent on the support of both the president and parliament.[10] In such systems conflict is more endemic, because presidents have much more leverage to maintain governments that do not actually have the support of a stable majority coalition in the legislature. Yet, the system still gives parliament the power to vote no confidence in the government and may force a showdown between the parliament and the president. The difficult relationship between executive and legislative branches in Russia often has been attributed to the fact that it employs a presidential-parliamentary constitutional system.[11]

CONSTITUTIONAL DESIGN AND DEMOCRATIZATION

Constitutional design has become a central theme in the burgeoning literature on democratic transition and consolidation. Juan Linz launched a flurry of scholarship on the relative merits of presidential and parliamentary systems for democratizing countries with a seminal article that

[8] See Shugart and Carey, *Presidents and Assemblies*, pp. 23–27. See also the discussion in Juan Linz, "Presidential or Parliamentary Democracy: Does It Make a Difference?", in Linz and Valenzuela (eds.), *The Failure of Presidential Democracy*, pp. 48–62.
[9] Ezra N. Suleiman, "Presidentialism and Political Stability in France," in Linz and Valenzuela (eds.), *The Failure of Presidential Democracy*, pp. 137–162.
[10] Shugart and Carey, *Presidents and Assemblies*, pp. 23–27.
[11] Matthew Soberg Shugart, "Executive-Legislative Relations in Post-Communist Europe," *Transition*, Vol. 2, No. 25 (1996), pp. 6–11.

outlined several defects in presidential systems that made them less conducive to democratization than parliamentary systems.

Linz's critique of presidentialism can be summarized in four main defects. First, the direct election of both the legislature and the chief executive creates a dual legitimacy in which both branches of government can claim a popular mandate. This enhances the possibilities for executive-legislative conflict, while at the same time failing to provide any mechanism for resolving conflicts by prioritizing one branch over the other. Parliamentary systems do not suffer from this dual legitimacy. Only the legislature is directly elected by the people. The chief executive has no claim to a direct mandate, and the no-confidence vote makes the parliament the ultimate power in the system. Second, the fixed term of office in presidential systems makes the system rigid and unable to adapt to changes in the political environment. A president who proves to be unpopular or incompetent cannot easily be removed from office, and the country is stuck with its choice until the next scheduled election, barring the very unusual step of impeachment. The no-confidence vote of parliamentary regimes allows the system to adapt to changing levels of support for the chief executive. Third, the system is very majoritarian in nature, making the election of the president a winner-take-all enterprise in which, regardless of whether he or she receives a majority of the popular vote, the winner of a presidential election takes over all of the executive branch. There is no mechanism for coalition government to reflect minority support for a president, nor is there a place in the system for losing presidential candidates. Fourth, the direct election of a president personalizes the contest, increasing the possibility that political outsiders can use charisma or mass disaffection with the political system to successfully run for the highest office in the land. This increases the possibility of demagoguery and incompetence on the part of the chief executive and increases the likelihood that the president will not have the support of a majority party or coalition in the legislature.[12]

A growing number of scholars have come to the defense of presidentialism, or at least of semi-presidential systems.[13] Defenders of presidentialism highlight the efficient representation provided by the stark choice of a directly elected executive and argue that the drawbacks of the system

---

[12] Linz, "Parliamentary or Presidential Democracy: Does It Make a Difference?" See also Scott Mainwaring and Matthew S. Shugart, "Juan Linz, Presidentialism, and Democracy: A Critical Appraisal," *Comparative Politics*, Vol. 29, No. 4 (1997), pp. 449–471.

[13] For a good overview of this debate, see Linz and Valenzuela (eds.), *The Failure of Presidential Democracy*; Shugart and Carey, *Presidents and Assemblies*; and Giovanni Sartori, *Comparative Constitutional Engineering* (New York: New York University Press, 1994).

commonly cited operate predominantly when the president faces a contrarian legislative majority.[14] Such an occurrence can be minimized with institutional engineering such as semi-presidential arrangements, electoral systems that constrain the number of parties in the system, and simultaneous presidential and parliamentary elections.[15] Moreover, attempts to systematically test the influence of constitutional design on democratization through quantitative cross-national analysis have produced conflicting or ambiguous results. The correlation between presidential or parliamentary systems and democratic stability seems to be greatly influenced by the cases examined.[16]

One of the most promising lines of research in this area looks at the interrelationship between constitutional design and the nature of the party system. Mainwaring has shown that the defects ascribed to presidentialism by its critics are actually attributable to the combination of presidential systems and multiparty systems. When party systems take on a two-party character, the president is more likely to have support of a majority party in the legislature and the system resists the interbranch conflict that has jeopardized democratization in states with presidential systems and multiple parties.[17] Sartori has argued that successful parliamentary systems rely on institutionalized and disciplined parties that can create and maintain majority coalitions. Without an institutionalized party system, parliamentary systems tend to produce assembly government that is wracked by instability, deadlock, and ineffective policy making.[18] Building on this scholarship, I will argue that an underdeveloped party system lies at the heart of problems in executive-legislative relations in Russia. A weak and fractionalized party system made it difficult for President Yeltsin to cobble together stable majority coalitions in parliament, pushing him to rule by decree rather than through the

[14] Scott Mainwaring, "Presidentialism, Multiparty Systems, and Democracy: The Difficult Equation," *Comparative Political Studies*, Vol. 26, No. 2 (1993), pp. 198–230.
[15] Shugart and Carey, *Presidents and Assemblies*, pp. 207–258.
[16] For a sample of conflicting findings regarding the impact of institutional design using cross-national analysis, see Alfred Stepan and Cindy Skach, "Presidentialism and Parliamentarism in Comparative Perspective," in Linz and Valenzuela (eds.), *The Failure of Presidential Democracy*, pp. 119–136; Shugart and Carey, *Presidents and Assemblies*, pp. 38–43; and Timothy J. Power and Mark J. Gasiorowski, "Institutional Design and Democratic Consolidation in the Third World," *Comparative Political Studies*, Vol. 30, No. 2 (1997), pp. 123–155.
[17] Mainwaring, "Presidentialism, Multiparty Systems, and Democracy: The Difficult Equation," pp. 198–230.
[18] Giovanni Sartori, "Neither Presidentialism nor Parliamentarism," in Linz and Valenzuela (eds.), *The Failure of Presidential Democracy*, pp. 112–115.

legislature. Moreover, weak parties have made it difficult for a coherent and stable opposition to form that can effectively resist the concentration of power in the executive branch. This may be the most salient problem of the post-Yeltsin era now that a young and ambitious president has taken power.

While the nature of the party system mitigates the effects of constitutional design, the party system is in turn influenced by constitutional arrangements. Presidentialism tends to have two effects on party formation. With regard to party performance in the state, directly elected presidents tend to promote weaker, less cohesive parliamentary parties, while parliamentary regimes tend to promote much more disciplined parties. This is due to the separate electoral constituencies of executive and legislative power under presidential systems, which fail to provide incentives for cohesive party discipline within the legislature. In parliamentary systems, executive power emanates from and is contingent upon majority confidence, thus requiring disciplined parties and coalitions to keep the executive in power. In presidential systems, legislators from the president's party can vote against the president without fear that the party will lose control over the executive branch.[19] In Russia, strong presidential powers and a weak legislature have contributed to the weakness of parties. When the legislature plays a marginal role in the composition or maintenance of the government and can easily be circumvented by the executive in the policy-making process, parties have fewer reasons to institutionalize. A vicious circle emerged in which the weakness of parties compelled President Yeltsin to circumvent the legislature and rule by decree, while these very actions maintained and increased the weakness of Russian parties in the political system.

However, in the electoral realm a directly elected executive tends to promote the consolidation of smaller party formations into larger coalitions by providing a single political prize that is typically the center of political competition. Consequently, depending upon the type of electoral system used in parliamentary elections, parliamentary systems tend to produce a greater fractionalization of the party system than presidential systems.

The electoral effect of presidentialism can best be understood in the context of scholarship on electoral systems in general. Single-member district elections tend to produce two-party systems (particularly when they are "first-past-the-post" systems), while multimember proportional

[19] Leon Epstein, *Political Parties in Western Democracies* (New York: Praeger, 1967), pp. 333–340. For a critique of this hypothesized relationship, see Sartori, *Comparative Constitutional Engineering*, pp. 94–97.

representational (PR) systems tend to produce multiparty systems.[20] The psychological effect of presidential elections is much like the assumed consolidating effect of single-member district electoral systems. Since the presidency can only be occupied by a single individual (except in cases of collegial presidencies), the district magnitude for a presidential race is necessarily one with the whole nation serving as the electoral district.[21] This produces a psychological effect on the strategies pursued by voters and elites. Voters will refrain from supporting marginal candidates out of fear of wasting their votes on a sure loser and will tend to support more popular candidates who are capable of winning, even if they are not the voters' first choice. Similarly, smaller parties and marginal candidates will tend to withdraw from competition and avoid expending resources on a campaign that is doomed to be a losing effort. Such parties are much better off joining together in broader coalitions with like-minded parties. The fear of splitting the vote within a specific ideological camp's potential electorate and allowing victory to a candidate from the opposite end of the political spectrum further reinforces such tendencies toward consolidation.

The mechanical effect of presidential elections also differentiates them from all types of parliamentary elections. Because only one individual can occupy the presidency, presidential elections are the ultimate winner-take-all elections. This means that even when a presidential candidate wins a majority, presidential elections leave a huge proportion of the electorate unrepresented. Usually, presidential elections produce winners with manufactured or negative majorities in which more voters than not rejected the winner (in plurality races) or chose him or her as the lesser of two evils (in two-round majoritarian races).[22] Thus, while parliamentary electoral systems may be more or less proportional in translating votes into seats, depending on district magnitudes and electoral formulas, they are always bound to produce less disproportionality than presidential elections, which offer nothing to losing parties.

---

[20] There is a wide body of literature that examines this relationship. The major works include: Maurice Duverger, *Political Parties: Their Organization and Activity in the Modern State* (New York: Wiley, 1963); Douglas Rae, *The Political Consequences of Electoral Laws*, 2nd ed. (New Haven: Yale University Press, 1971); Rein Taagepera and Matthew Shugart, *Seats and Votes: The Effects and Determinants of Electoral Systems* (New Haven: Yale University Press, 1989); Arend Lijphart, *Electoral Systems and Party Systems: A Study of Twenty-Seven Democracies, 1945–1990* (Oxford: Oxford University Press, 1994).

[21] Shugart and Carey, *Presidents and Assemblies*, p. 21.

[22] Rose and Tikhomirov claim that the 1996 election produced just such a negative majority for Yeltsin. Richard Rose and Evgeny Tikhomirov, "Russia's Forced-Choice Presidential Election," *Post-Soviet Affairs*, Vol. 12, No. 4 (1996), pp. 373–374.

HISTORICAL CONTOURS OF RUSSIAN EXECUTIVE-LEGISLATIVE RELATIONS

Russia's often tumultuous executive-legislative relations frequently have been attributed to the defects of presidentialism cited here. Yet, an overview of the post-Soviet period shows that executive-legislative relations in Russia have not been uniformly combative or solely driven by institutional incentives. Rather, the peaks and valleys of executive-legislative conflict are best explained by a confluence of factors, including institutional design, ideological conflict, and the relative strength of popular support for the competing sides. These three main factors have interacted to produce a variety of outcomes, ranging from constitutional crisis to conciliatory gestures and relative cooperation.

I want to suggest three major points that are born out in an overview of executive-legislative relations for the Yeltsin era and the beginning of Putin's presidency. First, constitutional crisis and systemic breakdown seemed to be caused primarily by ambiguity and contestation over the legal jurisdictions of the executive and legislative branches rather than by the distribution of powers themselves. There were ample opportunities for ideological conflict between President Yeltsin and a opposition-dominated State Duma to escalate to a constitutional crisis like the one experienced in the First Russian Republic. But the more clearly delineated powers of the new constitutional arrangements of the Second Russian Republic have thus far seemed to mitigate such an escalation. The fact that President Yeltsin and the State Duma have managed to agree on five different prime ministers since the introduction of the 1993 Constitution without resorting to the disbandment of parliament and the calling of new elections demonstrates a certain resiliency to the system that did not exist in the First Russian Republic.

Second, relations between the executive and legislature have involved instances of compromise as well as confrontation. When looking at the budget process or the composition of governments, one finds that the irreconcilable opposition has not consistently resisted Yeltsin's policies, nor has Yeltsin always pursued an agenda of radical reform in defiance of a majority of the legislature. Rather, Yeltsin has seemed to rule with the support of a tentative and shifting centrist coalition of progovernment factions, single-member district deputies, and certain opposition factions like the Agrarians and LDPR. This coalition has been based more on pork barrel politics than on ideology.[23]

---

[23] See Frank C. Thames, Jr., "Patronage and the Presidential Critique: Budget Policy in the Fifth State Duma," *Demokratizatsiya: The Journal of Post-Soviet Democratization*, Vol. 8, No. 1 (2000), pp. 46–64.

Finally, this relative peace has not been purchased solely by executive fiat, through the construction of a super-presidential system that endows the executive with such formidable powers that the president can effectively ignore the legislature. Compromise has come from both branches of government. Although possessing wide-ranging decree powers, President Yeltsin did not behave as the all-powerful ruler that such powers seemingly allow. His marginalization in late 1998, without a change in the Constitution, was testament to external constraints on his power.

The Rise and Fall of the First Russian Republic, 1990–1993

The democratic institutions of the First Russian Republic (1990–93) – the Congress of People's Deputies (CPD), the presidency, and the Constitutional Court – were grafted onto the preexisting Soviet-era RSFSR Constitution through amendments. There were attempts to write a new constitution to replace the 1978 RSFSR Constitution during this period. Oleg Rumyantsev headed a working group of a constitutional commission within the Congress of People's Deputies to design a new constitution that envisioned a parliamentary system. President Yeltsin and his advisors came up with their own versions of a new constitution that would produce a strong presidential system. Regional leaders weighed in with demands for regional autonomy. The process soon became mired in a political battle between opposing forces hoping to further their short-term political fortunes through the adoption of a constitutional structure that gave the bulk of powers to the institution under their control. As the ideological polarization between President Yeltsin and the Congress of People's Deputies widened, a conciliatory process that included all major political forces in the writing of a new constitution became further and further out of reach.[24]

Because democratic institutions were added by amendment to an undemocratic (or at best pseudo-democratic) constitution, the new democratic system based on popular election of legislative and executive bodies emerged gradually in reaction to external events and pressures. Initially, the regime was a pure parliamentary system. The Russian Congress of People's Deputies, elected in a two-round majoritarian election in March 1990, was the "supreme organ of state power." The 1,068-member legislative body met infrequently but had the power to amend the Constitution by a two-thirds majority vote. The CPD elected a smaller working legislature, the Supreme Soviet, which handled the day-to-day legislative duties of the state subject to review by the whole

---

[24] Richard Sakwa, *Russian Politics and Society* (London: Routledge, 1996), pp. 54–59.

Congress. Power within the Supreme Soviet was further concentrated in a presidium led by the powerful chairman of the Supreme Soviet, who was elected to a five-year term by the whole Congress.[25] The chairman acted as the head of state before the introduction of the presidency in 1991. The first chairman was none other than Boris Yeltsin, who won a very narrow victory after several attempts, reflecting the lack of a clear majority coalition either favoring or opposing a radical reform agenda at the time. Yeltsin used the position to great effect in his battles with Mikhail Gorbachev over autonomy for the Russian Federation.

A directly elected presidency was overlaid on this parliamentary system without significant constitutional changes to weaken the legislature's role as the supreme organ of state power or its hold over constitutional amendments. This would be the institutional source of conflict between the executive and legislative branches. At approximately the same time as the Congress introduced the presidency, it also established a Constitutional Court as a further check on presidential power. The Court could rule on the constitutionality of presidential decrees and adjudicate conflicts between branches of government. Thus, the system of the First Republic was an odd mix of a Congress with sole control over constitutional change and a president with a great deal of popular legitimacy as the representative of "all the people," but with limited constitutional powers.

Why did Russian elites introduce such a system? This fateful decision to institute a directly elected president without a well-articulated presidential system was the product of strategic maneuvers by powerful interests and political circumstance. Yeltsin and his reformist allies pursued this institutional change as a means to further consolidate political power and popular legitimacy through elections. Reformists pushed for a popularly elected president with the expectation that Yeltsin would win the post. But, as McFaul points out, there were enough conservative forces in the Russian Congress of People's Deputies and the Soviet power structures to block this institutional innovation. Political context and strategic miscalculation played a role in the reformist victory on the matter. The conflict between the Russian Federation and Soviet authorities broadened the appeal of a directly elected president to nationalist forces, who saw the president as a symbol of state sovereignty and an instrument in the struggle for autonomy from the Soviet Union. Moreover, democracy and popular elections had a strong resonance among the

---

[25] For good descriptions of the institutional context of the First Republic, see Scott Parrish, "Presidential Decree Authority in Russia, 1991–1995," in John M. Carey and Matthew Soberg Shugart (eds.), *Executive Decree Authority* (Cambridge: Cambridge University Press, 1998), pp. 64–68 and Robert Sharlet, "Russian Constitutional Crisis: Law and Politics under Yeltsin," *Post-Soviet Affairs*, Vol. 9, No. 4 (1993), pp. 314–336.

people that restrained vocal reaction against these ideas.[26] Furthermore, the disintegrating political and economic situation led to a push for a popularly elected president to strengthen executive power as a means of handling political and economic crises.[27]

Once the presidency was established, external pressures – the failed August 1991 coup and the continuing economic crisis – further exacerbated the chasm between the de jure and the de facto distribution of power in the system. Yeltsin's role in defying the August coup greatly enhanced his personal power and legitimacy. Energized by his personal popularity, Yeltsin increasingly used the powers of the presidency, solidifying it as the dominant institution of the system. As head of state, he decisively established Russian sovereignty by banning the CPSU on Russian soil, seizing control of enterprises, and ultimately dismantling the Soviet Union altogether along with the leaders of Ukraine and Belarus. During this period, the CPD would also grant Yeltsin sweeping decree-making authority to undertake radical economic reform. Thus, Russia's newly formed presidency was increasingly accumulating political power, but that power was not constitutionally grounded. When price liberalization and radical economic reform produced hyperinflation, the Congress of People's Deputies tried to reassert its authority. In the poorly defined system, the ideological battle over economic policy soon became a constitutional crisis over distribution of power in the system. The Congress, armed with the Constitution that named it the supreme organ of state power, confronted the president, who claimed a more recent and legitimate mandate from the people. The result was gridlock and ultimately extra-constitutional actions and violence on the part of both institutions.

The institutional context produced the potential for interbranch conflict that could escalate to a constitutional crisis. But ideological polarization and conflict over crucial policy decisions were essential to push the system to that outcome. Ideological polarization seemed to be a natural element of Russian politics during this period, given the revolutionary changes in the policy agenda and the divisions surrounding issues of ideology, statehood, and nationhood emanating from the collapse of

---

[26] Michael McFaul, "Institutional Design, Uncertainty, and Path Dependency during Transitions: Cases from Russia," *Constitutional Political Economy*, Vol. 10, No. 1 (1999), pp. 27–52. On the creation of the presidency in Russia and adoption of presidential regimes in post-communist states, see also Gerald Easter, "Preference for Presidentialism: Postcommunist Regime Change in Russia and the NIS," *World Politics*, Vol. 49 (January 1997), pp. 184–211 and Timothy Frye, "A Politics of Institutional Choice: Post-Communist Presidencies," *Comparative Political Studies*, Vol. 30, No. 5 (1997), pp. 523–552.

[27] Parrish, "Presidential Decree Authority in Russia," p. 65.

the Soviet Union.[28] But the battle between the president and Congress was more complex than the dichotomous conflict proclaimed by much of the (liberal) Russian and Western press, which depicted a struggle between a reformer with popular support (Yeltsin) and a chronically conservative Soviet-era institution out of touch with the popular will. The ideological conflict that animated the power struggle was not nearly this clear-cut, nor was it a static phenomenon. The domination of the CPD by anti-Yeltsin forces only emerged over time, and was due as much to Yeltsin's concentration of power and his neglect of coalition building in the legislature as it was to the inherent ideological composition of the legislature.

The Congress of People's Deputies was not elected with an antireform or even anti-Yeltsin majority. Analyses of roll-call voting in the CPD shows an evolution from a body marked by ideological diversity to one possessing an anti-Yeltsin majority. Remington and his colleagues show that roll-call voting in the CPD's first four congresses (May 1990–May 1991) were marked by a predominant left-right cleavage. In these early congresses there appeared two ideologically polarized camps of roughly the same size (about 40 percent each), with an amorphous centrist group that held the balance. Moreover, each bloc was about equally cohesive, which forced both to appeal to the more fluid center by moderating their proposals in order to gain passage. It was under this left-right dichotomy that Yeltsin and the "democrats" managed to secure their greatest legislative victories, such as Yeltsin's election as speaker of the Supreme Soviet and the establishment of the Russian presidency.[29]

Over time, this voting pattern changed substantially. During the crucial fifth and sixth congresses (July and October–November 1991 and April 1992) the left-right polarization of the initial congresses dissipated. Yeltsin would win his last major legislative victories in the fifth congress, gaining additional powers from the CPD to rule by decree and winning approval to postpone local elections. Surely, intervening events helped to secure these last victories, most notably, of course, Yeltsin's prominent role in defying the ill-fated coup attempt by conservatives in the Communist Party of the Soviet Union in August 1991. But Yeltsin's ability to turn his personal popularity into institutional power would

---

[28] Breslauer argues that the emotive issues of Russian nationalism and the collapse of the Soviet Union were a dominant source of the polarization that undermined the First Russian Republic. George W. Breslauer, "Roots of Polarization: A Comment," *Post-Soviet Affairs*, Vol. 9, No. 3 (1993), pp. 225–226.

[29] Thomas Remington, Steven S. Smith, D. Roderick Kiewiet, and Moshe Haspel, "Transitional Institutions and Parliamentary Alignments in Russia, 1990–1993," in Thomas F. Remington (ed.), *Parliaments in Transition* (Boulder, Colo.: Westview, 1994), pp. 163–170.

prove fleeting. By the last three congresses (seven through nine), a polarization returned, but this time around the question of support for Yeltsin himself and the powerful presidency he had built. Remington and colleagues argue that a pro-Yeltsin/anti-Yeltsin cleavage best explains the voting distribution in the last three congresses. Moreover, while the left-right cleavage of earlier congresses pitted two relatively equally matched groups against one another, the new pro-Yeltsin/anti-Yeltsin polarization clearly favored the opposition over the president. This is accounted for both by defections of reformists to the opposition and by departure of leading democrats to the executive branch. Remington and his colleagues figure that approximately 200 deputies changed their orientation from a pro-Yeltsin to an anti-Yeltsin position, and an additional 100 reformists left the CPD to take positions in the executive.[30]

Russian political scientist Alexander Sobianin makes a similar case. Sobianin examined the voting behavior of independent deputies who did not vote regularly for one of the two ideologically coherent groupings separated by the left-right cleavage described here. Sobianin found that it was the issue of presidential power, not economic reform, that led most of these deputies to oppose Yeltsin in later congresses.

[A]mong the centrist factions, all without exception have their lowest ranking [most contrary to the president] on the second issue, that is the division of power between the President and the legislature. The next lowest rating relates to the agenda and general political issues, and only in third position do we find opposition to the Government's performance and the course of economic reform.[31]

These analyses suggest an interesting interactive effect between institutional conflict over jurisdiction between the executive and legislative branches and ideological polarization. The conflict between President Yeltsin and the Congress of People's Deputies was born in an ideological battle over economic reform and the polarization surrounding the collapse of the Soviet Union. However, each branch's efforts to establish its own supremacy in the system exacerbated this ideological divide and pushed less ideological deputies into the reformist or (more often) anti-reformist camp. Institutional conflict heightened the ideological conflict over the future nature of the Russian state and, because opposing camps eventually gained control over the two major branches of government, this ideological battle became a constitutional one.

At the same time, the ideological polarization in Russian politics fueled the battle over institutional jurisdiction. Yeltsin's anticommunism

[30] Ibid., pp. 171–174.
[31] Alexander Sobianin, "Political Cleavages among the Russian Deputies," in Remington (ed.), *Parliaments in Transition*, pp. 200–201.

and the ideological fervor with which his economic policy makers pursued market reform made compromise with "antimarket forces" within the legislature morally repugnant to the executive branch. In response, the Congress of People's Deputies, which had originally been more ideologically diverse, became a bastion for nationalists and communists determined to thwart Yeltsin's political and economic agenda. Given the ideological currents that took control of the executive and legislative branches, it would have been extremely difficult, if not impossible, for some sustainable working relationship to materialize. It is difficult to imagine how Yeltsin could have put together a legislative coalition that would have supported his reforms in the form he envisioned. Under these circumstances, Yeltsin and his economic team decided that they could accomplish their policy goals only by circumventing the legislature. A popularly elected president, especially one embedded in a vaguely defined system like the First Russian Republic, allowed and even encouraged this behavior. Not needing a majority to sustain executive power, it was natural to neglect the difficult, time-consuming, and compromise-ridden process of coalition building that would have been necessary to promote a working relationship with the legislature in favor of ruling by decree, especially when the issues were viewed in such dichotomous, black-and-white terms.

Even when Yeltsin tried to work with the Congress, the absence of a well-institutionalized party system made cooperative engagement difficult. The lack of well-developed parties meant that the two branches could not be bridged by a common organization tying the president to a large group of legislators. This absence of intermediary organizations to facilitate compromise between the two branches could be seen in the failed attempts by Yeltsin and the Congress of People's Deputies to defuse the emerging constitutional crisis. In 1992, Yeltsin adopted a strategy of limited concessions designed to appeal to the newly emergent centrist bloc in the CPD, the Civic Union, which claimed to command the allegiance of up to 40 percent of the deputies. Yeltsin brought a number of industrialists into the government and ultimately sacrificed his acting prime minister, Yegor Gaidar, in favor of Soviet-era bureaucrat Viktor Chernomyrdin to satisfy the Civic Union. But the Civic Union failed to deliver a large contingent of votes, and a liberal-centrist coalition never materialized.[32] Gaidar's removal did not satisfy the Congress, and the crisis raged on.

---

[32] Sakwa, *Russian Politics and Society*, pp. 123–124. For a discussion of the Civic Union see Michael McFaul, "Russian Centrism and Revolutionary Transitions," *Post-Soviet Affairs*, Vol. 9, No. 3 (1993), pp. 196–222.

Institutional confusion and ideological polarization may have made conflict highly likely in this system, but it did not foretell its ultimate resolution by force or predict who would come out on top of the increasingly zero-sum game being played. This was determined by the ability of each branch to command the loyalties of important political actors (most notably the armed forces) and the relative legitimacy of the competitors among the people. As the comparative literature on presidentialism might predict, Yeltsin made much of the fact that his popular mandate was more recent than that of the Congress, characterizing the latter as a relic of the delegitimated Soviet system.[33] Moreover, the April 1993 referendum, which presented Russian voters with four questions reflecting relative support for President Yeltsin and the Congress of People's Deputies, clearly showed greater public support for Yeltsin. This show of popular strength, which arguably overestimated the extent of support for Yeltsin and his policies, gave the president confidence that dissolution of the less popular legislature would be welcomed (or at least passively accepted) by the population and that new elections would return a legislature with a more reformist composition.[34]

The interaction between elite decisions and public opinion remained important in the interim between the dissolution of the Congress in September and the violent resolution of the conflict in October. Many important political actors, including some regional leaders, the Constitutional Court, the Orthodox Church, and some notable democratic politicians, criticized the extra-constitutional actions taken by Yeltsin and came out in support of some form of negotiated compromise that involved simultaneous elections for parliament and the presidency.[35] It was only after the violent uprising of the parliamentary opposition in the streets of Moscow that the tide once again swung strongly in favor

[33] The institutional design of the legislature, with its membership of over 1,000, a smaller indirectly elected working legislature in the Supreme Soviet, and concentration of power in a Presidium dominated by the chairman lends some merit to this characterization. However, both the legislature and the presidency originated while Russia was still officially a part of the Soviet Union, and thus both could be considered "Soviet" institutions.

[34] Brown uses survey research to show that, despite the April referendum that showed majority support for Yeltsin and his policies among those who voted, actually a majority of Russians (56 percent) did not support the president on the eve of the dissolution of the Congress. Archie Brown, "The October Crisis of 1993: Context and Implications," *Post-Soviet Affairs*, Vol. 9, No. 3 (1993), p. 189.

[35] For example, see "Partiitsy ne ochen' dovol'ny prezidentom," *Nezavisimaya gazeta*, September 23, 1993, p. 2; Grigory Yavlinsky, "Minimal'noe vsaimodeistvie vlastei mozhet spasti situatsiyu," *Nezavisimaya gazeta*, September 28, 1993, p. 1; "Bol'shinstvo v prezidentskom sovete vystupilo za kompromiss," *Kommersant'-Daily*, October 2, 1993.

of Yeltsin, providing him with the legitimation to settle the conflict by force.[36]

A quick comparison to the economic crisis of 1998 shows the importance of political context in the process. In 1998, President Yeltsin possessed the same institutional advantages he had in 1993 and many more constitutional ones. Executive power remained constituted in a directly elected presidency that was independent of the confidence of a majority coalition in the legislature. He once again enjoyed a more recent electoral mandate with his 1996 reelection as president as compared to the 1995 elections to the State Duma. He also enjoyed much greater constitutional powers to subdue the legislature in 1998 than he had possessed in 1993. But by the fall of 1998 Yeltsin's public support had declined to the point that he was not willing to risk confrontation and early elections by pushing a third vote on his prime ministerial candidate, much less by resorting to violence in his battle with the legislature. Weakened by ill health and an economic crisis that wiped out all of the gains of his economic reforms, Yeltsin had more formal powers in 1998 than in 1993, but much less real power.

Peaceful Coexistence – The Second Russian Republic, 1994–1997

Unlike the First Republic, the institutional design of the Second Russian Republic represented a clear break with the Soviet past. A new Constitution replaced the old Soviet Constitution, establishing a whole new system of governance rather than the gradual introduction of single democratic institutions as occurred in the First Republic. But this new Constitution had rather inauspicious origins. The 1993 Constitution was not a series of compromises hammered out by an inclusive group of national and regional elites in a constitutional assembly. Rather, it was crafted and imposed by the victor of the violent struggle that had ended the previous regime. President Yeltsin claimed popular legitimacy for his constitution by virtue of its passage in a national referendum. But the referendum itself was marred by suspicions of vote fraud intended to artificially raise the turnout over the required 50 percent threshold to make the vote valid.

Perhaps this was the only way Russia was going to get a new constitution. Due to the polarization between reformist and antireformist forces, each occupying a rival branch of government, the conciliatory adoption of a new constitution seemed to be out of the question. Nevertheless, the legitimacy of such a constitutional project would be a major

---

[36] For the swing in opinion among democratic and centrist politicians in support of Yeltsin's use of force after the October insurrection, see "Deistviya prezidenta poluchayut podderzhku," *Nezavisimaya gazeta*, October 5, 1993.

concern. Thus, a major accomplishment for the Second Republic was its widespread acceptance among major political groups. Despite the lack of participation by key political forces in the formulation of the new constitutional order, the 1993 Constitution has enjoyed at least tacit legitimacy. All major parties have followed the rules laid out in the Constitution and have participated in elections for the new legislative and executive bodies.

Like the First Republic, the Second Republic is a semi-presidential system, with a president and legislature both directly elected and a government that is subject to presidential appointment and dismissal but that also requires the confidence of a majority in the parliament. Despite these similarities, the two systems differ dramatically in the amount of power wielded by the executive and legislative branches. The 1993 Constitution provides the president with key powers in two crucial areas – control over the composition of the government and decree powers – that make the executive branch in Russia one of the strongest among democratic polities.[37]

While the government is formally beholden to both the president (by appointment and power of dismissal) and the legislature (through the no-confidence vote), in practice the 1993 Constitution gives the president much greater control over the composition of the government and its survival in power. The president is given the power to appoint the prime minister with only the consent of the Duma. The president can propose his candidate three times for parliamentary approval. After a third unsuccessful vote, the president is empowered to dissolve the Duma, call new elections, and appoint an interim prime minister. Thus, while the Duma can block a president's prime ministerial candidate, by so doing they put their positions on the line and allow the president to appoint whomever he wants in the interim of presidential rule before new elections are held. Until the economic crisis of 1998, the Duma seemed unwilling to push confrontation with the president and risk dissolution. Viktor Chernomyrdin was approved after both the 1993 and 1995 parliamentary victories of antireformist forces despite his nonparticipation in the 1993 elections and his party's lackluster performance in 1995. Even more telling, the Duma gave its consent to Sergei Kirienko, who was widely distrusted by the communist-led Duma but was accepted by many deputies to prevent dissolution and new elections. This power over the appointment of the prime minister is augmented by exclusion of the Duma from other ministerial appointments. The members of the

---

[37] Alan Siaroff, "Semi-Presidential Government: An Increasingly Common – but Still Varied – Political System," paper presented at the annual meeting of the Midwest Political Science Association, Chicago, April 1998.

cabinet are appointed jointly by the president and prime minister without legislative approval.

Not only can the president push through his choice for prime minister, he can also dismiss the government or any particular minister at will without parliamentary approval. This control over the survival of the government is much greater than the Duma's power to vote no confidence in the government, because the risks facing the president if he decides to dismiss the government are negligible compared to those of the legislature. A vote of no confidence by the Duma can be ignored by the president the first time. But if the Duma passes another no-confidence vote within three months, the president is required to either replace the government or dissolve the Duma and call new elections.[38] Again, the threat of dissolution and the prospect of early elections has tended to constrain the legislature from exercising any real control over the survival of the government. As Orttung and Parrish have argued, "while the government formally needs the simultaneous confidence of both the president and a majority of the Duma to stay in office, in reality the president's support has proved sufficient."[39]

As will be discussed later, this assumption of timidity on the part of the Duma in its role in codetermining government composition and survival has been partly undermined by its assertive defiance of Yeltsin's attempt to reinstate Chernomyrdin after the five-month stint of the Kirienko government. But Yeltsin's removal of the popular Primakov in the midst of a legislative vote on impeachment, and his ability to secure approval of subsequent prime ministers most noted for their loyalty to Yeltsin, shows that the defiance of presidential power over the composition of government on the part of the State Duma was a temporary rather than permanent shift in power.

Presidential power in the Second Russian Republic was further strengthened through wide-ranging decree-making powers that allowed the president a decisive role in the legislative process. Article 90 of the 1993 Constitution grants the president the power to issue decrees that have the force of law. The only constraint on the president's decree-making authority is that decrees cannot contravene the Constitution or existing law.[40] The president's role in the legislative process is further augmented by other constitutional provisions. The president has the

---

[38] The three-month period between the first and second votes of confidence was dramatically shortened by the government in 1995 when it utilized a constitutional provision that allows the government to request a vote of confidence within ten days. The government used this provision to force an early second vote.

[39] Robert W. Orttung and Scott Parrish, "From Confrontation to Cooperation in Russia," *Transition*, Vol. 2, No. 25 (1996), p. 17.

[40] Parrish, "Presidential Decree Authority in Russia, 1991–1995," pp. 78–79.

power to veto legislation, which then needs a two-thirds majority in both houses of the legislature. Thus, if a war of laws versus presidential decrees were to break out, the president would have the upper hand, for he could veto contrarian legislation, and force the legislature to come up with super-majorities to override. Given the fragmented character of political forces in the legislature, attaining a two-thirds majority in both houses to overcome a presidential veto would be exceedingly difficult.

The 1993 Constitution also established an upper house, the Federation Council, made up regional executives and the leaders of regional legislatures.[41] This body was designed by Yeltsin as another instrument of legislative control but has developed into a more autonomous law-making body that serves the interests of Russia's regional elites, who have emerged as one of the most powerful political forces in the country. Originally, Yeltsin's influence over the Federation Council was secure, because he appointed the executive leaders of Russia's regions and therefore controlled the fate of one-half of that body's deputies. However, in 1996 Yeltsin relinquished his appointment power over regional executives and allowed them to be directly elected. This gave the upper house a greater degree of autonomy. Although it remained less confrontational than the lower house, the Federation Council defied President Yeltsin on several key issues, including the appointment of the powerful position of procurator general. Moreover, the Federation Council provided a national stage for powerful regional elites, some with presidential ambitions, such as Yuri Luzhkov and Alexander Lebed.

Finally, Yeltsin's Constitution protected these presidential prerogatives by making the president virtually impossible to impeach and the Constitution very difficult to change. Unlike the First Republic, where a simple two-thirds majority of the Congress of People's Deputies could accomplish both tasks, impeachment under the 1993 Constitution requires the support of extraordinary majorities in both houses, as well as agreement of both the Supreme Court and Constitutional Court that impeachable acts were committed and that all procedures were correctly followed. Amendments to the Constitution require super-majorities in both houses, the approval of the president, and support of two-thirds of regional assemblies.[42]

What did not change under Yeltsin's rule was the ideological polarization of the system. Contrary to reformers' hopes and expectations, Yeltsin was not faced with a more amenable, reform-minded legislature after 1993. Rather, the State Duma was marked by the same party frac-

---

[41] The deputies to the Federation Council were directly elected in 1993.
[42] Parrish, "Presidential Decree Authority in Russia, 1991–1995," pp. 79–80.

tionalization and ideological diversity found in the Congress of People's Deputies. Moreover, as in the CPD, the balance between reformers and antireformist opposition increasingly favored the latter. After the 1995 election, the Communist Party and its allies constituted a working majority in the Duma (221 out of 450 seats). While the institutional design of the Russian political system changed substantially in favor of executive power and of reformers by virtue of their occupation of this powerful office, the balance of ideological forces in the legislature did not.

Given these political realities, one might expect that the Second Russian Republic would have continued to experience the intractable interbranch conflict born of ideologically polarized groups dominating the competing branches. At best, constitutional crisis might be avoided because the new constitution provided such preponderant powers to the president that the conservative legislature would be powerless to resist the will of the reformist executive – stability purchased at the expense of virtual electoral dictatorship or delegative democracy, to use O'Donnell's term.

But the reality of the relative stability of the Second Republic (at least when compared to its predecessor) is much more complicated. The relationship between the executive and legislative branches has been more cordial since 1993. Moreover, the instances of cooperation between the two branches are not characterized solely by capitulation by the weaker State Duma. Yeltsin also had to compromise to accommodate what became a relatively effective and assertive lawmaking body, given its weak constitutional stature. There were a number of issues on which Yeltsin conceded to the will of the parliament to avoid costly confrontation and possible constitutional crisis. Almost immediately after the 1993 election inaugurating the new system, the State Duma used its power to grant amnesty to Yeltsin's most despised political opponents: the conspirators of the failed August 1991 coup and Ruslan Khasbulatov and Alexander Rutskoi, the recently imprisoned leaders of the October 1993 rebellion. Despite calls for the use of presidential powers to block the amnesty, President Yeltsin allowed the action to stand in order to preserve the fragile relationship between executive and legislature that had disintegrated into violence only months earlier.[43]

The president also had to give ground to parliament in the battle over the electoral law. Yeltsin tried to change Russia's mixed electoral system, which elects an equal number of deputies from a PR tier and single-mandate districts, to a system with 300 single-member district deputies and only 150 deputies elected according to PR party lists. After the

---

[43] Robert Sharlet, "The New Russian Constitution and Its Political Impact," *Problems in Post-Communism*, Vol. 42, No. 1 (1995), p. 6.

results of the 1993 election, Yeltsin had an interest in increasing the number of single-mandate district deputies, because these deputies tended to be less opposed to his policies and more easily swayed to support the president in exchange for personal favors or constituency pork. Indeed, a key element in the fluid pro-Yeltsin legislative coalition was single-mandate district deputies who ran as independents and formed their own parliamentary factions. However, a Duma majority in favor of an equal split between PR and single-mandate district seats managed to maintain the status quo.[44] In the process, the normally fractious Duma managed to mobilize the two-thirds majority necessary to override the Federation Council, which rejected its first version of the law. Yeltsin subsequently vetoed the law, but Duma representatives on the conciliation commission formed to hammer out a compromise managed to retain the equal split between PR and single-mandate district deputies, while conceding relatively minor points to the president over how the party lists were constructed.[45]

In this case, a determined Duma majority managed to navigate the many veto points stacked against it. Yeltsin's ability to change the electoral rules by decree was also hamstrung by larger questions of popular legitimacy. Had he blocked legislation on electoral arrangements and established electoral rules favorable to his interests by decree, the legitimacy of such elections would have been seriously questioned. This show of assertiveness on the part of the Duma was replayed in other legislative battles over the regulation of religious practice and the adoption of a criminal law code. In both cases, the laws were passed after Yeltsin called a conciliation commission to work out a compromise acceptable to both the executive and legislative branches. A law forbidding the repatriation of trophy art captured from Nazi Germany was passed over a presidential veto.[46]

---

[44] For an excellent explanation of the institutional and political factors producing this majority opinion in favor of the 225:225 ratio for Russia's electoral law, see McFaul, "Uncertainty, Path Dependency and Institutional Design during Transitions: Cases from Russia," pp. 27–52.

[45] The new law required party lists to be disaggregated into regional lists following a twelve-person national list. This was intended to alleviate the preponderance of representatives from Moscow who gained election on party lists in 1993. For a discussion of the debate over the electoral law, see Robert W. Orttung, "Battling over Electoral Laws," *OMRI Transition*, Vol. 1, No. 15 (August 1995), pp. 32–36. For an analysis of voting patterns among Russian parliamentary factions regarding the electoral law, see Thomas Remington and Steven Smith, "Political Goals, Institutional Context, and the Choice of an Electoral System," *American Journal of Political Science*, Vol. 40, No. 4 (1996), pp. 1253–1279.

[46] Eugene Huskey, *Presidential Power in Russia* (Armonk, N.Y.: M. E. Sharpe, 1999), p. 169.

While the previous examples show that on occasion the Duma successfully exerted power in the Second Republic despite its strong presidential powers, the budget process demonstrates how President Yeltsin
was able to assemble majority coalitions based on clientelism. Yeltsin
was able to pass his budget every year, relying upon a fluid coalition that
included independents, centrists, and key support from opposition factions in addition to his base among the pro-presidential parties.[47] Yeltsin
had to seek votes for his budgets outside his core support among
reformist parties. In addition to pro-presidential factions, the decisive
components of this coalition tended to be centrist deputies elected in the
single-member districts, centrist PR blocs like the Women of Russia and
the Democratic Party of Russia, and two parties of the "irreconcilable
opposition" – the Agrarian Party and Zhirinovsky's LDPR. Only the
most ardent representatives of the irreconcilable opposition (communists) and the democratic opposition (Yabloko) consistently voted against
Yeltsin's budgets, and even these parties did not always oppose them.[48]
Given the significant diversity in ideological orientation of these different elements of the Duma, this support had to be "purchased" with a
variety of resource allocations to key economic and regional interests.
Yeltsin managed to coopt the Agrarian Party by granting it control over
the Agricultural Ministry. For other parties, personal perquisites, what
Huskey calls "dacha politics," were used to sway individual deputies.[49]
Indeed, the more corrupt side of this manner of governing could be seen
in a report that up to $27 million was provided to communist and LDPR
deputies by interests close to the government in exchange for their
support in pushing through the 1997 budget.[50]

Finally, presidential control over the composition of the government
under Yeltsin was not absolute, even though the Constitution placed
most of the power for deciding the composition and survival of the government in the hands of the president. It cannot be denied that President
Yeltsin appointed and stuck with prime ministers and governments that
did not enjoy widespread support in the Duma – the return of the most
demonized reformer, Anatolii Chubais, in 1997 in a "young reformers"
government that included Nizhny Novgorod Governor Boris Nemtsov
being one of the more egregious examples. Yet, at times, President Yeltsin
also used his control over the composition of the government as an

---

[47] Thames, "Patronage and the Presidential Critique," pp. 56–61.
[48] The Communist Party voted in favor of the budget in 1994. Yabloko has never voted
in favor of a Yeltsin government's budget.
[49] Huskey, "Democracy and Institutional Design in Russia," p. 464.
[50] The report came from Igor Vandenko, "We Say 'Deputy' But Mean Broker," *Izvestiya*,
May 30, 1997, pp. 1–2, as cited in Huskey, *Presidential Power in Russia*, p. 172.

instrument for reacting to and placating negative public and legislative opinion, casting himself as the ultimate arbiter of the balance of political forces in Russia. Following electoral defeats at the hands of nationalist and communist opposition parties in 1993 and 1995, Yeltsin changed the composition of the government to reflect the diminished status of reformers.

Moreover, nonpartisanship and political pragmatism were viewed as the most prized attributes of the prime minister, who was seen as more of a technocrat than a politician. Before being pushed to form a centrist electoral bloc for the 1995 election, Chernomyrdin fit this mold of nonpolitical manager.[51] The same was true for Yevgeny Primakov. The "young technocrat" Sergei Kirienko was also said to have no partisan attachments. But this appointment more closely resembled the confrontational push for radical economic change of the "young reformist" government of Chubais and Nemtsov (Kirienko was a Nemtsov protégé) than any conciliatory gesture to appoint a prime minister acceptable to a wide range of political forces in the Duma.

This balancing of forces through appointment made executive-legislative relations a bit easier, as pragmatic prime ministers like Chernomyrdin could work with all ideological groups within parliament, and more ideological and unpopular ministers like Anatolii Chubais could be sacrificed as a concession to the opposition at times of confrontation or rising popular disenchantment with reforms.[52] However, this was hardly an invitation to the Duma to be a partner in government. Power within the government and other executive positions remained highly contingent upon cultivating favor with Yeltsin; it was not any accurate reflection of public support as conveyed in parliamentary elections. Indeed, the reappointment of Chernomyrdin following the 1993 elections was a bit ironic considering that centrist parties, and particularly those representing large industrial interests, were the big losers in the election, whereas parties gaining a much larger share of the PR vote – nationalists, communists, and more radical reformers – found themselves largely excluded from government.

[51] For a discussion of Chernomyrdin's technocratic style, see Elena Chinyeava and Peter Rutland, "A Prime Minister without Politics," *Transition*, Vol. 3, No. 4 (March 1997), pp. 32–38.

[52] Hahn describes the replacement of Chernomyrdin by Kirienko in precisely these terms. Yeltsin, dissatisfied with the failure to clear wage arrears and the corrupt interference by oligarchs in the Chernomyrdin/Chubais government, dismissed the government in order to broaden the benefits of economic reforms to more of society and to ensure the election of a democratically minded successor in the next presidential election. Gordon Hahn, "From Chernomyrdin to Kiriyenko," *Problems of Post-Communism*, Vol. 45, No. 5 (1998), pp. 3–16.

This personalization of power had its most detrimental effects in the backroom power struggles among Yeltsin's appointees, particularly as health problems removed Yeltsin from daily engagement in the affairs of the state. Erratic appointment changes designed to reestablish Yeltsin's control over the executive branch upon returning from long health-related absences were further evidence that restraint in personnel management was contingent on the person occupying the office rather than on the rules governing the institution. As long as Yeltsin was in power, the government was never safe from unexpected reshuffling or removal driven by Yeltsin's own insecurities and power struggles within his inner circle.

Under Yeltsin, the constitutional arrangement of the Second Russian Republic provided a great deal more stability than the First Republic. The ideological foundation for conflict did not changed greatly under Yeltsin. The two branches of government remained dominated by contradictory ideological forces. But the institutional context changed. The establishment of a "super-presidential" system can be credited in part for the increased stability under Yeltsin, as it removed the ambiguity that drove leaders of both institutions to pursue contradictory visions of a new Russian system. The division of powers in the 1993 Constitution deterred confrontation by the Duma through the threat of dissolution. Other institutional innovations also fostered accommodation, including a partisan-dominated legislature, conciliation commissions, and presidential liaisons to parliament.[53] But this stability was fragile, based in large part on the behavior of individual politicians and their willingness to avoid confrontation and accept defeat rather than use the full arsenal of constitutional powers at their disposal. The potential for exacerbation of confrontation into constitutional crisis was mitigated by the unambiguous preference given the executive branch in the system. But the cooperation that began to develop over time was contingent upon individuals and particular political contexts. The lack of well-institutionalized political parties, the primary institution necessary for sustained inter-branch cooperation, remained a huge obstacle to stable executive-legislative relations and democratic consolidation in general.[54]

---

[53] For a discussion of the interaction between internal parliamentary organization and executive-legislative relations, see Joel Ostrow, "Institutional Design and Legislative Conflict: The Russian Supreme Soviet – A Well-Oiled Machine, Out of Control," *Communist and Post-Communist Studies*, Vol. 29, No. 4 (1996), pp. 415–433 and Joel Ostrow, "Procedural Breakdown and Deadlock in the Russian State Duma: The Problems of an Un-Linked Dual-Channel Institutional Design," *Europe-Asia Studies*, Vol. 50, No. 5 (1998), pp. 793–816.

[54] Mainwaring argues that "[o]ne of the most difficult obstacles facing the new post-1974 democracies in their efforts at democratic consolidation is weakly institutionalized party

Economic Collapse and Political Crisis, 1998

The fragile stability of the system was shattered with a demonstration of Yeltsin's personalized grip on power. In March 1998, Yeltsin flexed his political muscle by unexpectedly dismissing his loyal Prime Minister Viktor Chernomyrdin after more than five years in office and replacing him with a thirty-five-year-old political neophyte, Sergei Kirienko. It was rumored that Yeltsin had become suspicious of Chernomyrdin's growing status, both domestically and internationally. Like so many other potential rivals to Yeltsin's authority, Chernomyrdin was removed. This move sparked a spiral of political and economic crises that temporarily left a physically frail Yeltsin marginalized to a mostly symbolic role, having ceded daily control over political decision making to Prime Minister Yevgeny Primakov, a compromise candidate who was forced upon him by the State Duma. This process demonstrates that even in a strong presidential system a president who is severely politically and physically weakened cannot remain at the center of the political system.

This surprising turn of events began with an all-too-familiar exercise – Yeltsin reshuffling personnel in the government. Although politically weakened by health problems and continued wage arrears, Yeltsin still sat at the center of the political system. He had already taken steps to challenge Chernomyrdin's power a year earlier by bringing in Boris Nemtsov and Anatolii Chubais as deputy prime ministers. When he suddenly dismissed Chernomyrdin and replaced him with the obscure Sergei Kirienko, the move met with a mixed reaction. The opposition decried the nomination of the political neophyte, but liberal circles and Western governments and media welcomed the change as the (latest) best chance for radical reform to get on track. (The new government would secure a large IMF bailout loan in part because of its "reformist" credentials.) The coming economic collapse had yet to materialize, so Yeltsin was reasonably secure in launching another attempt at radical reform that was finally to tackle Russia's chronic tax collection problems and rein in the oligarchs and their robber-baron capitalism. The Duma put up a fight but capitulated in the confrontation over the Kirienko appointment, as expected. After two negative votes it was decided to hold the third and decisive vote by secret ballot, allowing members of the communist opposition, particularly those elected from single-member districts and thus most vulnerable to the risk of new elections, to defect.

systems." Scott Mainwaring, "Party Systems in the Third Wave," *Journal of Democracy*, Vol. 9, No. 3 (July 1998), p. 67.

Economic crisis and collapse intervened to bring a hasty end to the Kirienko government. A confluence of forces outside the young prime minister's power pushed the system to collapse. Poor tax collection (a legacy of the previous government), the Asian crisis, a drop in world oil prices, and the collapse of the state treasury-bill pyramid combined to create a crisis of confidence that sent foreign investors fleeing, removing a chief source for continued financing of the budget deficit. Despite promises to the contrary, the Kirienko government was forced to devalue the ruble and default on international loans, bringing the financial crisis home to the average Russian. Yeltsin responded by firing Kirienko and trying to bring back Chernomyrdin as a force of calm and stability.[55] But in the midst of an economic crisis rooted in the policies and practices of the previous regime, the zig-zag from Chernomyrdin to Kirienko was taken as further evidence of erratic, bankrupt leadership. Despite this, there seemed to be a good chance that Chernomyrdin would be able to gain approval through the formation of a coalition government. Yeltsin also offered a power-sharing agreement by which he would grant the Duma the power to approve and remove individual ministers in exchange for acceptance of Chernomyrdin as prime minister. The deal also included a "nonaggression pact": Yeltsin promised not to dissolve parliament for a year, and the Duma agreed to refrain from impeachment and votes of no confidence for the same period.[56] The agreement was accepted by all parties but broken by Gennady Zyuganov on the eve of the first vote on Chernomyrdin, when Zyuganov called for Yeltsin's resignation in exchange for Chernomyrdin's confirmation.[57]

Yeltsin, who had dared the Duma to defy him three times on the Kirienko appointment only months before, was now the disadvantaged party, more fearful of fresh elections than the emboldened Duma opposition. The Communist Party and its allies now managed to hold together and along with Yabloko controlled the votes necessary to block Chernomyrdin's confirmation.[58] When Grigory Yavlinsky publicly offered

---

[55] Interestingly, on the eve of Yeltsin's dismissal of the Kirienko government the Duma seemed split on the appropriate action to be taken against the government in reaction to the economic crisis. Zyuganov and Yavlinsky called for the government's resignation and a no-confidence vote. Zhirinovsky argued that some ministers should be replaced but that dismissing the whole government would not accomplish anything. Shokhin and the Our Home is Russia faction were against a no-confidence vote. Gennady Seleznev and Yegor Stroev, the leaders of the Duma and Federation Council, also came out against resignation of the government. *RFE/RL Daily Report*, Vol. 2, No. 161 (August 21, 1998).

[56] *RFE/RL Daily Report*, Vol. 2, No. 166 (August 28, 1998).

[57] *RFE/RL Daily Report*, Vol. 2, No. 167 (August 31, 1998).

[58] For a breakdown of the vote against Chernomyrdin, see Reuters, August 31, 1998, cited in *Johnson's Russia List*, No. 2338 (August 31, 1998).

Yevgeny Primakov as a pragmatic, nonpolitical compromise candidate, Yeltsin seized the opportunity to avoid a devastating third vote on Chernomyrdin and offered Primakov in his place. He was quickly approved by the Duma and proceeded to form a government of majority confidence with a member of the Communist Party, Yuri Maslyukov, in charge of the economy.

Three aspects of the decline of Yeltsin's political power during the 1998 economic crisis need to be highlighted. First, as in the constitutional crisis of 1993, public opinion and the strategic actions of political elites mattered as much or more than constitutionally defined powers. The economic crisis and the debilitating effect it had on the legitimacy of Yeltsin's whole legacy of economic reform was surely a necessary condition for the demise of Boris Yeltsin. Yet, strategic decisions helped to determine the timing and character of Yeltsin's decline. Yeltsin was discredited not only for these systemic failures but also for his erratic behavior in discarding Chernomyrdin in an effort to jump-start reform, only to bring him back to reestablish confidence and stability. In a sense, he had expended too much political capital in pushing through Kirienko to have any chance of forcing the return of Chernomyrdin. One can speculate about how differently the crisis might have unfolded had Yeltsin stuck with Chernomyrdin. Had he not pushed through a new government (that quickly failed) five months earlier, would Yeltsin have been able to push through his first choice for prime minister even in the midst of economic crisis? Although this surely depends on his choice, I think the answer is probably yes.

Second, while Boris Yeltsin was weakened, the powers of the presidency were not changed. The Duma accepted a compromise candidate rather than exchanging support for Chernomyrdin for changes in the Constitution. This had huge consequences for subsequent executive-legislative relations, because it allowed Yeltsin to recover from the crisis in time to name a successor endowed with the same vast constitutional powers he enjoyed. At the time of the crisis, President Yeltsin suggested that he was willing to introduce changes in the Constitution, but the content and implications of these changes remained ambiguous. A popular war, Yeltsin's resignation, and early presidential elections intervened. The new occupant of the office, buoyed by a new electoral mandate, dropped any suggestion of constitutional reform intended to bring greater balance between the executive and legislative branches. Instead, President Putin has made fuller use of executive powers as a means to strengthen the state. Constitutional changes were never institutionalized, and thus the economic crisis of 1998 weakened President Yeltsin but did not weaken the presidential republic he had done so much to create.

Third, unlike the collapse of the First Russian Republic, the temporary shift in power toward the legislature brought on by the economic crisis occurred within the bounds of the Constitution. The same president who had taken extra-constitutional steps to dissolve the Congress of People's Deputies rather than see that body strip the presidency of its powers compromised on the composition of the government with the Duma. He later voluntarily ceded even more authority to Prime Minister Primakov, essentially retreating from the political scene. However, when the opportunity arose, Yeltsin and his advisors in the executive branch managed to peacefully regain the upper hand. By the end of 1999, Yeltsin managed to exit from the political stage with the full powers of the presidency intact and a handpicked successor poised to be elected as the second president of Russia.

The End of the Yeltsin Era and the Rise of Putin, 1999–2000

The political and economic crises of 1998 were not the death knell of the Yeltsin era that many considered them to be. Yeltsin reemerged as a powerful and unpredictable factor in the spring of 1999, with the advent of the NATO military campaign against Serbia, among other things, spurring his renewed activity. Sensing the rising popularity of Primakov, Yeltsin removed him in the middle of a battle over his own impeachment in the State Duma. He managed to avoid impeachment by threatening a new constitutional crisis that endangered the positions of Duma deputies and raised the possibility of emergency rule and delayed parliamentary and presidential elections. Yeltsin won quick and overwhelming approval for his choice for prime minister, Sergei Stepashin, a loyal supporter who had spent his political career in the security services.

However, Stepashin quickly fell out of favor in the face of an attack by Chechen rebels against Dagestan and his failure to thwart the formation of the powerful new alliance of regional elites, Fatherland–All Russia, led by Moscow mayor Yuri Luzhkov, which threatened to take over the executive branch through the ballot box at the next general election. In August 1999, Stepashin was removed and replaced by another member of the security services, Vladimir Putin, without much resistance from the Duma.

Despite successfully reestablishing control over the composition of the government, Yeltsin was still quite weak and unpopular. The Kremlin seemed to be in disarray, frantically going through prime ministers in an effort to find a successor who could win the upcoming presidential elections in 2000 and guarantee immunity from prosecution for Yeltsin and members of his inner circle. Opposition forces in the State Duma were content to sit back and watch the apparent self-destruction, being very reluctant to challenge Yeltsin on the eve of parliamentary and presidential elections and thereby provide him with an excuse to disband parliament, postpone or cancel elections, and impose emergency rule.

Yeltsin declared that the unknown Putin was his preferred successor to the presidency immediately upon nominating him for prime minister. This endorsement was met initially with derision, since Putin had no independent political base, and association with Yeltsin was deemed a severe liability in the upcoming election. The Kremlin also hastily assembled a new political bloc called Unity, led by Emergency Minister Sergei Shoigu. Neither Putin nor Unity seemed to have much chance to win in the fast-approaching elections, given the widespread disillusionment with the Yeltsin administration.[59] Meanwhile, the Fatherland–All Russia bloc was leading in public opinion polls after convincing former Prime Minister Yevgeny Primakov to lead its party list in the parliamentary elections. At the beginning of the parliamentary campaign, it looked as though this bloc of regional governors would win the parliamentary election as the new "party of power" and provide a springboard for a strong run at the presidency by Primakov or Luzhkov.[60]

However, as McFaul showed in Chapter 1, all of this changed with the second military intervention in Chechnya.[61] Unlike the first Chechen war, this campaign enjoyed strong social support. Putin's determined execution of the military campaign established him as the decisive leader of action that the Russian public seemed to crave. According to opinion polls conducted by VTsIOM, Putin's approval rating soared from 31 percent in August 1999 to 78 percent by November.[62] Putin publicly endorsed Unity, enabling the bloc to rise from obscurity to a close second place finish in the last month of the campaign. The reformist bloc Union of Right-Wing Forces also performed well beyond expectations by associating itself with Putin and the Chechen war. Conversely, support for noncommunist opponents of the Kremlin, Fatherland–All Russia and Yabloko, declined dramatically before the vote.

Striving to capitalize on the popularity of the Chechen campaign to secure Putin's succession, Yeltsin resigned from office at the end of 1999

---

[59] Initial commentary centered on whether Unity would overcome the 5 percent threshold to win seats in the PR tier of the election. See Nikolai Petrov and Alexei Makarkin, "Unity (Medved)," in Michael McFaul, Nikolai Petrov, and Andrei Ryabov (eds.), *Primer on Russia's 1999 Duma Elections* (Washington, D.C.: Carnegie Endowment for International Peace, 1999), pp. 121–124.

[60] Boris Makarenko, "Fatherland," in McFaul, Petrov, and Ryabov (eds.), *Primer on Russia's 1999 Duma Elections*, pp. 61–75.

[61] For a fuller discussion of the 1999 parliamentary election, see Chapter 1 of this volume.

[62] VTsIOM survey results can be found at the Russia Votes website, www.russiavotes.org.

in a dramatic New Year's Eve address. Putin became acting president and received all the electoral benefits of being the head of state. More importantly, the resignation moved the presidential election from June to March, which undermined the ability of other candidates to mount credible campaigns and lessened the chance that the Chechen campaign might worsen, souring public opinion. The tactic worked well. Major presidential contenders, such as Primakov and Luzhkov, decided not to run against Putin, who continued to enjoy 80 percent approval ratings through the presidential electoral campaign. Putin won election easily in the first round.[63]

A substantial change in the nature of executive-legislative relations was brought about by the personal popularity of Vladimir Putin and the sequence of elections. Elections were held at the height of Putin's popularity, producing a large legislative contingent that supported the president. For the first time, post-communist Russia had a president who enjoyed majority support in the legislature. This is a critical difference from the Yeltsin era. As Fish notes in the concluding chapter of this volume, Yeltsin failed to call new elections at the height of his popularity following the failed August 1991 coup and thus always faced a legislature dominated by the opposition.[64]

Putin has made great use of this improved relationship with the State Duma. He managed to push through the long-delayed ratification of the START II treaty and introduced a package of legislation that includes dramatic changes in federal relations. In his first set of draft laws to the State Duma, Putin proposed that regional governors and legislators not sit on the Federation Council and be replaced by representatives elected by regional legislatures through a secret ballot. He also sought legislative approval for the power to dismiss governors if a court determined that their actions contravened federal law. Both measures passed the first reading by wide margins (362–34 and 357–28, respectively), suggesting that the State Duma may be a strong ally in Putin's campaign to rein in the powers of regional governors, an alliance hard to imagine under Yeltsin.[65]

The reversals of fortune between the two branches of government during the late 1990s highlight the interaction between political context and constitutional powers in determining the balance of executive-legislative relations in Russia. Yeltsin's political weakness in 1998 was not institutionalized into a lasting redistribution of power between the executive and legislative branches. Consequently, talk of constitutional

---

[63] For more discussion of the 2000 presidential election, see Chapter 1 of this volume.
[64] See conclusion by Steven Fish in this volume.
[65] *New York Times*, June 1, 2000, P. A9; *RFE/RL Newsline*, June 1, 2000.

reform quickly dissipated as the political context changed. A popular war in Chechnya and the dramatic surge in popular support of Vladimir Putin allowed Yeltsin to escape the crises of 1998, handpick a successor, and retain the full powers of the presidency intact. Having handily won the 2000 presidential election in the first round, President Putin towered over the Russian political system at the beginning of his term with a combination of dominant constitutional powers, popular support, and a cooperative legislature that even exceeded the height of Yeltsin's power in the wake of the failed August 1991 coup. How Putin uses this power and whether he can maintain it will be decisive factors determining the fate of Russia in the post-Yeltsin era.

CONCLUSIONS

This chapter has shown that confrontation and conflict between the executive and legislative branches have been a major part of post-communist Russian politics. However, the degree of this conflict has changed substantially over time. With the introduction of the 1993 Constitution, President Yeltsin and the legislature found ways to defuse conflicts before they led to collapse of the system. His successor, Vladimir Putin, began his tenure on an even more conciliatory note. Institutional design of the system has been important in this process, but so have learning and a degree of ideological moderation on both sides of the political spectrum. The development of some measure of conciliatory interaction between the two branches in the Second Republic provides some reason for hope that Russia's democratic experiment, undoubtably flawed and unstable, may survive. However, the current consensus between the two branches of government also threatens to increase the authoritarian tendencies of the system if power becomes too concentrated in Putin's hands.

During the Yeltsin era, conflict in Russia's executive-legislative relations was fueled by a consistent ideological division between a "reformist" executive and an "antireformist" legislature. This ideological divide between the two branches of government survived the collapse of the First Russian Republic and three elections, two parliamentary and one presidential. In Chapter 1, Michael McFaul argued that the institutional design of presidential and parliamentary elections can explain the seemingly contradictory outcomes in parliamentary and presidential elections. Parliamentary elections produced a fractionalized Duma in which the Communist Party was the dominant force, while the consolidating nature of presidential elections pushed the latent anticommunist majority, which was split among many parties in parliamentary elections, to coalesce behind one noncommunist candidate in the second round of the presidential election.[66]

This dynamic was not evident in the latest round of elections that launched the post-Yeltsin era. In the 1999 parliamentary elections, parties associated with the executive branch did much better than in 1993 or 1995. Although the Communist Party remains the largest party in the State Duma, opposition forces comprise a much smaller proportion of the Duma, and a majority coalition supporting President Putin has emerged. Two developments help to account for this dramatic change in executive-legislative relations. First, the ideological distance between opposing camps has become much smaller. Economic developments since the collapse of the Soviet Union have produced a narrowing of the political spectrum by default. The failure of the Soviet command economy still resonates, forcing all major parties, including the Communist Party, to abandon calls for a return to a command economy. At the same time, the recent economic collapse, coming after seven years of economic contraction, has delegitimized the neoliberal reforms of the Yeltsin years to such an extent that all of the major political blocs in the 1999 parliamentary campaign offered voters a centrist message.[67]

Second, Putin is likely to have an easier time dealing with the legislature simply by virtue of the fact that he is not Yeltsin. Yeltsin was so stigmatized by the opposition and by many erstwhile supporters for dismantling the Soviet Union, bombing the White House, and starting the first war in Chechnya that he could not possibly develop a working relationship with the legislature based on mutual trust. Despite his close association with the Yeltsin regime, President Putin has been able to begin with a clean slate and has been able to build on the conciliatory practices that began to emerge in the Second Russian Republic. Ironically, although handpicked as Yeltsin's successor, Putin has benefitted from an image of being everything Yeltsin was not – young, healthy, professional, and capable of working with all political forces.

The post-Yeltsin era that is now emerging has offered some relatively propitious conditions for executive-legislative cooperation, given Putin's enormous popularity and the timing of elections. Yet, the cooperative atmosphere is personalistic in nature, based solely on the political stature of Vladimir Putin. As the initial years of the Yeltsin presidency demonstrate, a president's popular support is often fleeting and can weaken

---

[66] See also Robert G. Moser, "The Electoral Effects of Presidentialism in Russia," *The Journal of Communist Studies and Transition Politics*, Vol. 14, No. 1/2 (1998), pp. 54–75.

[67] Mikhail Dmitriev, "Party Economic Programs and Implications," in McFaul, Petrov, and Ryabov (eds.), *Primer on Russia's 1999 Duma Elections*, pp. 37–40.

quickly in the face of the complex challenges facing Russia. The ambitious programs to strengthen federal power and restructure the economy
that Putin has begun to pursue will no doubt engender some opposition.
It will take more than personal charisma for Putin to retain his current
favor with the State Duma.

A stable, well-established party system will be vital for any future
institutionalization of cordial relations between Russia's two branches of
government. Political parties offer a cost-effective means of producing
stable, long-term majority coalitions in the legislature and provide crucial
organizational linkages between the president and the legislature.[68] While
parties remain weak, party development has been taking place in Russia.
Proportional representation, which is used to elect half the seats in the
Duma, has forced the creation of parties. The extreme fractionalization
of the party system witnessed in 1995 began to subside in 1999, as voters
and elites heeded the incentives of the 5 percent legal threshold. But consolidation and institutionalization of the party system is most reliant
upon political elites. Well-known politicians, especially contenders for
the presidency, must form parties rather than run as independents. Such
parties could have a contagious effect on the rest of the political spectrum, much as the Gaullist party did in France during the Fifth Republic. Its electoral success pushed the left to consolidate in order to remain
electorally competitive.[69]

It is still too early for a final judgement on Putin's commitment to
party building. But, unfortunately, initial signs suggest that Putin will
follow Yeltsin's tradition of avoiding strong affiliation with a single party.
Putin has supported the transformation of Unity from an electoral
bloc to a political party and called upon the party to be the basis of a
legislative majority supporting reform. But he has stopped short of
fully embracing the party as his own.[70] Moreover, he has advocated the
removal of proportional representation from the electoral system,
because, like Yeltsin, Putin can use patronage to curry support from independents elected in single-member districts. While this may enhance his
influence over the State Duma in the short term, such a move would be
a severe blow to long-term party development.[71] The early post-Yeltsin

[68] John H. Aldrich, *Why Parties? The Origin and Transformation of Political Parties in America* (Ann Arbor: University of Michigan Press, 1995).
[69] Ezra Suleiman, "Presidentialism and Political Stability in France," in Linz and Valenzuela (eds.), *The Failure of Presidential Democracy: Comparative Perspectives*, pp. 137–162.
[70] Itar-Tass, "Russian President Calls on Unity to Become Political Bulwark of Reforms," May 27, 2000, cited in *Johnson's Russia List*, No. 4330 (May 27, 2000).
[71] Interfax, "Putin Favors Change in Russia's Electoral System," May 6, 2000, cited in *Johnson's Russia List*, No. 4289 (May 6, 2000).

experience suggests that presidential elections will continue to have a dual impact on Russian party development. On the one hand, presidential elections have allowed politicians to run independent of partisan attachments, undermining the role of parties in the electoral and governing process, as both Yeltsin and Putin's desire to be "above parties" has shown. On the other hand, presidential elections constrain the number of viable contenders, which could help consolidate the party system if there were greater congruence between presidential and parliamentary electoral dynamics.

Finally, the balance of constitutional powers between the executive and legislative branches will have a profound effect on the future stability of the system. Comparative experience suggests that in semi-presidential systems with dual executive power, conflict is less endemic and less likely to escalate into a crisis of regime when one branch is given priority in the system. The experience of the First Russian Republic provides further evidence of the danger of housing two popularly elected bodies under one constitutional roof without establishing the prerogatives of one over the other.

Many would welcome the weakening of the Russian presidency, given Yeltsin's erratic use of power and signs that Putin will centralize power to such an extent that the fragile democracy will degenerate into an electoral autocracy. But, while critiques of Russia's current system imply that a different institutional arrangement would work better, this may not be the case. The alternatives to super-presidentialism may actually increase the potential for institutional conflict and regime instability in Russia. One must remember that in countries with weakly institutionalized party systems, parliamentary systems pose their own risks to democratic consolidation. As Sartori reminds us, successful parliamentary government requires "parliamentary fit parties."[72] The likely result of parliamentary democracy in Russia's underdeveloped party system would be more akin to the fractious instability of France's Third Republic than to the efficiency of the Westminster model, or even to the multiparty coalitions of consolidated Western European states.

The emergence of Putin has removed any serious consideration of constitutional reform that would weaken the presidency. Moreover, even if the balance of power swings once again toward the legislature, it is unlikely that constitutional reform in Russia would mean the introduction of a parliamentary regime. Rather, any constitutional change would likely retain Russia's semi-presidential system but incorporate the

---

[72] Giovanni Sartori, "Neither Parliamentarism Nor Presidentialism," in Linz and Valenzuela (eds.), *The Failure of Presidential Democracy: Comparative Perspectives*, pp. 106–118.

legislature more fully into the origination and survival of government. This type of arrangement poses its own dangers. Presidential control over government personnel produced frequent turnover under Yeltsin, and one can only presume that giving both branches the power to remove ministers will produce even greater instability in the composition of the government. Such a constitutional arrangement may produce the type of instability found in the First Russian Republic, when a more constitutionally powerful legislature entered into protracted struggle for supremacy with the president. This would transform Russia from a super-presidential system, which produced poor policy but relatively stable governance under Yeltsin, to a system that resembles even more the worst elements of the "presidential-parliamentary" system that has been shown to be so unstable worldwide. Super-presidentialism may not have been very conducive to democratization in Russia, but, unfortunately, it may be preferable to the available alternatives.

Perhaps the most beneficial constitutional change for Russia would be greater separation of powers and a move toward a pure presidential system. The greatest threat to regime stability has been posed by conflicts over the composition of the government. If the government were replaced by a cabinet solely under the control of the president, this source of conflict would be removed. Many might object that this would further concentrate power in the presidency by taking the Duma completely out of decisions over who heads executive ministries. While this may be true, it is clear that the Duma has little influence over the make-up of the government under the current system, except in extraordinary situations such as the economic collapse of 1998. Moreover, this reform would entail a significant weakening of the presidency as well – the removal of dissolution power over the parliament. This is a particularly attractive element of pure presidentialism in the current political climate, given the potential for abuse of power by President Putin, who has already shown a relatively weak commitment to such pillars of democracy as human rights and freedom of the press.[73]

---

[73] Of course, the military campaign in Chechnya provides the greatest example of human rights abuses. Putin's disregard for freedom of the press has been displayed in the May 2000 attack by federal forces on Media-Most, among other things. See Brian Humphreys, "Commandos Raid Media-Most," *Moscow Times*, May 12, 2000, cited in *Johnson's Russia List*, No. 4295 (May 12, 2000); Fred Weir, "A Kremlin Warning to Media?", *Christian Science Monitor*, May 15, 2000, cited in *Johnson's Russia List*, No. 4300 (May 15, 2000); and Micheal Steen, "Moscow TV Cries Foul on Free Speech in Permit Row," *Reuters*, May 19, 2000, cited in *Johnson's Russia List*, No. 4314 (May 19, 2000).

3

The Russian Central State in Crisis: Center and Periphery in the Post-Soviet Era

Kathryn Stoner-Weiss[1]

The close of the twentieth century and the dawn of the twenty-first has brought ever-greater uncertainty for Russia. On the one hand, following the collapse of the Soviet Union in December 1991, citizens of a new Russia gained previously unprecedented freedoms: speech, association, assembly, and choice of leaders. Russians also gained access to foreign-made products, and market relations (although primitive at times) flourished. On the other hand, however, after almost ten years of transition, Russia is neither a consolidated democracy nor a finely tuned market economy.[2] Political, social, and economic problems abound. Among the most pressing of Russia's challenges, however, and a challenge that is at the root of virtually all of the others, is the crucial task of constructing a state capable of extending coherent authority into the eighty-nine provinces that comprise the Russian Federation. This chapter provides some initial insight into the weakness of the Russian central state. I emphasize that autonomy taken de facto by provincial authorities has damaged the administrative capacities of the central state and thus threatens the center's ability to pursue its policy goals in the periphery. This has become so significant a problem for Russia's future economic and political development that within days of his May 7, 2000, inauguration as Russia's second president, Vladimir Putin proposed tough legislative solutions in the hopes of creating a strong, effective central state.

His efforts come not a moment too soon. Over the last ten years, the federal government's ability to govern across the Russian expanse has

[1] Funding support for this research was provided by the National Council for Eurasian and East European Research, Contract No. 811–16, and by the Smith Richardson Foundation. The author is grateful to Eric McGlinchey, Svetlana Tsalik, Alexei Sitnikov, and Alexander Sokolowski for research assistance, as well as to Steven Solnick, Kathleen McNamara, and Sheri Berman for useful comments on this paper.
[2] Anders Aslund, *How Russia Became a Market Economy* (Washington, D.C.: Brookings Institution, 1995).

been severely eroded. The economic crisis wrought by the collapse of the ruble and unilateral government debt default in August, 1998, presented yet another opportunity for provincial leaders to threaten the federal center's already tenuous ability to rule Russia. The imposition of price controls, trade restrictions, and threats of tax withholding in the fall of 1998 made some analysts and observers harken back to the early 1990s, when the survival of the Russian state appeared to be at serious risk.[3] Certainly, the "August events" presented regional leaders with new opportunities to further challenge central authority. But their abilities and propensities to avail themselves of central weakness should be viewed as part of a steady march toward a more decentralized Russian Federation and a weakened central state that predates the disastrous financial events of August 1998 and has extended far beyond them.

What follows is a brief examination of the formal and informal processes by which expanding spheres of political and economic autonomy have devolved to the Russian provinces over the last decade. I define autonomy as "the freedom regions have for discretionary decision making unimpeded by central control."[4] The greater the regional autonomy that is wrested from the central state, the less capacity the center has to penetrate the periphery, mobilize the population there to its causes, and have its authority recognized as legitimate.

The mechanisms by which Russia's provinces gained increased autonomy include bilateral negotiations and the signing of bilateral treaties and agreements with the center. But a rather striking amount of the autonomy gained by the provinces was simply taken de facto, rather than negotiated and delegated by the federal center de jure. This has severely eroded Russian central state strength. I adopt Joel Migdal's definition of state strength as the ability a state has to

---

[3] For a small sampling of the kinds of aggressive actions regional leaders have taken since the collapse of the Russian economy in August 1998, see, for example: Oleg Odnokolenko, "Repetitsiia razvala Rossiiskoi Federatsii," *Segodnya*, September 15, 1998, p. 2; Igor Sas'kov, "Lebed' prikazak tsenam ne rasti," *Segodnya*, September 2, 1998, p. 1; "Russian Regional Leaders Taking Anti-Inflation Measures," *Foreign Broadcast Information Service Daily Report*, September 8, 1998; Pavel Avramov, "Lebed's Brother Publicly Defies Yeltsin, Launches Tax Mutiny," *Institute for East–West Studies, Russian Regional Report, Internet Edition*, Vol. 3, No. 34 (August 27, 1998); "Many Local Governments Setting Up Their Own Security Councils," *Institute for East West Studies, Russian Regional Report, Internet Edition*, Vol. 3, No. 34 (August 27, 1998); Irina Morozova, "Stavropol Imposes Price, Export Controls Despite Legal Protests," *Institute for East–West Studies, Russian Regional Report, Internet Edition*, Vol. 3, No. 38 (September 23, 1998).

[4] Robert Putnam, Roberto Leonardi, and Rafaella Nanetti, "Devolution as a Political Process: The Case of Italy," *Publius*, Vol. 11, No. 1 (1981), p. 95.

penetrate society, regulate social relationships, extract resources, and appropriate or use resources in determined ways. Strong states are those with high capabilities to complete these tasks, while weak states are on the low end of a spectrum of these capabilities.[5]

In the post-Soviet era, the Russian state was supposed to succeed where the Soviet state had failed. Where Soviet institutions gradually diminished in their ability to provide the population with services, and the economy ceased to provide enough quality goods, the hope was that the new democraticized and marketized Russia would do better. It has not. At the end of the twentieth century, approximately 35 percent of Russians lived below the official poverty line; average life expectancy for males was fifty-nine years, and for females seventy-three years. Pension arrears and wage arrears persisted throughout Russia in the late 1990s, partly because regional government officials simply redirected federal funds intended to pay off these arrears. This was despite the fact that federal state agencies were abundant in both center and periphery, and the state's participation in social and economic life was very significant on paper. Indeed, Russian state expenditures at all levels of government (federal and regional) comprised between 38 and 42 percent of official gross domestic product from 1995 to 1998. This translates into 56 to 61 percent of real legal gross domestic product.[6] But despite this high degree of penetration into the periphery, the central state did not govern authoritatively in the Russian heartland. That is, although the central state had a presence on paper in a wide variety of policy areas through the 1990s, it lacked power in practice.

The eroding authority of the federal center is especially worrisome given the developmental task that the Russian state faced over the last decade and will continue to face in the twenty-first century. Moreover, as President Putin himself immediately recognized, the center's waning ability to ensure that its will is fulfilled poses an extremely serious threat to the country's further political and economic development.

The aims of this chapter are threefold. First, I examine how far central state capacity has eroded in governing the Russian provinces by exploring the degree to which the provinces have gained increased de facto and de jure autonomy. Second, I identify, if only preliminarily, the key causes of weakened central state capacity in ruling Russia. Third and finally, I provide an initial evaluation of the consequences of a weakened Russian central state for future economic and political development.

---

[5] Joel Migdal, *Strong Societies and Weak States: State-Society Relations and State Capabilities in the Third World* (Princeton: Princeton University Press, 1988), pp. 4–5.
[6] Andrei Illarionov, "What Went Wrong in Russia: The Roots of the Economic Crisis," *Journal of Democracy*, Vol. 10, No. 4 (1999), p. 76.

My approach is somewhat distinct from previous work on center-periphery relations in Russia. Other scholars have focused more on the center's impact on the periphery in terms of fiscal federalism and strategic bargains aimed at lending predictability to the center's relations with the provinces. Daniel Treisman, for example, argues that the center used budgetary subventions strategically to buy off some regions so that they stopped their pursuit of autonomy or independence, while effectively punishing other regions who were (ironically) more loyal by not extending similar subventions. In other words, he finds a correlation between regional separatist activism in the early 1990s and central budgetary fiscal flows.[7] But his theory envisions a relatively consolidated central state capable of responding quickly and resolutely to aggressive regional demands. The evidence garnered at the regional level presented here challenges this picture, as well as casting doubt on the idea that the center, by opening and closing the tap of fiscal flows at certain times, effectively ended other equally serious regional challenges to its authority.

Steven L. Solnick, while critical of Treisman's conclusions, also envisions a coherent federal center that is capable of strategically bargaining with selected regions so as to prevent the most powerful regions from acting collectively to extract even more benefits from the center.[8] While I do not dispute that this may be at least partially correct, my perspective challenges the notion that the central state is strong enough or unified enough regarding its policy goals to act in this directed manner. Further, I argue that it is the de facto autonomous action of many regions that has done particular damage to the administrative capacities of the central state and has served to steadily erode the center's ability to fulfill its own developmental goals. The evidence presented here suggests that, in fact, the central government's "containment" strategy (through the signing of bilateral treaties or strategic use of budgetary transfers) was not particularly effective in stemming further autonomy taken by regions de facto. Thus, where previous scholarship has more heavily emphasized the center's impact on the periphery, I look at both the formal and informal ways in which regional government action has affected the abilities of agencies at the federal center.

In adopting this approach, my perspective has much in common with some of the recent theoretical work on the developing world that exam-

[7] Daniel Treisman, "The Politics of Intergovernmental Transfers in Post-Soviet Russia,"*British Journal of Political Science*, Vol. 26, No. 3 (1996), pp. 299–336; Daniel Treisman, "Russia's Ethnic Revival: The Separatist Activism of Regional Leaders in a Postcommunist Order," *World Politics*, Vol. 49, No. 2 (1997), pp. 212–249.

[8] Steven L. Solnick, "Federal Bargaining in Russia," *East European Constitutional Review*, Vol. 4, No. 4 (1995), pp. 52–58.

ines the causes and consequences of weak states.[9] I want to emphasize that there are obviously certain advantages politically and economically to keeping the Russian central state weak. The Soviet state was overly intrusive into people's daily lives, and a democratic Russian state should obviously allow far greater political and economic freedom. To encourage thriving markets and a lively democracy, the Russian state should be smaller and weaker than its Soviet predecessor. Further, experience from other transitional contexts demonstrates that strong states faced with weak societies can do great damage to the development of markets and pluralistic politics. At most, some would argue, the state should regulate certain key aspects of markets in order to keep transaction costs low and ensure the free flow of goods. But doing even this requires some degree of state strength, and it requires recognition of the authority of the central state in certain key policy areas.

As Migdal, Kohli, and others have argued in other contexts, chronically weak states present a host of dangers for developing countries. They cannot provide even the most minimal protections to their citizens; they cannot ensure the free flow of goods across the country; they cannot provide basic health and educational services; and they cannot prevent unfettered rent seeking and pilfering by self-serving bureaucrats.[10] Moreover, relative to the monumental developmental goals that the Russian state set for itself at the start of the 1990s, its weakness is all the more problematic and pressing for the country's future political, economic, and social development.

THE SOVIET PAST: THE INSTITUTIONAL UNRAVELING OF A STRONG CENTER

During all but the final few years of the Soviet system, central dominance over the periphery was ensured by a multilayered and overlapping system of institutional subordination. The four institutional cornerstones of the center's control over the periphery were: the Communist Party, the unitary system of soviets, the vertical organization of ministries, and the planning mechanisms of the economy.

Under the Soviet system, the Communist Party of the Soviet Union (CPSU) exercised overarching control of the center over the periphery.

---

[9] Migdal, *Strong Societies and Weak States*; Joel S. Migdal, Atul Kohli, and Vivienne Shue (eds.), *State Power and Social Forces: Domination and Transformation in the Third World* (New York: Cambridge University Press, 1994).

[10] Stephen Holmes, "What Russia Teaches Us Now: How Weak States Threaten Liberty," *The American Prospect*, No. 33 (July–August 1997), pp. 30–39; Migdal, *Strong Societies and Weak States*; Samuel P. Huntington, *Political Order in Changing Societies* (New Haven: Yale University Press, 1968); Peter Evans, *Embedded Autonomy: States and Industrial Transformation* (Princeton: Princeton University Press, 1997).

The Soviet Union itself was comprised of fifteen separate union republics, of which the Russian Socialist Federated Soviet Republic (the RSFSR), the predecessor of the Russian Federation, was the largest. The RSFSR was further subdivided into eighty-eight territorial units, divided into three categories: (1) sixteen autonomous republics; (2) forty nine oblasts and six *krais*, plus the two special status cities of Moscow and Leningrad (now St. Petersburg); and (3) fifteen autonomous oblasts and autonomous *okrugs* (geographically located within the borders of some autonomous republics, oblasts, and *krais*). The autonomies (autonomous republics, autonomous oblasts, and autonomous *okrugs*) were organized around one or several of the hundred or so ethnic groups located on the territory of the RSFSR (thus the Tatar Autonomous Republic, the Buryat Autonomous Republic, etc.). Oblasts and *krais* were essentially administrative units. Oblasts, primarily populated by ethnic Russians, were not attributed any particular ethnic character, whereas *krais* combined characteristics of both oblasts and autonomous republics.

Fourteen of the fifteen union republics had their own Party organizations. The RSFSR, however, was included in the All-Union Party structures until 1990, when a Russian Communist Party was founded. Within the RSFSR, the CPSU had provincial party organs in all of the eighty-eight subnational units. These began at the autonomous republic and oblast levels and descended to the district or county (*raion*) level, city level, village level, all the way down to the Primary Party Organizations that were present in all places of work. Each level was dominated by the next highest level, with the oblast and autonomous republic Party organizations at the top of the territorial hierarchy. In the RSFSR, oblast and autonomous republic Party organs were subordinate only to the Central Committee of the CPSU. The first secretary of the oblast or autonomous republican Party committee (*obkom*) was therefore the undisputed political boss of the region – termed "prefect" by Jerry Hough in the late 1960s.[11] Since party organizations were designed to parallel state organs of power, the basic state legislative units were (in descending order of administrative authority) autonomous republican and oblast soviets, *raion* soviets, city soviets, and village soviets. Despite modest attempts at reform during the 1960s and 1970s, "administration at the local level was effectively an extension of central authority."[12] Further buttressing

---

[11] Jerry F. Hough, *The Soviet Prefects: The Local Party Organs in Industrial Decision-Making* (Cambridge, Mass.: Harvard University Press, 1969).

[12] Ronald J. Hill, "The Development of Soviet Local Government since Stalin's Death," in Everett M. Jacobs (ed.), *Soviet Local Politics and Government* (Boston: Allen and Unwin, 1983), p. 18, as cited in Kathryn Stoner-Weiss, *Local Heroes: The Political Economy of Russian Regional Governance* (Princeton: Princeton University Press, 1997), p. 64, note 24.

the hierarchical system of top-down control was firm center-periphery linkage through the "unitary system of soviets" or legislatures, such that each was subordinated to the next highest level.

Just as importantly, the soviets were dominated by the corresponding Party organizations. The second-longest-serving general secretary of the Communist Party (after Stalin), Leonid Brezhnev, modernized the original Bolshevik principle (initiated under Lenin during the Civil War) of Party supremacy in Article 6 of the 1977 Constitution of the Soviet Union. Article 6 identified the Communist Party as "the leading and guiding force of Soviet society and the nucleus of its political system, of all state organizations and public organizations." In practical terms, this meant that the Party maintained control over local soviets, often supplanting their authority. The Party dominated the soviets through a range of instruments, not the least of which was control over the nominations of deputies to sit in regional legislatures. These deputies, in turn, elected an executive committee of the soviet (*ispolkom*), and generally the overlap between the chief functionaries of the local party organization and the *ispolkom* was significant, if not perfect.

Finally, the vertical structure of the myriad ministries that ran practically all aspects of social, cultural, political, and economic life in the Soviet Union ensured further centralization. Administrative agencies at the regional and local levels were subordinated to the department or ministry at the next highest level:

Thus the city education department [was] subordinated to both the executive committee of the city soviet and the oblast education department. The oblast education department in turn [was] responsible both to the executive committee of the oblast soviet and the republican ministry of education. The executive committee itself [was] subordinated to both the local soviet and the executive committee (or Council of Ministers) at the next territorial level.[13]

The dictates of the planned economy meant also that local soviets had virtually no independent authority to establish their own spending priorities – this was essentially decided by central bureaucrats in Moscow. In sum, the Soviet system of multi-institutional subordination ensured a high degree of centralization and rendered regional governments little more than administrative, not policy-making (and certainly not central policy–flouting) organs.

As the Soviet system began to unravel in the late 1980s, however, so too did this vertical system of central control over the periphery. This was in part hastened by the holding of free elections to regional soviets

[13] Jerry F. Hough and Merle Fainsod, *How the Soviet Union Is Governed* (Cambridge, Mass.: Harvard University Press, 1979), p. 490.

(or legislatures) in the spring of 1990, thus damaging the unitary system of soviets and loosening the stranglehold of the CPSU on the machinery of government. The Party itself collapsed following the attempted August 1991 coup against then-president of the Soviet Union Mikhail Gorbachev, although its death knell had been sounded when Gorbachev lifted Article 6 in the spring of 1990, just as Russians elected new regional legislatures in popular contests. In the summer of 1991, the new president of Russia, Boris N. Yeltsin, took the extraordinary step of banning the Party in all places of work in his republic. This was later declared unconstitutional, but at the time it seriously damaged the authority of the Party across Russia and further helped to weaken central control over regional political and economic actors in the periphery.

The gradual erosion of the power of central ministries over the economy in particular was brought about initially through a series of half-baked reforms under Gorbachev, also in the late 1980s. Throughout the late 1980s, the staffs of the huge bureaucracies were slashed and the ministries were subjected to a series of ill-conceived reorganizations.[14] This led to a reduced role for planning agencies and federal bureaucracies in regional economies, and contributed to the emerging independent authority of powerful enterprise directors.[15]

Finally, Yeltsin's political jockeying with Gorbachev in 1990 and 1991 for Russian supremacy over the unraveling USSR also undoubtedly hastened the devolution of power. His now infamous exhortation to regional leaders within Russia to "take as much autonomy as you can swallow"[16] paralleled his own struggles against union supremacy and Gorbachev's desperate attempts in 1991 to hold the Soviet Union together.

Yeltsin likely did not anticipate, however, just how much autonomy Russia's regional governments would grab through the 1990s. Nor did he anticipate the effect their efforts would have on the Russian central state's ability to govern. In 1990 and 1991 the autonomous republics of Russia changed their names to republics to denote what they considered to be their newly elevated status. Four (Adigai, Gorno-Altai, Karachia, and Khakassia) of five autonomous oblasts similarly declared themselves sovereign and also unilaterally raised their status to that of republic. This too was the beginning of a dangerous precedent. By declaring themselves

---

[14] Peter Rutland, *The Politics of Economic Stagnation in the Soviet Union: The Role of Local Party Organs in Economic Management* (New York: Cambridge University Press, 1993), p. 208.

[15] For more on the breakdown of hierarchical control in Soviet institutions, see Steven L. Solnick, *Stealing the State: Control and Collapse in Soviet Institutions* (Cambridge, Mass.: Harvard University Press, 1998).

[16] *Komsomolskaya Pravda*, March 14, 1991.

republics, these autonomous oblasts grabbed increased jurisdiction over their own territories. As a result, the Russian Federation is currently comprised of twenty-one republics, forty-nine oblasts, six *krais*, the two special status cities of Moscow and St. Petersburg (both of which have oblast status), ten autonomous *okrugs*, and one autonomous oblast. The Chechen republic, of course, declared itself independent and waged a partially successful war of independence with the Russian Federation from 1994 to 1996. A second Chechen conflict began in the fall of 1999 and remains unresolved at the time of this writing. The government of the Chechen republic does not consider Chechnia to be a part of the Russian Federation today, but it is usually still counted as such since its formal relationship with Russia has yet to be decided conclusively.

NEGOTIATED AUTONOMY: THE BILATERAL TREATY PROCESS

In part, the particularly confrontational years of center-periphery relations (in particular, from 1990–91 through 1993) stemmed from divergent views regarding the appropriate distribution of power among levels of government. The center favored a national federal system – a type of "federalism from above" – where the central government would clearly take the lead in determining the distribution of power between itself and the federation's constituent units; whereas regional leaders advocated (and continue to advocate) a more contractually based federal system.

Contractual federalism foresees each subnational unit entering the federation on a negotiated basis, such that the center's power would be deemphasized relative to that of the federation's constituent parts. The center's failed *zemli* proposal (according to which Russia would have been redistricted into fifty regions rather than eighty-nine), the "war of laws" of the early 1990s between the federal center and a number of regions, and the regional practice of temporarily withholding federal tax revenues should all be viewed in the context of these conflicting perspectives on the shape of the Russian state.[17] The compromise that eventually emerged was a result of regional government action that, since 1994 in particular, has forced the center to cede more political and economic control. The economic crisis of autumn 1998 merely extended this process. The result was that by the early spring of 2000, President Putin resorted to sweeping legislative proposals designed to tighten Russia's federal structure.

Conflicts in center-periphery relations in Russia arose early in the reform process. The legislatures created through popular election in 1990

[17] For more on these examples of center-regional conflict, see Stoner-Weiss, *Local Heroes*, Chapter 3.

introduced the notion of accountability to local politics. Not unreasonably, if regional legislators were to be held responsible by constituents for the political and economic conditions of their regions, then they wanted more control over key policy instruments. This early period was punctuated by the frequent practice of regional governments' withholding tax revenues from federal authorities, and periodic refusals on the part of some regions to follow central policy prescriptions in areas such as privatization.[18]

Initial steps toward negotiated autonomy included the three federative agreements of 1992 (which were long on promise, but short on meaningful transfer of power from center to periphery), and then an initial set of bilateral treaties in 1994.[19] These included the treaty between the federal center and the Republic of Tatarstan in February 1994, and similar bilateral treaties between the center and six other republics by the end of the same year. Eventually, however, the central government moved far enough away from its initial conception of "federalism from above" to sign additional treaties with thirty-three other constituent units of the federation in 1996 and 1997.[20] At the time of this writing there were reportedly forty-seven treaties in all.[21]

Despite this penchant for cutting bilateral deals with particular regions, the central government authorities also intended for the 1993 Constitution of the Russian Federation to serve as the defining document for center-periphery relations. It incorporated two articles (71 and 72) enumerating exclusive federal and shared federal and regional areas of jurisdiction, but did not include an article enumerating or exclusively reserving certain powers for the regions. In the wake of the breakup of the Soviet Union and the violent showdown between the president and the Supreme Soviet of October 1993 (in which many regional govern-

---

[18] Natalyia Gorodetskaya, "Irkutsk Refuses to Pay Taxes into the Federal Budget," *Nezavisimaya gazeta*, May 22, 1992, p. 2.

[19] Stoner-Weiss, *Local Heroes*, pp. 85–87.

[20] Nikolay Petrov and A. Titkov, "Geokhronologiya" (Geochronology), in *Politicheskii Landshaft Rossii* (The political landscape of Russia) *Biulleten'* No. 2–3 (Moscow: Carnegie Endowment for International Peace, 1997), p. 13.

[21] Full texts of the treaties and agreements signed from February 15, 1994, through June 13, 1996, are published in M. N. Guboglo (ed.), *Federalizm vlasti i vlast' federalizma* (Moscow: State Duma of the Russian Federation, Committee on Federal and Regional Policy, and the Russian Academy of Sciences, Institute of Ethnology and Anthropology, 1997). Those treaties and agreements signed in 1997 are most easily available, I have found, through signatory regional government and republican administrations. See also V. N. Lysenko, "Razdelenie vlasti i opit Rossiiskoi Federatsii" (Division of power and the experience of the Russian Federation), in Guboglo (ed.), *Federalizm vlasti i vlast' federalizma*, pp. 166–193.

ments supported the latter), President Yeltsin and his team of constitutional drafters thought that by not enumerating the exclusive rights of regions, they were limiting what Yeltsin would later term "political" agreements with errant regions, like Tatarstan.[22]

Tatarstan, therefore, established its relationship with the federal center on a unique basis – "contractual" rather than constitutional.[23] The Tatarstan treaty was signed only a few weeks after the adoption of the Russian Constitution in December 1993. Sergei Shakhray (then chair of the Presidential Commission for the Preparation of Treaties on the Division of Powers and Authorities between the Federal Organs of State Power and the Organs of State Power of the Subjects of the Federation, the body charged with signing bilateral agreements on behalf of the federal government), explained that the Tatarstan treaty was not intended to serve as a model for other regions. It "was politically necessary to eliminate the separatist tendencies that existed in the republic between 1990 and 1993, to establish a legal path to resolving the problem of stability and to normalize the relations of power."[24] The problem, of course, was that signing such an agreement with one constituent unit opened the door to further demands for special treatment by other regions. In sum, the Tatarstan treaty set a dangerous precedent and had the effect of raising the status of one member of the federation, although the Constitution explicitly states that all members are of equal status (Article 5, point 4).

Naturally, other regions sought to rectify this situation, and it is here that we see the center becoming more reactive than proactive in its relations with many of the eighty-nine regions of Russia. For example, as Shakhray himself described it, "[b]eginning in 1994–5, gradually the procedure arose of preparing and signing agreements on the division of subjects and authority between federal and regional organs of state power."[25] Although he insisted that the basis of federal relations in Russia was constitutional and not contractual, noting that the Constitution of 1993 foresaw the possibility of such agreements,[26] Shakhray's own account of the process by which bilateral agreements have been signed indicates that the practice was not intended to be as widespread as it became. In sum, while key central officials like Shakhray continue to pay lip service to their conception of "federalism from above,"

[22] B. N. Yeltsin, radio address, October 31, 1997.

[23] Lysenko, "Razdelenie vlasti i opit Rossiiskoi Federatsii," p. 172.

[24] Sergei Shakhray, "Rol' dogovorniikh protsessov v ukreplenii i razvitii rossiiskogo federalizma" (The role of the treaty processes in the strengthening and development of Russian federalism), in Guboglo (ed.), *Federalizm vlasti i vlast' federalizma*, p. 152.

[25] Ibid., p. 153.   [26] Ibid., p. 156.

established on a national-constitutional basis, their actions indicate that in fact they have now come to favor a contractually based conception of the Russian Federation.

A brief examination of the process by which the treaties were formed and an analysis of their content, and that of their accompanying agreements, further supports this perspective. It is important to note at the outset that the impetus for the treaties came from the regions themselves and not from the center.[27] A commission appointed by the president was responsible for negotiations with the regions on behalf of the federal government. The treaties (*dogovora*) themselves are relatively general statements regarding the nature of the division of powers and shared powers between the particular subject of the federation and federal institutions. All the treaties are slightly different, although they contain some common elements. They are accompanied by a series of agreements (*soglasheniye*), which can be signed any time after the conclusion of the treaties.

The agreements are far more detailed than the treaties with respect to specific policy purviews and are, therefore, rather wildly different for each region depending on particular policy concerns and resource endowments. Sverdlovsk, for example, signed eighteen agreements, ranging from the region's investment policy, to use of natural resources, to health and cultural policies, in addition to its original treaty. By contrast, Kaliningrad signed only three agreements: one on education and science, another on cultural questions, and a third on maintaining law and order in the region.[28]

Further, regions were able to propose additional agreements after they had signed their original treaties.[29] Many, but not all, of the agreements were made for set periods of time (generally two to five years). According to the terms of these time-bound agreements, they may be canceled by either party (the region or the federal center), provided that each side provides the other with notice at least six months prior to the expiration of the agreement of its intention to do so. If no such notice is provided,

---

[27] Ibid., p. 157.

[28] See the "Treaty on the Division of Power and Authority between the Organs of State Power of the Russian Federation and Organs of State Power of Sverdlovsk Oblast" as well as the eighteen *soglasheniye*. All are published in Guboglo (ed.), *Federalizm vlasti i vlast' federalizma*, pp. 313–19 and pp. 652–690. Kaliningrad's agreements are in Guboglo (ed.), *Federalizm vlasti i vlast' federalizma*, pp. 642–648.

[29] For example, Sverdlovsk oblast concluded its agreement on the regulation of land relations and the administration of land on May 29, 1996, although its original treaty with Moscow and other agreements were signed on January 12, 1996. See Guboglo (ed.), *Federalizm vlasti i vlast' federalizma*, p. 870.

the agreements are automatically renewed for an additional two to five years.[30]

According to the presidential decree (no. 370) of March 12, 1996, the treaties and accompanying agreements were not to violate the constitution of the Russian Federation; could not change the status of a subject of the Federation; could not add to or change what is enumerated in Articles 71 and 72 of the Constitution; and were to respect the supremacy of the Constitution.[31] On this basis, in the view of central officials, the treaties and agreements were not intended to be extra-constitutional documents; they were merely supposed to "concretize areas of joint jurisdiction specific to each subject of the Russian Federation, taking into account the specific peculiarities of each region."[32]

In reality, however, a number of the treaties and agreements actually did either contradict the Constitution or go beyond what was envisioned in Articles 71 and 72. For example, areas that in the Constitution of the Russian Federation are ascribed to the federal government exclusively (Article 71) appeared as areas of joint authority in many treaties. This type of constitutional violation appeared in the treaties of North Ossetiya (Article 4, point 3), Kabardino-Balkariya (Article 4, point g), Tatarstan (Article 3, point 2), and Bashkortostan (Article 4, point 2), where the treaties granted these regions the right to defend state and territorial integrity. Another notable example is the authority both Sverdlovsk and Udmurtiya gained in their treaties over the functioning of enterprises in the defense complex (Article 2, point g of the Sverdlovsk Treaty; Article 2, part 7 of Udmurtiya's Treaty).[33]

Further, in a number of agreements, areas that were again to be exclusively reserved for the Russian Federation government were included in lists of authorities for subjects of the Federation. For example, participation in international relations, the establishment of relations with foreign states and conducting agreements with them (Tatarstan, Article 2, point 11); the establishment of national banks (Tatarstan, Article 2, point 12; Bashkortostan, Article 3, point 11); and questions of republi-

---

[30] A statement to this effect appears at the end of all the agreements between Sverdlovsk oblast and Moscow, although no such statement appears at the end of the agreements with Kaliningrad, and only a few other regions' agreements contain this statement. See Guboglo (ed.), *Federalizm vlasti i vlast' federalizma.*

[31] Shakhray, "Rol' dogovorniikh protsessov v ukreplenii i razvitii rossiiskogo federalizma," p. 157.

[32] Ibid., p. 158.

[33] These and almost twenty other areas where many of the treaties violate the Constitution are cited in Lysenko, "Razdelenie vlasti i opit Rossiiskoi Federatsii," pp. 184–185.

can citizenship (Tatarstan, Article 2, point 8; Kabardino-Balkariya, Article 3, point k; Bashkortostan, Article 3, point 1).[34]

Finally, areas that in the Constitution are identified as spheres of joint jurisdiction between the federal government and the subjects of the Federation at times appeared in the treaties as the apparently exclusive authority of several of the subjects of the Federation. Such areas include the defense of the rights of citizens (Tatarstan, Article 2, point 1; Kabardino-Balkariya, Article 3, point j; Bashkortostan, Article 3, point 1); formation and use of a republican precious metals and stones fund (Yakutiya, Article 1, point j); and a system of state organs, their organization and activities (Tatarstan, Article 1, point 7; Kabardino-Balkariya, Article 3, point g; Bashkortostan, Article 3, point 2), to name but a few.[35] It remains unclear whether a June 1999 federal law ("On the principles and ordering of the division of areas of jurisdiction and authority between organs of state power of the Russian Federation and organs of state power of the subjects of the Russian Federation") was intended as a mechanism by which to resolve these violations of the Russian Constitution retrospectively (that is, applying to treaties signed prior to June 1999), or merely applied to any treaties and agreements signed in the future.[36]

In sum, the treaties and agreements, despite central government declarations to the contrary, were not always based on the Constitution and supportive of the principles of the supremacy of federal law and the establishment of a single political and economic expanse. They have served to establish Russia's federal relations more on a contractual than on a national-constitutional basis, carving out far more freedom of action for the subjects of the Federation than the drafters of the 1993 Constitution had intended. On one level or another, some treaties contradicted the Constitution rather directly. Indeed, the treaties and agreements in general contradicted the declared intention of the Constitution to render all subjects of the Federation equal to one another.

There is also evidence that the treaties and agreements are themselves examples of autonomy taken by the regions rather than autonomy granted by the federal center. For example, in some important ways the

---

[34] Again, more examples can be found in Lysenko, "Razdelenie vlasti i opit Rossiiskoi Federatsii," p. 185, and through careful comparison of the treaties and the Constitution.

[35] Lysenko, "Razdelenie vlasti i opit Rossiiskoi Federatsii," p. 186; treaties of the respective regions in Guboglo (ed.), *Federalizm vlasti i vlast' federalizma*.

[36] Natalia Vladimrova Valamova, "Konstitutsionnaia model' rossiiskogo federalizama," and Tatiana Andreeva Vasilieva, "Stanovlenie federativnikh otnoshenii i praktika Konstitutsionnogo Suda Rossiiskoi Federatsii," both presented at the conference Rossiiskii federalizm, konstitutsionnie predposilki, i politicheskaia real'nost', Irkutsk, Russia, October 1–2, 1999.

1994 treaty with Tatarstan and the accompanying twelve agreements codified what was already in place in the republic. In the area of foreign trade and external ties, Tatarstan had begun to carve out its own policies before the republic gained the de jure right to do so in its treaty.[37] In addition, the republic had embarked on an ambitious need-based social assistance program as early as 1993 – well before the authority to do so was codified in the treaty.[38]

The 1996 Sverdlovsk treaty and accompanying agreements borrowed from the Constitution of the short-lived Urals Republic (in existence officially from November 1, 1993, through November 10, 1993) and served to codify many of its rather ambitious provisions regarding relations with the center.[39] These included, for example, the establishment of the region's own civil service (outside of the provisions in Article 72 of the constitution), the right to establish internal legal regulation of areas of joint regional and central jurisdiction, and the right to approve the appointment and removal of the leaders of the territorial divisions of federal organs of power in agreement with the responsible federal organs of executive power. Perhaps most striking, however, is the provision in the treaty (Article 8) that allowed the oblast to suspend the normative acts of ministries and departments of the federal government. This is a softened version of a section of the Constitution of the Urals Republic that provided for the suspension of federal law more generally. In the treaty, the oblast was given the authority to apply to the courts or to ask the Russian government directly to suspend the normative act in question. If the federal government failed to act within a month, the oblast had the right to unilaterally suspend the federal normative act.[40]

Although the treaties may have served to calm the more rebellious and demanding regions of Russia (Tatarstan and Sverdlovsk chief among them) in some respects, this came at considerable cost to the federal government. The empirical evidence indicates that the treaty-signing process worked more to the advantage of the regions than of the center. Addi-

---

[37] Agreements were signed in early 1994 that had existed in draft form prior to the February 1994 bilateral treaty. See John Slocum, "Russia's Regions and Republics as International Actors: The Case of Tatarstan," mimeo, 1997.

[38] Lyudmila Nikolayevna Kolesnikova, director of section on social guarantees, State Committee on Labor and Social Questions, and Marina Vladimirovna Shishigina, division head, Division of Social Protection, Ministry of Social Welfare, Republic of Tatarstan. Interviews conducted by Svetlana Tsalik on behalf of the author in April 1997 in the Republic of Tatarstan. The references are taken from transcribed tapes of the interviews.

[39] For more on the Sverdlovsk case and the Urals Republic, see Gerald M. Easter, "Redefining Centre-Regional Relations in the Russian Federation: Sverdlovsk Oblast," *Europe-Asia Studies*, Vol. 49, No. 4 (1997), pp. 617–635.

[40] Lysenko, "Razdelenie vlasti i opit Rossiiskoi Federatsii," p. 178.

tionally, in some areas of joint competency enumerated in a number of the treaties and agreements and in Article 72 of the Constitution, no federal law existed (for example, private ownership of farm land). The result, then, is that many regions, through their treaties and agreements, gained the legal authority to act unfettered by any central regulation or oversight whatsoever in these policy areas.

DE FACTO AUTONOMY: EXPANDING SPHERES OF REGIONAL AUTONOMY

The economic crisis wrought by the August 1998 ruble devaluation served to underscore the fact that in practice many regions exercise autonomy beyond what is provided for in the bilateral agreements, the Constitution, or existing federal law. That is, the treaties did not afford much predictability to center-periphery relations, nor did they reliably ensure the implementation of and adherence to central policy at the provincial level.

Increased autonomy is sometimes simply taken by republics and oblasts alike.[41] Over the last ten years, regions have been punished infrequently by central authorities for doing so. President Putin's most aggressive legislative innovation, however, allows for the removal from office of governors and the dissolution of legislatures that issue legislation judged to be in contradiction to federal law and the Constitution.[42]

De facto autonomy arose in the latter half of the 1990s in particular because the center had simply defaulted on many of its jurisdictional responsibilities. Regions, to the degree that they were able, were left to fill the empty policy space as best they could. Others could not afford to

---

[41] Further study is required to determine whether certain types of regions and republics tend to be more aggressive in seizing policy autonomy from the center. It is clear that this behavior takes place in both oblasts and republics, but in some oblasts and republics more than in others.

[42] Putin's original package of legislative proposals appears in *Nezavisimaia gazeta*, May 20, 2000. The package included two key pieces of legislation. The Duma formally adopted this legislation (with some amendments) in July 2000. The laws include a change in the composition of the Federation Council such that regional governors and heads of regional legislatures do not automatically gain seats. Instead, the governor nominates a representative to the Federation Council whose tenure coincides with his own. The regional duma also nominates and appoints a representative whose term coincides with its own. A second legislative change outlines the mechanisms by which regional governors may be removed from office and regional legislatures might be dissolved should they pass regional laws or decrees that have been ruled in court to be direct violations of the Constitution of the Russian Federation or federal law. While this is a strong stick for the federal government to wield, given that the regional legislatures and governors are popularly elected, it is likely that this power will be used rarely if at all. At time of writing, this law had yet to be tested.

implement central policy and so carved out for themselves a different sort of autonomy – the freedom to do nothing.

Examples of policy autonomy taken (as opposed to granted or formally acknowledged by the federal center) in the face of central state incapacity come from a whole host of regions and policy areas. In the mid to late 1990s, the continuing problem of wage arrears that persisted in many regions (despite central government avowals to end such practices) is but one of many notable examples. Regional governments, in many cases, simply appropriated the funds transferred by the center for the payment of wages to public sector workers and used these funds in other areas of their cash strapped budgets. Earlier in the reform process, many regions refused to free the prices of basic consumer goods, delayed the implementation of the state privatization program, and continued to hamper small business development.[43]

De facto policy autonomy was also particularly evident in the area of social welfare – a sphere of the utmost importance in a country whose economy has all but collapsed. According to Article 72, point j of the Constitution, social welfare is under the joint jurisdiction of the regions and the federal government. As already mentioned, as early as 1993, before it concluded its bilateral treaty with the federal center, Tatarstan embarked independently on its own need-based set of social assistance programs (prior to the conclusion of the republic's bilateral treaty or the adoption of the federal Constitution). Social assistance at the federal level has not yet been established as a need-based system (although there are plans to do so). As a result, in the 1990s, certain categories of citizens received assistance from the state regardless of whether they actually had a financial need for the assistance (e.g., all single-parent families received benefits, rather than only those who met a certain income requirement). According to the officials in Tatarstan's Ministry of Social Welfare, however, national policy in this regard was essentially unimplementable, since the federal government was not providing sufficient funds to support such an approach to social assistance. Tatarstan's approach, then, was simply to seize the initiative and adopt a need-based system regardless of central policy dictates at the time.

Autonomy taken in social welfare policy yielded relatively positive results for the constituents of the Tatarstan government, but this proved more the exception than the rule. Evidence that the central government defaulted on its responsibilities in this area, and the sad consequences, come from two much poorer regions – Kostroma and Ivanovo. As a result of central inaction, these regions attempted to assume such policy

---

[43] Darrell Slider, "Russia's Market-Distorting Federalism," *Post-Soviet Geography and Economics*, Vol. 38, No. 8 (1997), pp. 449–451.

responsibilities regardless of whether they had the legal authority or economic capacity to do so effectively. The seemingly unintended consequence was that more autonomy fell to these regions de facto. They were held responsible by constituents, but had few resources to act.

In Kostroma, for example, the head of the oblast Department of Social Welfare explained that the federal Ministry of Labor and Social Development provided almost no support in coordinating or supporting regional programs: "I would not say that we get a lot of support from Moscow. We receive mainly methodological support."[44] In Ivanovo oblast, the head of the Department of Social Welfare was more pointed in her criticism of federal authorities:

We get no money, no information . . . nobody comes here and teaches our staff [about new federal legislation or normative acts] . . . We have been forgotten and deserted . . . We do not even receive anything apart from the occasional brochure on recent legislative innovations.[45]

Frequently, regional governments simply did not have the funds to implement federal law but were still held accountable by their constituents. In Kostroma, for example, the head of the Department of Social Welfare explained,

[W]e are sued several times a month for not implementing federal law. Pensioners do not sue the President or the Chairman of the State Duma, they all come here and sue our department . . . So far the law making activity of the federal center is aimed at making politically popular statements and has nothing to do with the real situation in the country.[46]

Indeed, the department head himself was sued in a civil court for the equivalent of 200 minimum wages for not giving a car to a disabled person.[47]

In the face of this kind of pressure from constituents and an absence of federal leadership in implementing the law, regional governments often took drastic and creative measures in desperate attempts to fill in policy space. In Kostroma, officials resorted to rather creative ways of

[44] V. I. Balyberdin, head of Kostroma Oblast Administration Department of Social Welfare. Interview conducted by Alexei Sitnikov on behalf of the author, Kostroma, July 1997. The quotations here come from transcribed tapes of the interview.

[45] L. A. Fomina, head of Ivanovo Oblast Administration Department of Social Welfare. Interview conducted by Alexei Sitnikov on behalf of the author, Kostroma, July 1997. The quotations come from transcribed tapes of the interview.

[46] Interview with Balyberdin, 1997.

[47] I. M. Nynyk, deputy head, Division of Pensions and Invalids, Kostroma Oblast Administration Department of Social Welfare. Interview conducted by Alexei Sitnikov on behalf of the author, Kostroma, July 1997. The quotations come from transcribed tapes of the interview.

financing social assistance programs in response to failed promises to deliver funds by federal authorities. One official described the following example:

We made an agreement with a car manufacturer that produces specially equipped cars for invalids. It agreed to provide us with vehicles we need if we paid its energy debt to Mosenergo. It was obvious that we could not pay it, and so we were left with no cars for our disabled . . . So we looked for other possibilities and discovered them. We made agreements with plants that supply the car manufacturer with parts. We came up with 760 million rubles a month in spare parts [which we sold to the auto producer in return for a few cars].[48]

In Ivanovo, the head of the Social Welfare Department explained that in an effort to get legally required funds from federal ministries, "we have contacted the federal agencies, written letters, sent in our analysis of the situation, but so far have not received a coherent response. It seems as though nobody in Moscow has any idea of what is going on in the regions."[49] As a result, the oblast did what it could to provide the social assistance that is guaranteed by federal law – and that is supposed to be paid for with federal funds – with what help it was able to squeeze from local enterprises and its own limited budgetary funds. Often, however, federal law went unimplemented, and often with impunity from central government authorities. Policy autonomy amounted, in these cases, to the freedom to opt out of central policy initiatives altogether.

Finally, regions continued to carve out more de facto autonomy through their legislative efforts. For example, *Izvestiya* reported in 1997 that the Justice Ministry examined 44,000 regional legal acts, including gubernatorial orders, and found that "nearly half [i.e., almost 22,000!] of them do not correspond with the Constitution of the Russian Federation." For example, North Ossetiya, Voronezh, Samara, Arkhangelsk, Irkutsk, Tyumen', and Omsk have all apparently passed legislation restructuring their judiciaries, a right exclusively reserved to the federal government by Article 71 of the Constitution. Further, Altay *krai* and Sverdlovsk oblast, among others, have passed hard currency, credit, and customs laws, also in violation of the Constitution. Other regions have even introduced illegal taxes (Kareliya, Volgograd, and Nizhnyi Novgorod).[50] More recently, a similar report was issued indicating that during the first three quarters of 1998, 30 percent of regional acts were found to violate the Constitution and federal law.[51] Governor Mikhail

---

[48] Interview with Nynyk, 1997.   [49] Interview with Fomina, 1997.
[50] See the *Izvestiya* report, November 4, 1997, as reproduced in the *Institute of East–West Studies Russian Regional Report*, Vol. 2, No. 38 (November 6, 1997).
[51] *Russian Regional Report* (New York: Institute of East–West Studies, October 1998).

Prusak of Novgorod oblast explained in detail how his region carved out its own policy autonomy in order to attract increased foreign investment. Prusak explained: "We understood that to wait for ideal laws in the near future in Russia was hopeless." As a result, Novgorod found ways of circumventing the Russian legislative process to establish its own land code, which leases land to foreign investors for a period of forty-nine years. Prusak noted, "we hope that when that period is up, a Russian land code will be in place."[52] In the latter 1990s, in particular, Prusak and other governors (both progressive and conservative) agreed that "Russia's movement forward today comes from what is happening in the regions. It is not the center making demands on the regions, but regions demanding decisions from the federal government."[53]

All of this is not to argue that the center has been utterly powerless vis-à-vis Russia's regions. Nonetheless, the foregoing should serve to demonstrate that the center's ability to enforce its authority and implement its policies was extremely weak and that the center was outpaced in policy efforts by regional governments in a wide variety of policy areas. Throughout the 1990s, regional governments were able to, and sometimes did, simply take on policy responsibility and act autonomously (for better or worse), often without any federally recognized legal authority to do so. Why has this happened and what are the consequences?

THE INSTITUTIONAL CAUSES OF CREEPING REGIONAL AUTONOMY

There are a number of explanations regarding why the regions have determined the pace of decentralization in Russia. Gone are the institutional bulwarks of vertical integration – in particular, the CPSU and the institutions of the planned economy – that served to keep the regions in check in the Soviet past. They have not, however, been replaced by the kind of buttressing institutions that might better bind the periphery to the center.

To a certain extent, the introduction of representative government and the election of governors, coupled with efforts to establish a market economy, clash with the center's vision of "federalism from above." Democratization, therefore, naturally leads to some degree of decentralization. The introduction of representative government in the regions has

[52] Prusak's remarks were made to guests of the Institute of East West Studies at a luncheon the author attended on March 3, 1998, in New York City.
[53] Remarks by Prusak, 1998. Novgorod is not alone in preempting a land law. Since November 1997, Saratov, Tatarstan, and Samara have all adopted similar measures. See *RFE/RL Newsline*, June 26, 1998.

created a line of accountability between regional officials and their local constituents. It has shifted their point of political reference from the federal center in Moscow to the locality, in effect. After the election of governors across Russia in 1996 and 1997, they became difficult for the federal executive branch to discipline. Indeed, Yeltsin's furtive attempts to oust Primorskiy *krai*'s Yevgeny Nazdratenko failed completely, and even the center's attempt to strip him of power and influence in the region by transferring authority to a federally appointed presidential envoy, Viktor Kondratov, did not serve to disempower Nazdratenko fully. Indeed, Kondratov even requested that this authority be returned to Nazdratenko.[54]

In addition, the disbanding of the command structure of the economy and the gradual establishment of even weak market relations has encouraged the increased devolution of power away from the federal government as private interests continue to grow. Beyond these general processes, however, is the weakness of potentially unifying national institutions in Russia and the overall under-institutionalization of Russian center-periphery relations. That is, where under the Soviet system, central-provincial relations were hyper-institutionalized, in the post-Soviet period, institutions that might buttress and promote central authority in the provinces are weak or simply nonexistent.

Parties

In other national contexts, like the United States and Germany, a strong party system is often a key element in maintaining a well-integrated and stable federal state. Strong emphasis is usually placed on the ability of political parties to aggregate social classes and interests, while the integrative function of parties is sometimes overlooked. In a stable federal state, it is important to remember that parties are "primary and necessary parts of the machinery of government, essential vehicles to convey men's loyalties to the State."[55] Peter Ordeshook argues that "[e]ven when salient local and national issues do not coincide, and even if personalities distort the relationship between national and local political outcomes, the fates of national and local politicians cannot be wholly separate."[56]

[54] *RFE/RL Newsline*, February 13, 1998.

[55] Richard Hofstadter, *The Idea of a Party System* (Berkeley: University of California Press, 1969), pp. 70–71, as cited in Peter C. Ordeshook, "Russia's Party System: Is Russian Federalism Viable?" *Post-Soviet Affairs*, Vol. 3, No. 4 (1996), p. 205.

[56] Ordeshook, "Russia's Party System: Is Russian Federalism Viable?" p. 205. See also William Riker, *Federalism: Origin, Operation, Significance* (Boston: Little Brown, 1964).

Parties are instruments of aggregation, but also of integration, and can help to constrain local politicians so that they more reliably adhere to the will of national governments. A truly national party organization can run candidates in elections in a wide number of regions across the country. The truly national organization provides financial and technical support during the election and has strong ties to local party organizations. Indeed, "candidates for local office rely on national political figures to give meaning to the party labels attached to their names."[57] Relatedly, a national party is able to rely on some basic level of programmatic discipline among its candidates and officeholders. In this way, parties are often important ties that bind states together.

In the contemporary Russian case, however, in contrast to the overbearing role played by the Communist Party of the Soviet Union in the Soviet system, there is little evidence that national political parties exist that are capable of performing such unifying functions. Most of the political parties running candidates in the 1993, 1995, and 1999 elections to the State Duma have little institutional presence outside of Moscow.[58] The (new) Communist Party of the Russian Federation (CPRF) is perhaps an exception, but even it appears unable to provide a great deal of assistance to local candidates, or to evoke strong programmatic support from candidates running under its banner. In the 1996–97 gubernatorial elections, for example, CPRF leader Gennady Zyuganov boasted that his party had supported thirty-six of the fifty-two elected governors.[59] Even if one accepts this figure unambiguously, the effect has not been a "red-oppositionist takeover" of Russia's regions as was initially feared. Many of these allegedly communist governors have pursued their own, as opposed to the Party's, programmatic interests. This has often meant cooperating with the Yeltsin government even when CPRF leaders in Moscow oppose doing so. Indeed, even Alexander Rutskoy, former vice president of Russia (and one of President Yeltsin's political archenemies), upon winning the governorship of Kursk oblast abandoned his sharp criticism of the government, and moderated the more radical aspects of his platform.[60]

---

[57] Ordeshook, "Russia's Party System: Is Russian Federalism Viable?" p. 205.

[58] Support for this point comes from M. Steven Fish, "The Advent of Multipartism in Russia, 1993–1995," *Post-Soviet Affairs*, Vol. 11, No. 4 (1995), pp. 340–384. Despite the lack of representation of "national" political parties in regional legislatures, however, Fish argues that Russia is developing a consolidated party system. See also Kathryn Stoner-Weiss, "The Limited Reach of Russia's Party System: Underinstitutionalization in Dual Transitions," mimeo, 2000.

[59] Slider, "Russia's Market-Distorting Federalism," p. 448.

[60] Jeffrey W. Hahn, "Regional Elections and Political Stability in Russia," *Post-Soviet Geography and Economics*, Vol. 38, No. 5 (1997), p. 261.

Nezavisimaya gazeta reported that even many governors who ran officially in the 1996 gubernatorial elections as candidates from Our Home Is Russia, (the so called "party of power") promptly dropped their affiliations.[61] Moreover, on both the opposition and reform sides of the Russian political spectrum, one is hard pressed to find cases where leaders of supposedly national political parties in Moscow are capable of having programmatic influence on elected governors in the provinces.

Party penetration in regional legislative elections appears to be even worse. Generally, the representation of national parties in the provinces is comprised of two or three individuals, amounting to little more than "two sisters and Uncle Vanya."[62] More often than not, candidates to regional legislatures either run (and win) without any party affiliation whatsoever, or run as part of a regional party having no ties to national parties.[63] Indeed, most regional assemblies are populated by elected deputies with no party affiliation whatsoever. The Central Electoral Commission of the Russian Federation reported that in elections to regional legislatures between 1995 and 1997, only 336 deputies, or 10.1 percent, were elected from the twelve largest parties in Russia. Another 10 percent ran as members of regionally based parties, leaving approximately 80 percent of the newly elected deputies unaffiliated with any party or movement – regional or national.[64]

This is unlikely to change in the immediate future, given the degree of antiparty sentiment among provincial politicians. In a not untypical view, for example, Governor Prusak of Novgorod noted that no parties have developed in his province's legislature. He argued that this was all to the good, as "parties cause problems" for effective governance.[65] Finally, undoubtedly contributing to the legitimacy of parties as electoral institutions, throughout his two terms as president of Russia, Boris Yeltsin never joined a political party. Significantly, his successor, Vladimir

---

[61] *Nezavisimaya gazeta*, January 21, 1998, as cited in the *Russian Regional Report*, Institute for East-West Studies, January 29, 1998.

[62] Vladimir Gel'man and Grigorii Golosov, "Regional Party System Formation in Russia: The Deviant Case of Sverdlovsk Oblast," *The Journal of Communist Studies and Transition Politics*, Vol. 14, No. 1 (1998), p. 4.

[63] For an insightful and interesting description of one of the few regional party systems in Russia, see Gel'man and Golosov, "Regional Party System Formation in Russia: The Deviant Case of Sverdlovsk Oblast."

[64] Vybory v zakonodatel'nie (predstavitel'nie) organi gosudasrstvennoi vlasti sub'ektov rossiiskoi federatsii 1995–1997: elekrotal'naia statistika (Elections to the legislative [representative] organs of state power of the subjects of the Russian Federation, 1995–1997: electoral statistics, 1998) (Moscow: Ves' Mir, 1998), pp. 625, 632.

[65] Remarks by Prusak, 1998.

Putin, handily won election on March 26, 2000, also without any party affiliation. In sum, the lack of a national party system not only places the consolidation of Russian democracy in jeopardy, but also exacerbates the problem of developing a well-integrated Russian state.

The State Duma

Relatedly, the State Duma is weak relative to the federal executive; factions are relatively poorly organized; and party links to regional legislatures and leaders are tenuous. Aside from this, however, the Duma has not succeeded in devising the necessary legislation governing center-periphery relations. V. N. Lysenko, chair of the Duma Subcommittee on the Development of Federal Relations (part of the Duma Committee on Regional Policy), noted that the Duma had not been able to pass legislation in key areas of joint federal-regional jurisdiction. These include, for example, the establishment of principles of taxation assessment and collection; a law on lawyers and judges; the establishment of general principles of organization of state organs; questions regarding the ownership, use, and sale of land, natural resources, and water; and the defense of the rights of national minorities, among others.[66]

Further, the Duma has a poor track record in drafting and adopting laws that would provide a coherent basis for center-periphery relations. Lysenko reported that in 1997, the Duma proposed to accept nearly 100 laws in the area of joint jurisdiction between the subjects of the federation and the federal government. Drafts, however, were prepared in parallel by a number of committees, and several key areas (for example, the demarcation of state property) were ignored altogether.[67] Even if laws could be drafted that would more effectively regulate center-periphery relations, the foregoing evidence indicates that implementation of legislation limiting regional autonomy would be highly problematic.

The Federation Council

The upper house of the Russian Parliament, the Federation Council, has become an increasingly powerful institutional stronghold of regional interests since its inception in December 1993. As of 1995, regional governors and heads of regional legislatures automatically received seats in the upper house. Granting regional government leaders roles as both national and local political actors was initially thought to be a way in which President Yeltsin could demobilize provincial voices in national politics, since work in the council would be only part-time, given repre-

---

[66] Lysenko, "Razdelenie vlasti i opit Rossiiskoi Federatsii," p. 168.
[67] Ibid., p. 169.

sentatives' duties and responsibilities back home.[68] In fact, however, the council became an additional way in which provincial politicians participated collectively in national government and further limited its incursions into provincial affairs. The council, for example, supported individual governors in disputes with federal authority, the most notorious case being that of Y. Nazdratenko in his struggle to retain his authority in Primorskiy *krai* in 1997.[69] It also defied the president in such matters as twice refusing to accept the forced resignation of the head federal prosecutor, Yurii Skuratov, in the spring of 1999.

As a result, shortly after his inauguration in May 2000, President Putin proposed to remove governors and heads of regional legislatures from the Federation Council. The State Duma accepted this legislation in the summer of 2000 such that governors and heads of regional legislatures will no longer automatically receive seats in Russia's upper house. Instead, they will be replaced by two permanent representatives – one proposed and voted upon by the regional legislature and the other by the governor – from each region of Russia. From President Putin's perspective, this should have the effect of reinstating a more effective division of legislative and executive branches of power, and most importantly, of removing governors as powerful, often contradictory, voices in national politics.[70]

The Constitutional Court

Briefly, the Constitutional Court, the legal body charged with adjudicating infringements of the 1993 Constitution, has thus far not served as a strong check on the rising tide of regional government autonomy. Russia suffers from the communist legacy of a weak legal system and enduring low levels of legitimacy for legal institutions.[71] The Constitutional Court was relatively active in adjudicating cases from 1991 through 1993, but its behavior under its former chair Valeriy Zor'kin during Yeltsin's dispute with the old Russian parliament served to discredit it, at least temporarily, as an impartial and effective arm of the state.

Since 1994, the Court has adjudicated an array of disputes regarding regional and republican government constitutional infringements, but implementation of its decisions has been sporadic. A notorious example

---

[68] Ordeshook, "Russia's Party System: Is Russian Federalism Viable?" p. 211.

[69] Hahn, "Regional Elections and Political Stability in Russia," p. 260, and *RFE/RL Newsline*, July 8, 1997.

[70] See Putin's speech on Russian television, May 17, 2000, BBC monitoring, as well as a draft of the law published in *Nezavisimaia Gazeta*, May 20, 2000.

[71] Peter H. Solomon, Jr., "The Limits of Legal Order in Post-Soviet Russia," *Post-Soviet Affairs*, Vol. 11, No. 2 (1995), pp. 89–114.

of noncompliance with the Court's rulings was the fate of its decision regarding the constitutionality of the city of Moscow's residency permit (*propiska*) system. The Court twice ruled that requiring such a permit violated the constitutional right of Russian citizens to freedom of movement. Moscow's mayor, Yuri Luzhkov, however, refused to accept and implement the ruling, announcing that the city would define its own residency requirements, not the Court.[72] Moscow's residency permit endures as a result. In Udmurtiya, leaders of the republic refused to implement a court ruling that struck down a republican law that would have enabled the leaders of the republic to name heads of city and *raion* administrations, rather than their standing for popular election. Udmurtiya relented only when President Yeltsin issued a decree ordering republican authorities to comply with the court ruling.[73] Similarly, the leader of the Republic of Komi, Yuri Spiridonov, refused to implement a ruling striking down provisions in Komi's Constitution and law on appointing executive authorities. Spiridonov argued that "only the Komi legislature may decide whether republican laws should be changed."[74]

Thus, while a legal culture that might support implementation of the Court's decisions may develop over time, without stronger assurances that its decisions will be followed, the Court cannot reliably stem the rising tide of regional autonomy.

The Presidential Representative

In the face of legislative inertia, weak political parties, and an ineffectual Constitutional Court, the federal executive has made several attempts to devise institutions to place center-regional relations on a more predictable footing. Foremost among these is the presidential representative. There have been no less than three attempts from 1991 through May 2000 to make this institution the front line in the battle for central control over the regions.

President Yeltsin's first attempt to introduce this institution at the local level was largely a failure. Under this first iteration, the role of the presidential representatives appointed to every region beginning in 1991 was to ensure that federal legislation was reliably implemented and to provide information about the political situation in each region. The office of presidential representative was described by some of its detractors as "the emperor's eyes in the localities."[75] Significantly, however, Yeltsin claimed that the job of the presidential representative would not be to

[72] Petrov and Titkov, "Geokhronologiya," p. 10.
[73] *RFE/RL Newsline*, February 3, 1998, and Petrov and Titkov, "Geokhronologiya," p. 11.
[74] *RFE/RL Newsline*, February 3, 1998.   [75] Stoner-Weiss, *Local Heroes*, p. 75.

interfere in the business of local governance. The decree that he signed in August of 1991 officially creating the position stated simply: "Leaders and officials of ministries, departments and other organizations of the RSFSR [as it was still then called], and organs of executive power are instructed to assist the RSFSR presidential representatives in the fulfillment of the functions vested in them."[76] These "functions" were described merely as fulfilling the president's instructions. What this meant in practice was not even clear to many of the men Yeltsin appointed to these positions. Some of Yeltsin's appointees, usually already residents of the region to which they were assigned, construed their functions as merely reporting the goings-on of the local legislature and executive. Others, however, claimed that they had the power to remove local political actors from office if they persistently defied federal authority.[77]

In reality, this original incarnation of the office of presidential representative did not carry with it much influence in local affairs. In Yaroslavl' oblast, for example, the presidential representative had no real influence in local governance. In the first eighteen months after his appointment, he revealed that there had been two instances where local authorities had failed to implement presidential decrees. He dutifully reported these transgressions to his superiors in the presidential administration, but no action whatsoever was taken against the local officials in question. In terms of technical support, he had been in office for more than a year before he received a photocopier and a fax machine.[78]

To the extent that presidential representatives came to have any influence over politics in their provinces, this had little to do with the office itself. Rather, in some cases, because he made his appointments so quickly in the fall of 1991, President Yeltsin inadvertently put former local Communist Party officials into positions as presidential representatives. For example, in Saratov oblast, the presidential representative had previously been the first secretary of the city of Saratov Communist Party committee. Because he was able to simply transfer the apparatus and authority of his previous position to his new office as presidential representative, he used his new position to further his own political interests and not those of the president.[79]

Following the election of governors in the regions, Yeltsin sought to recast and strengthen the role of presidential representative to maintain some degree of central influence over regional politics. In July 1997, therefore, a second regulation was issued establishing the authority of

[76] Ibid., p. 76.   [77] Ibid.   [78] Ibid., p. 77.   [79] Ibid., p. 78.

presidential representatives to reorder the cooperation of the center and
the regions in three areas: oversight of the fulfillment of the federal
budget, use of federal property in the regions, and the strengthening of
the cadres of federal organs of power at the regional level.[80] In practice,
this meant that the presidential representative was to oversee and coordinate the work of virtually all federal bureaucrats at the regional level.
To add some perspective to this, on average there are between thirty and
fifty federal government structures in any given region of Russia, employ-
ing hundreds of people.[81] While granting this sweeping new authority to
the presidential representative was intended to serve as a counterweight
to the sizable gubernatorial administrations in the regions, it is difficult
to see how in practice a single individual (even with the help of his own
apparatus) could effectively coordinate and control such a large number
of bureaucrats in such a wide variety of policy areas. Nor is it clear why
the leaders of federal organs in the regions would submit to the authority of the newly empowered presidential representative. As the empirical
examples of continued regional noncompliance to federal policy presented in this chapter indicate, this second version of the presidential representative did little in practice to strengthen the influence of the center
in the periphery.

As a result, President Putin, as one of his first acts in office, issued a
decree on May 13, 2000 establishing a new incarnation of the presidential representative. In this third version, he created within his presidential administration seven "federal districts" that encompass all
eighty-nine of Russia's regions. He assigned each of the seven districts a
presidential representative. The old office of presidential representative
has been abolished, although many of the former occupants of these
offices have become "regional inspectors" who report directly to each of
the seven new presidential representatives. As in the last two iterations
of the office, the new presidential representative is subordinate to the
president of the Russian Federation and is a member of the presidential
administration. As a result, the presidential representative can only be
removed by the president of the Russian Federation. Also, as in the two
previous versions, this new presidential representative is charged with a
startlingly wide array of responsibilities. These include analyzing the
effectiveness of the activity of law enforcement organs, overseeing the
legislative activity of regional governments, organizing oversight of
the fulfillment of federal laws and presidential decrees and the realiza-

---

[80] See *Rossiskaya gazeta*, July 16, 1997, as cited in Petrov and Titkov, "Geokhronologiya,"
   p. 14.
[81] Petrov and Titkov, "Geokhronologiya," p. 13.

tion of federal programs, as well as coordinating federal offices within his federal district.[82]

It is difficult, at this early stage, to see exactly how this new version of the presidential representative is likely to be more successful in ensuring that the center's policies are followed in the regions. For despite the fact that the representatives have been given seats on the Security Council of the Russian Federation, and are apparently to have larger staffs and greater resources afforded to them, the breadth of their responsibilities is daunting. Further complicating matters, Putin's representatives are responsible for a group of oblasts and republics (approximately fifteen, on average, per federal district). Considering the complexities and sheer geographic size of some of these regions, it is hard to see how the presidential representative (even with a more sizable apparat of his own) will be able to discharge the functions assigned to him. Even with a staff of 100 to 200 officials, the apparatus of each presidential representative will be little match for fifteen regional bureaucracies, led by independent-minded (and popularly elected) governors. As in the past, tensions between the president and regional governors are likely to arise in the future if the (unelected) presidential representatives attempt to seriously infringe on regional governance.

As in previous iterations, the office has been hastily constructed and the presidential representatives' exact tasks left poorly defined in the founding decree, relative to those of regional governors and legislatures as well as federal agencies at the regional level. Finally, the new presidential representatives, and the seven new federal districts that they oversee, appear to create yet another new layer of federal bureaucracy at a time when the Russian state can ill afford to grow.

Popular Support for Regional Autonomy

Aside from a weak institutional framework for linking center and periphery in Russia, public support for local institutions over national institutions may also contribute to the further devolution of power to the provinces, despite central preferences. In a 1993 survey conducted in four regions among almost 4,000 respondents, Josephine Andrews and Kathryn Stoner-Weiss found that "respondents in all four regions – Nizhnii Novgorod, Saratov, Tiumen' and Yaroslavl' – were more supportive of governmental institutions at the regional level than at the

---

[82] Prezidentskii Ukaz 2000-05-13-002, "O polnomochnom predstavitele Prezidenta Rossiiskoi Federatsii v federal'nom okruge" (Soobshenie Press Sluzhbi Prezidenta Rossiiskoi Federatsii, www.president.kremlin.ru).

national level."[83] More recently, a panel survey of more than 2,500 respondents across Russia indicates the same pattern of support for sub-national over national institutions. For example, when asked which level of government should decide the bulk of policy questions, 37.9 percent of respondents answered that "Most or all questions should be decided in the regions," while only 11.1 percent responded that "Most or all questions should be decided in Moscow" (i.e., by federal authorities). Further, in the same national survey, 44.6 percent of respondents said that they were trustful of their regional and local administrations, as opposed to 42 percent who declared themselves mistrustful of their regional administrations. By comparison, 39.5 percent declared themselves trustful of the central government, and 51.3 percent were mistrustful of the center.[84] Respondents across the country were, therefore, more consistently mistrustful of the federal government than of regional governments.

In the United States, popular support for regional autonomy historically has proved to be an important factor in imposing limits on federal incursion into local affairs.[85] Now that political actors are accountable to their electorates in Russia, and if market relations strengthen, public opinion may well encourage regional leaders to seek more autonomy from federal authority. The force of public opinion, therefore, may serve to further embolden regional leaders to act autonomously and beyond the strict letter of the law.

CONCLUSIONS – THE RUSSIAN STATE AT RISK?

What then are the implications of the under-institutionalization of center-periphery relations and the resulting weakness of the central state for Russia's continued political and economic development?

In theory, the comparative politics literature tells us that the promises of decentralization (whether led by center or periphery) for economic growth and the consolidation of democracy are many. These include the idea that democratic decentralization is an effective way of meeting local needs, and the belief that participation in local governments has an educating effect, in the sense that it trains local people as leaders and also

---

[83] Josephine Andrews and Kathryn Stoner-Weiss, "Regionalism and Reform in Provincial Russia," *Post-Soviet Affairs*, Vol. 11, No. 4 (1995), p. 384.

[84] I am grateful to Timothy J. Colton of Harvard University for providing me with this data from his 1996 national panel survey of voting age respondents, randomly chosen from across Russia.

[85] See, for example, Barry Weingast, "The Economic Role of Political Institutions: Market-Preserving Federalism and Economic Development," *The Journal of Law, Economics and Organization*, Vol. 11, No. 1 (1995), pp. 1–31.

enhances civic consciousness, reducing apathy and building support for democracy.[86] While these are the political and economic promises of decentralization, the variation is considerable regarding the extent to which its promised benefits are realized.

Indeed, as the Canadian example demonstrates, the very existence of a federal state can be at risk when too much decentralization takes place. As provincial governments have taken more of the lead in defining center-periphery relations over the last century, the country's political stability and territorial integrity have become increasingly threatened. These threats come not just from ethnic enclaves like Quebec, but also from other economically powerful provinces in the West. This also has had negative ramifications for the health of the Canadian economy.

In contemporary Russia, the empirical evidence indicates that the process of devolution of authority may now be largely self-sustaining, despite President Putin's best efforts. That is, even if the center persists in attempting to slow or control provincial autonomy, many provincial leaders, in the face of weak and inconsistent central institutions that are incapable of imposing meaningful negative sanctions, will continue to act beyond their de jure rights when necessary. This could have very negative implications indeed for overall Russian state integration, as policy between regions will continue to vary radically and federal programs will go unimplemented.[87]

The empirical evidence of regional noncompliance with federal authority adds further nuance to some recent interpretations of center-periphery relations in Russia. It is difficult to reconcile the picture of a rather incapacitated central state presented here with that of a center nimble enough to strategically and consistently pay off some regions, while punishing others. In addition, it is increasingly unlikely that this will prove a wholly accurate picture of the capacity of the central state in the near future.

Perhaps of more comparative significance, however, are the dilemmas that unchecked provincial policy autonomy, and the under-institutional-

---

[86] See, for example, Brian Smith, *Decentralization: The Territorial Dimension of the State* (London: Allen and Unwin, 1985).

[87] I am not arguing, however, that variation in policy or development across regions – asymmetrical federalism – is inherently bad for state integration or causes political instability. On the contrary, it may encourage competition between regions for investment. Such competition might encourage the further development of markets for both labor and capital. Further, there is some degree of asymmetry in all federal states, and it can be a source of stability. My claim is merely that when the federal government acts in its constitutionally defined sphere of competency, however defined, its actions must be viewed as legitimate and authoritative by subnational governments. This ensures that the state remains in essence a coherent political and economic expanse.

ization of center-periphery relations more generally, may present for further political and economic development. While Russian territorial integrity does not appear to be at serious risk, the de facto decentralization and continued erosion of central oversight over the periphery is an insidious and equally menacing problem for Russia's future.

4

Russian Economic Reform, 1991–1999

Yoshiko M. Herrera

At the end of 1998, seven years of Russian economic reform seemed to come to a denouement in which the conditions of life were in many respects worse than when the new state began in 1991. The late summer financial crisis and currency collapse, which resulted in shortages and breakdowns in nearly every kind of transaction – from wire transfers and ATM withdrawals to simple mail deliveries and grocery purchases – were remarkable not only for the velocity and depth of the crisis, but also for the lack of surprise or outrage with which the crisis was met by the population. Russians had, tragically, been there before.

However, within only a year, the sense of despair has given rise to renewed optimism. As it turns out, the Russian government's default and the swift devaluation of the ruble in 1998 were followed in 1999 by the first real signs of economic recovery, namely, positive growth and especially gains in industrial production. For those studying economic reform in Russia, the surprising post-1998 economic progress was even more remarkable because it followed what seemed like the total collapse of the economic reform program of the 1990s. Thus, rather than resolving doubts about of how economic reform in Russia has proceeded, the post-1998 turn of events has raised new questions and suggests the need for further research.

Just as it would be unwarranted to judge the Russian economic reform program only by the post-1999 results, so would it be unwise to judge the program only by the crisis of 1998. Unfortunately, on the basis of meager gains in efficiency, investment, and production, as well as epidemic crime, corruption, and social catastrophes including rising income inequality, poverty, and public ill-health, the Russian economy during most of the 1990s was a picture of despair even before the crisis of 1998. Moreover, despite recent improvements in growth, many negative effects of the transition, such as corruption and the lack of the rule of law, continue unabated. In understanding or evaluating the Russian economic reform program, we must consider not only recent successes, but also the long-term negative effects that the reform program may have had on the Russian economy.

By 1998, Russian GDP was still only at 55 percent of the 1989 GDP level, and for the 1989–98 period, foreign direct investment per capita in Russia was three times less than the per capita average for Eastern Europe and the Baltics.[1] Also, by the end of 1999, over 25 percent of Russia's population was living below the subsistence level,[2] and in 1997 a Russian government report ranked the country 135th in the world in terms of male life expectancy.[3] The steep decline in life expectancy was largely attributable to a record-breaking mortality rate, which had increased over 40 percent since 1989 and was the worst in over a century for Russia, at 15.1 deaths per 1,000 people.[4] The 1997 annual mortality rate was higher than in any European, American, or Asian country, except for Cambodia and Afghanistan (the rate in the U.S. is 8.8 deaths per 1,000 people). Moreover, the birth rate declined by 60 percent from 1989 to 1995, and from 1990 to 1996 the number of deaths by contagious diseases increased by 70 percent.[5] In addition to societal malaise, according to the Heritage Foundation/Wall Street Journal's "index of economic freedom," which rates countries according to ten factors supposed to be indicators of economic promise, in the year 2000 report Russia ranked number 122 out of 161 countries.[6]

What explains the extreme difficulties experienced by Russia during the process of economic reform? And, perhaps more importantly, what does the Russian experience with reform teach us about transitions from state to market-based economies? Several scholars have argued that the reform program upon which Russia embarked in late 1991 was itself sound, but the problem was that the reforms were not implemented quickly or comprehensively enough – the medical advice was appropriate, but the patient, alas, was too incompetent or weak (willed) to follow the advice of the doctors and take the medicine as prescribed. However, in the analysis that follows, I argue that it was not the lack of imple-

[1] *Transition Report 1999* (London: European Bank for Reconstruction and Development, 1999), pp. 73, 79.
[2] "Excel Database," *Russian Economic Trends*, May 2000.
[3] "Russia Death Rate Soars," Associated Press, May 14, 1997.
[4] Michael Specter, "Deep in the Russian Soul, a Lethal Darkness," *New York Times*, June 8, 1997.
[5] "Russia Death Rate Soars," Associated Press, May 14, 1997.
[6] Gerald P. O'Driscoll, Jr., Kim R. Holmes, and Melanie Kirkpatrick, *2000 Index of Economic Freedom* (New York: The Heritage Foundation/Wall Street Journal, 2000). The factors include, for example, trade policy, privatization and property rights, state regulation and taxation, monetary policy, and the extent of the black market.

mentation of reforms or a lack of speed that ruined the reform effort. Rather, I argue that the failures of Russian economic reform program were the result of a fundamental misunderstanding of the relationship between political and economic reforms in the context of a weak Russian state, and a consequent inattention to the development of the state institutions necessary for supporting a market economy. That is, we gravely misunderstood the patient.

In light of the prevalence of dichotomous metaphors used in the analysis of economic reform in Eastern Europe and the states of the former Soviet Union, I must emphasize that the argument presented here is neither an "anti–shock therapy" argument nor an argument for "big government." Instead of being about *speed* or *size*, this is an argument about the *content* of the Russian economic reform program and the economic ideas that influenced that content. Specifically, the argument addresses the lack of attention to political institutional development during the course of economic reforms in Russia.

Although the analysis of reform choice is sometimes framed in terms of either market-oriented reforms or state institution building, the conceptualization of an "either/or" choice should be put to rest. When we argue for the necessity of the development of state institutions *as market infrastructure*, we certainly are not suggesting that market reforms should have been delayed indefinitely until institutions were consolidated. Rather, we are suggesting that successful states and markets work in concert with one another, and that the working out of a market-oriented reform program should not be separated from the state context in which it is to be implemented. By setting aside the question of state institutional development, in the mistaken belief that institutional reforms would develop endogenously as a result of economic reforms, neoliberal reformers misread the central puzzle facing Russia and proved ill-equipped to chart Russia's course through marketization and democratization.

In the pages that follow, I develop this argument by first presenting a brief discussion of the ideas behind the Russian economic reform program. Following this theoretical discussion, I outline the actual Russian economic reform program by analyzing the reforms in terms of liberalization, stabilization, and privatization. I follow the discussion of policies with an evaluation of the results of the reforms according to efficiency, investment, growth, crime, and social consequences, including income inequality and poverty. In the third section I outline how Russia's experience has informed our understanding of economic and political reform in general. In particular, I discuss the inadequacy of the neoclassical model for handling information problems, the debate over privatization, the necessity of state capacity and institutions, and the importance of the political process in an economic reform program. Finally, I discuss comparisons to neoliberal economic reform programs in other post-socialist contexts. I suggest that although neoliberalism may have been effective in countries where state capacity was relatively high, the weakness of Russian state institutions rendered neoliberalism an ineffective reform choice for Russia.

THE IDEAS BEHIND RUSSIAN ECONOMIC REFORM

If we accept that under communism the state officially controlled nearly all political and economic activity, then the introduction of markets, which would play a major role in the distribution of goods and services, necessitated taking certain functions away from the state. Second, if we understand that state functions are not discrete units that can be seamlessly added or subtracted, then we would have to conclude that at the heart of the debate over any type of "reform" in the post-communist world was the question of what to do with the institutions and actors that comprised the communist state. At the moment of Russian economic reform in the early 1990s, there was widespread agreement on the these propositions. For example, in a book-length report on the challenges facing Russian economic reform published in 1992, the World Bank repeatedly stressed the need for state institutional reforms to support market reforms.[7] However, as is also evident in the World Bank's report, there was little agreement on how reform of the Russian state could be accomplished.

In answer to the question, "What should be done?", Anders Åslund portentously responded, "The choice of economic system is profoundly ideological."[8] In fact, the theoretical understanding of the nature of institutional change turned out to be crucially important to how reformers dealt in practice with the question of state institutional reform. Reformers in Russia embraced a set of neoliberal assumptions regarding political and economic development that suggested that political reforms should only come after economic reforms.[9] The theory was that the right economic system would by itself drive the development of desirable political institutions. Drawing the practical implications of this efficiency-based theory of institutional change, reformers reasoned that the only way to rectify the weaknesses and problems of the Russian state was to

---

[7] *Russian Economic Reform: Crossing the Threshold of Structural Change* (Washington, D.C.: World Bank, 1992).

[8] Anders Åslund, *How Russia Became a Market Economy* (Washington, D.C.: Brookings Institution, 1995), p. 5.

[9] On the idea that economic liberalization makes political reform possible, see Åslund, *How Russia Became a Market Economy*, p. 10.

concentrate as much as possible on reforming the economic system.[10] The introduction of markets and private ownership was to be the first step, while political institutions, including the legal system, were expected to spontaneously develop later, in response to the efficiency-based demands of the market.[11]

In addition to ideological motivations, the choice to focus on economic reforms before institutional reforms was also partly driven by practical considerations and experiences. The idea of reconfiguring the Russian state was an *enormous* task even to think about, much less to implement. And, in the transition from the USSR to the Russian Federation at the end of 1991, the emasculation of state functions coupled with selected strategic political alliances appeared to be a potentially successful means of carrying out reform. The fact that there existed a small group of reformers who were, in some sense, above politics, fueled the hope that the problem of state institutions could be ignored in the short term without consequence. That is, because reformers were already in power, economic reform was conceptualized as something that could be accomplished separately from institutional reform. Consequently, rather than getting bogged down in the problem of "building institutions," neoliberal reformers seized the moment for economic rather than political reform.

The building of the market under the neoliberal reform program was divided into three elements: liberalization, stabilization, and privatization. The theoretical goals of liberalization centered on the idea that, by introducing markets, liberalization would enhance efficiency. Liberalization was to include the freeing of both prices and trade, and the theoretical foundation of liberalization was neoclassical economics.

The centerpiece of neoclassical economic theory is that a competitive economy, based on prices and markets, allocates scarce resources efficiently, minimizing waste. Allocation is efficient when no additional

---

[10] See, for example, Anders Åslund, "The Russian Road to the Market," *Current History*, Vol. 94, No. 594 (1995); Åslund, "Has Poland Been Useful as a Model for Russia?", in Anders Åslund (ed.), *Economic Transformation in Russia* (New York: St. Martin's Press, 1994); and Vitaly A. Naishul, "Economic Reforms: A Liberal Perspective," in Åslund (ed.), *Economic Transformation in Russia*, pp. 174–181.

[11] Åslund makes this point explicitly. The logic is not that a legal system is unnecessary per se, but that policy makers should not devote their attention to developing a set of workable laws, because legal development is a long, slow process, and moreover by pursuing economic reform policy makers can create demand that will itself drive the development of an efficient legal system. See Åslund, *How Russia Became a Market Economy*, pp. 7–8 and Anders Åslund, "Economic Causes of Crime in Russia," in Jeffrey Sachs and Katharina Pistor (eds.), *The Rule of Law and Economic Reform in Russia* (Boulder, Colo.: Westview Press, 1997).

output can be produced without increasing at least one input, and no input can be decreased without decreasing at least one output. A corollary to the neoclassical emphasis on prices and markets is that government intervention in the competitive market often creates inefficiency and therefore should be reserved for market failures. The logic behind price liberalization was that without state controls, in the form of price setting as well as subsidies, prices would reflect the balance between supply and demand. One effect of free prices is that shortages of goods, so common in planned economies, should be eliminated, because shortages are said to result from prices being set too low, creating demand that exceeds supply. And, because according to neoclassical economics price is the primary conveyor of information in a market economy, by introducing prices the reformers hoped to introduce better information, which would also improve efficiency.

However, in addition to efficiency gains, some Russian reformers also argued that liberalization would produce political reform by limiting the power of groups opposed to reform. In response to the argument that a legal system and political institutions should have been developed before or during the economic reform program, Anders Åslund asserted that such measures are easier to take after liberalization, because it is only through liberalization that the power of antireform political groups can be broken.[12] Thus, according to reformers, the theoretical goal of liberalization was both to increase efficiency and to create the conditions for political reform.

In regard to stabilization, the theoretical goal was to control inflation and improve the financial position of the state. Control of inflation was necessary because inflation has a negative impact on investment as well as on consumption. Attempts to improve the financial position of the state under the neoliberal program were largely aimed at decreasing state spending and debt in order to reduce the role of the government in the economy. This reduction of the role of government was supposed to make the economy more efficient.

While the theoretical goals of liberalization and stabilization were clear, the goals of privatization were vague and controversial. Even accounts by those reformers directly involved in the process were not entirely consistent in terms of goals. Efficiency, depoliticization, better corporate governance, and restructuring were all suggested as possible outcomes of privatization, but a consistent theoretical argument for the Russian privatization program was not advanced. This confusion among

[12] Åslund, *How Russia Became a Market Economy*, p. 10. For evidence against this perspective see Joel Hellman, "Winners Take All: The Politics of Partial Reform in Postcommunist Transitions," *World Politics*, Vol. 50, No. 2 (1998), pp. 203–34.

Russian reformers reflects the broader lack of consensus on privatization programs among economists.

While liberalization, stabilization, and privatization, per se, were not a recipe for disaster, the initial conceptual separation of economic and institutional reform had serious negative consequences. As we will see in the sections that follow, in the end what defined the Russian economic reform program was not so much the emphasis on efficiency or markets, but rather a simplistic view of markets and states that appreciated neither the complexity of real existing markets and states in capitalist economies and the relationship between them, nor the legacy of Soviet-era state institutions. Neoliberal reformers treated the existing Russian state as simply an undifferentiated source of inefficiency and corruption that must be dismantled. The economic reforms in Russia degenerated into a process of *destatization*, that is, a set of policies designed to thwart the development or support of state institutions for governing the economy. The belief that good state institutions would spontaneously develop following economic reform meant that the existing configuration of Soviet-era state and social institutions, including communist elite networks, could be ignored. Finally, and most significantly, the growth of corruption and illegal activity in private economic transactions, coupled with incompetence and weakness in government regulation, was justified by reformers as a short-term phenomenon that was a necessary step on the road to market reform.[13] As the following discussion will demonstrate, the neoliberal belief that the pursuit of economic reforms alone would allow political institutions to develop endogenously, turned out to be wrong.

REFORMS IN ACTION

On liberalization and stabilization, the Russian government worked closely with the International Monetary Fund. The Russian government and the IMF discussed and easily agreed on price liberalization: this included immediate liberalization of prices of consumer goods, and more gradual liberalization of prices of housing rents, public utilities, and public transportation.[14] A notable exception was in the energy sector, where prices were debated but no early commitments were made.

---

[13] See especially Maxim Boycko, Andrei Shleifer, and Robert Vishny, *Privatizing Russia* (Cambridge, Mass.: MIT Press, 1995). For a laudatory account of corrupt macroeconomic policy, see Andrei Shleifer and Daniel Treisman, *The Economics and Politics of Transition to an Open Market Economy: Russia* (Paris: Development Centre, OECD, 1998).

[14] Alexei V. Mozhin, "Russia's Negotiations with the IMF," in Anders Åslund and Richard Layard (eds.), *Changing the Economic System in Russia* (London: Pinter Publishers, 1993), p. 66.

In the fall of 1991, the government announced its intention to set prices free as of January 2, 1992. The government then set most prices free on that date, and almost all remaining prices were lifted by presidential decree on March 7, 1992.[15] The immediate effect was the elimination of shortages of most consumer goods, since prices came to reflect the balance between supply and demand. However, the rapid price increases made many goods too expensive for the majority of the population. The few price controls which remained were supposed to be on only a limited number of basic consumer goods such as bread, and on goods produced by monopolies; these included natural gas, electricity, transportation systems, postal services, municipal services, and arms. The price controls took three forms: (1) actually setting prices (supposedly according to inflation levels), (2) state subsidization of market prices, and (3) state mandated subsidization of producer prices for certain consumers.[16]

Energy prices were intensely debated, but in the end energy prices were not fully liberalized, export quotas were not eliminated, and the much-discussed export taxes, which would have covered the price differential between domestic and world prices, were not put in place. The existing export taxes were kept low; this policy worked to the extreme benefit of the energy sector, which could buy inputs at fixed below-market prices and then sell its products abroad at world prices.[17] As of 1998, the cost of domestic fuel oil was still only 75 percent of the world market price, although this was up from 7–10 percent of the world price in 1992.[18]

Regarding foreign trade, the state monopoly on foreign trade was largely eroded during the perestroika reforms of 1987. By November 1991, Russian enterprises were allowed to engage in foreign trade without special registration; however, foreign trade was still controlled by numerous import and export quotas and tariffs.[19] Beginning in 1992, importing was largely freed from both licensing requirements and quotas but was still subject to tariffs. Exports, however, remained subject to quotas and licensing requirements until 1995. Tariffs on exports

[15] Mozhin, "Russia's Negotiations with the IMF," p. 66.

[16] Expert Institute, "Russia toward the Year 2000," *Problems of Economic Transition*, Vol. 39, No. 5 (1996), pp. 28–29, reprinted from *Voprosi Ekonomiki*, No. 2 (1996), pp. 4–50.

[17] Mozhin, "Russia's Negotiations with the IMF," pp. 66, 67.

[18] "Commercial Overview of Russia: Part 1 – Economic Profile," *BISNIS (Business Information Service for the Newly Independent States, U.S. Department of Commerce)*, March 1999.

[19] Natalia Tabatchnaia-Tamirisa, "Trade Liberalization and Industry Protection in Russia during 1992–1995," *Hitotsubashi Journal of Economics*, No. 38 (1997), p. 81.

continued throughout the reform period. Meanwhile, illegal importing and exporting represented a large portion of Russian foreign trade; the Russian State Customs Committee estimated that in 1994, for example, 25–30 percent of exported and imported goods had been smuggled into or out of the country.[20]

Stabilization

The fiscal policy discussions with the IMF in early 1992 centered around the idea of a balanced budget, where the deficit would be kept within 1 percent of GDP. On tax issues, the VAT was to be introduced, tax privileges were to be reduced, and energy production and consumption were to be taxed.[21] Although the IMF demanded a progressive income tax, there was no commitment to an income tax policy. With regard to monetary policy, the IMF insisted on raising Central Bank interest rates, at least to positive real levels, and the IMF demanded limitations on Central Bank lending to the government and to commercial banks. Commercial banks and the government used Central Bank funds to provide "credits" to industry and agriculture. These credits were unlikely to be repaid, and in any case the funds were being lent to banks and the government at negative real interest rates. Money supply was difficult to address in the IMF discussions because the ruble zone extended beyond Russia, and other republican central banks were enacting their own policies. On external policy, a unified exchange rate was the key priority for the IMF. There was also supposed to be the development of a foreign exchange market, and the elimination of all export quotas (except on energy). Finally, there was little discussion of a social safety net. With regard to social safety net issues, the IMF argued only that unemployment benefits were too high.[22] The Russian government agreed to implement a new unemployment benefits program on June 1, 1992, but it did not actually do so.

The IMF agreements formed the theoretical core of the reform program regarding liberalization and stabilization. It is significant that the agreements are marked by a lack of attention to reconfiguring the inherited Soviet state institutions. This lack reflects the neoliberal conception of reform, in which political institutions are a consequence of positive economic reforms rather than a symbiotic component of economic reform. Second, the discussions with the IMF are interesting for the way in which they were conducted. For example, it is notable that an official reform program was not published. There were bits and pieces

---

[20] Ibid., p. 84.
[21] Mozhin, "Russia's Negotiations with the IMF," pp. 67–70.
[22] Ibid., p. 67.

of the plans published in newspapers, but as was the case with the well-known memorandum to the IMF published in *Nezavisimaya gazeta* in March 1992, public announcement came only after deals had already been accepted by the government.

At the beginning of 1992, as the liberalization program began, stabilization was aimed mainly at controlling the budget deficit and inflation through extensive cutting of government expenditures. This tight stabilization program showed some results in terms of money supply growth and inflation, but by mid-1992 the country was also suffering from a massive interenterprise nonpayment problem. There is little evidence that firms reacted to cuts in government spending by beginning restructuring. Instead, it appears that enterprises went on with business as usual, except that to a remarkable degree, supplies, when actually delivered, were not paid for. In July 1992, Victor Gerashchenko became chairman of the Central Bank. Because the government had given the Central Bank few options for financing its deficit besides printing money, Gerashchenko responded to the nonpayment crisis by authorizing credits to the budget as well as to enterprises, farms, and even former Soviet republics. This rise in expenditures, which was paid for by printing rubles, resulted in high inflation by the fall of 1992.

In mid-1993, Boris Fedorov, as finance minister, tried to limit inflationary credits from the Central Bank and tried to get the Central Bank to raise its refinance rate to positive real levels. Fedorov also ended credits to former Soviet republics. In the fall of 1993, after President Boris Yeltsin's violent showdown with the parliament, Yegor Gaidar came back into the government, and he and Fedorov managed to raise the Central Bank's refinancing rate to positive real levels and to control the granting of inflationary credits. However, by January 1994, after the huge political defeat in the December 1993 elections, both Gaidar and Fedorov left the government. By April 1994, credits were growing rapidly, inflation was on the rise, and the Central Bank's refinancing rate had again become negative.

Another attempt at controlling inflation occurred in March of 1995, when the government finally agreed to limit its spending to what it could raise in taxes or borrow. In comparison to a level of approximately 75 percent in 1994, only 7 percent of the deficit was financed with Central Bank credits in 1995.[23] Meanwhile, the federal government deficit in 1995 was also kept in check; it decreased from the 1994 level of 11.4 percent of GDP to 5.4 percent in 1995.[24] In addition, inflation and the exchange rate had stabilized considerably by 1996.

[23] *Financial Times*, April 10, 1995, as cited in Shleifer and Treisman, *The Economics and Politics of Transition to an Open Market Economy: Russia*, p. 29.
[24] *World Economic Outlook* (Washington, D.C.: IMF, 1998), p. 100.

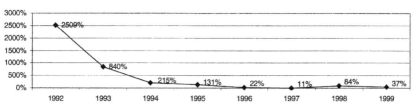

Figure 4.1. Annual rate of growth in Consumer Price Index, 1992–1999. *Source*: Calculated from "Excel Database," *Russian Economic Trends*, May 2000.

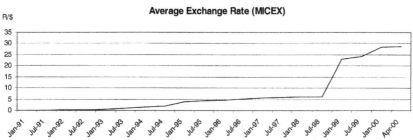

Figure 4.2. Average exchange rate, 1991–2000. *Source*: Calculated from "Excel Database," *Russian Economic Trends*, May 2000.

From Figures 4.1 and 4.2 it appears that, at least in terms of the exchange rate and inflation, the stabilization efforts of 1995 and 1996 resulted in dramatic improvement of the fiscal position of the state as compared to 1992. In order to understand later events, it is necessary to analyze the seemingly successful stabilization efforts of 1995–96.

Russia achieved temporary stabilization in 1996 through apparently ordinary means; the government stopped printing money in order to finance the deficit. However, this stabilization policy brings up two questions: first, how did the government handle the deficit in the absence of Central Bank credits, and second, why was this strategy successful only in 1995–96 rather than earlier? Regarding the first question, the budget deficit was handled mainly through borrowing. New methods for financing the deficit included the issuance of short-term treasury bills (called GKO) and some longer-term treasury bills (OFZ), as well as loans from the IMF.[25] Federal government expenditures did decrease, from 26.0 percent of GDP in 1992 to 17.6 percent of GDP in 1995. But, during the same period, revenues also decreased, from 15.6 percent of GDP to 12.2 percent of GDP.[26]

The answer to the second question, concerning why this seemingly uncomplicated stabilization strategy was adopted only in 1995, is much more complex. Daniel Treisman has uncovered a plausible answer by investigating the politics of the stabilization effort.[27] The first part of the stabilization story concerns how the government was able to finally cut expenditures. Commercial banks were profiting from processing and using government credits granted to industry and agriculture. Banks received fees for handling such credits, and they also held onto funds in order to speculate on the ruble – this partially explained nonpayments to enterprises by the government. By ending the system of government subsidization of industry, commercial banks stood to lose their main source of income.

Treisman argued that in exchange for ending credits, the government offered banks high-interest, virtually guaranteed short-term bonds. By buying these bonds, the banks got out of the business of speculating on the ruble, which greatly helped in the fight against inflation, and banks were guaranteed high, safe profits. The government was also able finally to make significant cuts in expenditures, which was also supposed to improve the state's financial position. However, when government expenditures in the form of credits to farms, enterprises, and state organizations were officially cut, many of these organizations were left in perilous financial circumstances. Under conditions in which bankruptcy or restructuring are possible, the cutting of subsidies might have resulted in the shutting down of inefficient enterprises and organizations. However, for reasons that will be discussed below, restructuring occurred only to a limited extent after the ending of state credits.

Instead, what followed the ending of state credits was another round of the nonpayment crisis. This time, however, the nonpayment occurred in the energy sector on a massive scale. Farms, enterprises, and govern-

[25] Barry Ickes and associates point out that it is unclear how many GKO were purchased by the Central Bank of Russia itself. If this is the case, the government may not have moved as far away from monetary financing of the deficit as is commonly thought. Barry Ickes, Peter Murrell, and Randi Ryterman, "End of the Tunnel? The Effects of Financial Stabilization in Russia," *Post-Soviet Affairs*, Vol. 13, No. 2 (1997), p. 110.
[26] *World Economic Outlook*, p. 100.
[27] See Daniel Treisman, "Fighting Inflation in a Transitional Regime: Russia's Anomalous Stabilization," *World Politics*, Vol. 50, No. 2 (1998), pp. 235–65; see also Shleifer and Treisman, *The Economics and Politics of Transition to an Open Market Economy: Russia*.

ment organizations (schools, offices, etc.) stopped paying electricity and fuel bills. Treisman and Shleifer estimated that the net increase in credit to clients by the fuel and electricity sectors for 1994 to 1996 was close to $5 billion. They correctly point out that "the non-payment crisis masked a covert redistribution of credit."[28] That is, instead of credits coming to enterprises from the central bank and the government through commercial banks, credits came from the energy sector industries in the form of nonpayment.

The energy companies, in response, threatened to cut off supplies, but were prevented from doing so by the government. In the end, the energy sector agreed to take such losses because, as compensation for accepting nonpayment by the public, the government allowed energy companies not to pay taxes, and energy companies were granted extremely lucrative export privileges. Treisman and Shleifer provide data on tax indebtedness to the government as well as data on the rates of profit of the energy sector as evidence for their argument. These data show that at the same time that arrears from the public to the energy sector were amassing, energy sector tax indebtedness and energy sector profits were increasing.[29]

This argument by Treisman and Shleifer suggests that in essence there was a shift from funding of government expenditures (which had profited banks) to a failure to collect taxes (which profited energy companies). In addition, instead of simply printing rubles, as it had done in the past, the government borrowed heavily from banks to finance the deficit. This argument suggests that inflation was "conquered" by making an agreement with the energy sector and banks (1) to borrow heavily from banks at high interest rates and (2) to allow the energy sector to profit enormously from exports in exchange for the energy sector's taking over government subsidization of industry and agriculture.

Although this stabilization policy did bring down inflation, it did not address the corrupt political practices that had so often been the cause of fiscal imbalance. For example, during the presidential campaign in 1996, the federal government deficit rose again to 9.1 percent of GDP.[30] Although the deficits in 1997 and the first half of 1998 were lower than those in 1996, they remained too high for the Russian economy to support. In addition, wage and payment arrears rose sharply during this time, in part because the Ministry of Finance was using tax revenues to repay domestic debt.

[28] Shleifer and Treisman, *The Economics and Politics of Transition to an Open Market Economy: Russia*, pp. 48–49.
[29] Ibid., pp. 49–52.
[30] *World Economic Outlook*, p. 100

Beginning in the spring and summer of 1998, as it became more difficult for the government to repay or roll over its domestic short-term debt, the government decided to borrow in foreign currency. Andrei Illarionov reports that "in the first eight months of 1998, Russia's foreign debt increased by $18.5 billion."[31] The accumulation of foreign-currency-denominated debt significantly raised the government's foreign currency obligations at a time when the government also needed its foreign currency reserves to support the ruble. Rather than helping the situation, the emergency rescue package from the IMF approved on July 20, 1998, only made matters worse. The first $4.8 billion tranche went to the Central Bank, rather than to the Ministry of Finance, and was used up by mid-August in a vain attempt to save both Russian banks and the ruble. The culmination of this expensive policy was the financial crisis on August 17, 1998, in which the Russian government devalued the ruble, defaulted on domestic government debt, and declared a moratorium on debt principal payments to foreigners. Despite complicated explanations for the crisis, economists such as Illarionov are correct in arguing that the economic causes of the financial crisis in Russia were simply too much government debt and an overvalued exchange rate.[32] However, the history of Russia's stabilization efforts suggests that the political causes of the crisis stem from the fact that the political and institutional bases of Russian state fiscal irresponsibility never self-corrected – this despite the apparent success of macroeconomic reforms a few years before.

Another point that must be emphasized in understanding Russia's efforts at stabilization is that although government spending decreased overall during the 1990s, there was no successful strategic realignment of government obligations. Rather than cutting unnecessary spending programs and supporting other ones deemed useful, most government programs were simply continued with reduced budgets.[33] In such a situation, all critics of the government were correct: in general, any government spending was wasteful; at the same time, all state institutions were woefully underfunded. Unfortunately for those involved in economic reform, the solution to productively cutting government expenditures was a political one; specifically, it involved coming up with a politically acceptable reconfiguration of state institutions. However, as we shall see,

---

[31] Andrei Illarionov, "What Went Wrong in Russia? The Roots of the Economic Crisis," *Journal of Democracy*, Vol. 10, No. 2 (1999), p. 75.
[32] Illarionov, "What Went Wrong in Russia? The Roots of the Economic Crisis," pp. 74–75.
[33] Vladimir Popov, "The Political Economy of Growth in Russia," *Program on New Approaches to Russian Security*, Working Paper, No. 17 (2000), p. 4.

the neoliberal economic reform program did not actively focus on the reform of the Russian state.

Privatization

The privatization of Russia actually began when Russia was still part of the Soviet Union. The perestroika-era laws had transferred de facto control over enterprise resources and assets to directors and other *nomenklatura* economic elites. However, after the breakup of the USSR, this de facto control over enterprise resources by the *nomenklatura* became increasingly legitimized and legal. In July 1991, the All-Union Law on Destatization and Privatization allowed for the conversion of state enterprises to different forms of property, including leased, collective, cooperative, joint stock, and private property.[34] Although enterprise directors continued to seek greater juridical rights of control over their enterprises, there were no laws implementing the Law on Destatization and Privatization, and so, at the beginning of 1992, although there were over 3,000 leased enterprises and almost 1,000 nonstate enterprises, state-owned enterprises still accounted for 96 percent of production.[35] However, delays in privatization prolonged the de facto control over enterprises by directors; they did not reverse this control.

Among a few small and medium-sized enterprises, privatization proceeded with the Law on Leasehold and Law on Cooperatives, whereby labor collectives of employees were able to buy shares in the enterprise.[36] Often employees were offered shares at a discounted rate, or credits were made available to employees to purchase the shares. A large block of shares would be reserved for later sale, with the voting block of those unsold shares going to the management. The dispersion of shares among employees and various incentives held by the management effectively worked against organized employee resistance to management initiatives. This early privatization, characterized by easily gained legal control by mangers over enterprises, was to be a foretaste of later large-scale privatization. However, the transition was not easy. The freeing of prices in January 1992 erased the foundation of those nonstate enterprises, which had been profiting by purchasing products at state-controlled prices and then selling at market prices. At the same time, the position of state enterprise directors was strengthened, in the sense that they could now profit directly because they no longer had to go through intermediary enterprises.[37]

---

[34] Simon Clarke, "Privatisation: The Politics of Capital and Labour," in Stephen White, Alex Pravda, and Zvi Gitelman (eds.), *Developments in Russian and Post-Soviet Politics* (Durham, N.C.: Duke University Press, 1994), p. 170.
[35] Ibid., p. 171.   [36] Ibid., pp. 172–173.   [37] Ibid., p. 176.

Official privatization began in 1992. One of the first steps was to divide enterprises into categories, largely according to size. Small shops immediately were given to local property committees to be sold or auctioned for cash as proprietorships. The proceeds of this small-scale privatization were to go to local governments. A second aspect of the first phase of privatization was the issuance of vouchers. All Russian citizens received vouchers in the fall of 1992, which they could either sell for cash, invest in an investment fund, or use to buy shares in an enterprise. The voucher distribution coincided with the privatization of most medium- and large-scale enterprises. These enterprises, supposedly through their labor collectives, were given a choice among three privatization options. The option that proved most popular was the second, whereby the workers would receive 51 percent of the shares for almost nothing; the remaining 49 percent would be sold at auction and were usually bought up by management. This option was popular because it removed state ownership at very little cost to the enterprise directors, while providing an opportunity for directors to later purchase shares from the employees, which would consolidate directors' control over the firms.

Some scholars, such as Maxim Boycko, Andrei Shleifer, and Robert Vishny, celebrated the alliance with enterprise directors, so-called stakeholders, because they claimed that it broke the old Soviet central ministries, created open corporations with tradable shares, and created, via the voucher system, more shareholders as well as a concentration of shareholdings.[38] The first point, regarding the breaking of the Soviet central ministries, is questionable, since the central ministries were largely dismantled by Gorbachev under perestroika.[39] The other two points turn out to be true in name only. In responding to criticisms of the alliance with stakeholders, Boycko and his colleagues wrote, "to secure political support, Russia's privatizers had to make compromises and give in to the demands of major interest groups. Local governments, managers, and workers all got much more out of privatization than most observers would consider reasonable."[40] But the question is, what did the major interest groups get, and how did they get it? It is significant that stakeholders did not get a set of rights defined by law and upheld in the courts. Managers got control of firms' assets without having to take responsibility for debt, investment, or restructuring. Workers got shares in firms in which, as shareholders, they were practically and legally unable to influence management. Local governments got the

---

[38] Boycko, Shleifer, and Vishny, *Privatizing Russia*, pp. 94–95.
[39] Clarke, "Privatisation: The Politics of Capital and Labour," p. 169.
[40] Boycko, Shleifer, and Vishny, *Privatizing Russia*, p. 93.

privilege of exerting unpredictable power over business in their territories, leading to unstable enforcement of federation laws. Nevertheless, some of those involved in privatization have justified giving in to stakeholders in order to achieve the greater goal of depoliticization.

In the end, after the first phase of privatization, as of January 1, 1994, 11,000 out of 14,500 medium- to large-scale enterprises in Russia had been privatized, and by mid-1994, 80 percent of small enterprises had been privatized.[41] The second phase of privatization began in July 1994, and it consisted of three main objectives: (1) the consolidation of shares in enterprises, which was accomplished largely through limitations on workers' rights to increase their shareholdings; (2) the continuation of the sale of vouchers in securities markets; and (3) the selling off of some of the largest Russian enterprises. In November and December of 1995, the infamous "loans-for-shares" auctions began. According to this concept, banks would provide long-term loans to the government, and the government would provide controlling share blocks in large Russian enterprises as collateral. The value of the shares would be determined by auctions. This process was extremely controversial because of widespread instances of fraud and corruption in the process of auctioning the shares. In the conclusion of this volume, Steven Fish discusses the implications of the loans-for-shares auctions on democratization in Russia. Finally, the third phase of privatization began at the end of 1995. In this third phase, the approximately 136 large enterprises were to be auctioned off on a case-by-case basis.[42] This process is ongoing and consistently fails to meet government revenue targets.

THE RESULTS OF ECONOMIC REFORM IN RUSSIA FROM 1991 TO 1998

Despite the triumphant declarations throughout the 1990s of several of those involved in the reform process, accumulating evidence suggests that marketization has been largely unsuccessful in Russia. Moreover, the post-1998 gains appear to have occurred despite the reform program of the 1990s rather than because of it. Here I consider how the reform program actually impacted efficiency, investment, growth, crime and corruption, and social welfare in Russia.

Efficiency

Because of the lack of serious restructuring of enterprises and the lack of a competitive environment, the neoliberal economic reform program in Russia did not result in greater efficiency. An important reason why

---

[41] "Commercial Overview of Russia," *BISNIS*, March 1999.
[42] Ibid.

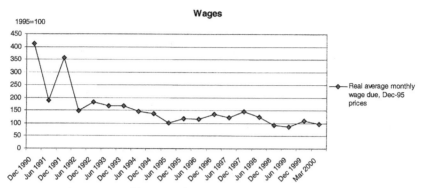

Figure 4.3. Average monthly wages due, 1990–2000. *Source*: Calculated from "Excel Database," *Russian Economic Trends*, May 2000.

restructuring was limited was that despite the liberalization of prices and trade, there was a severe lack of investment. The neoliberal plan curtailed any possibility for government-led investment programs, while at the same time private banks were unable or unwilling to extend long-term loans. Moreover, the privatization program brought almost no new capital for restructuring to firms. Thus, firms were constrained in any fundamental restructuring attempts, despite changes in prices and ownership.

In addition, despite the fall in output, efficiency-oriented change in employment has been extremely limited. Until the end of 1998, there had been only meager reorganization of firms through layoffs and other changes in the structure of employment. During most of the 1990s, unemployment increased gradually, but there were no massive layoffs; generally speaking, falling output was absorbed instead by falling real wages, as illustrated in Figure 4.3.[43]

Reductions in work time, unpaid vacations, and delayed wage payments under inflationary conditions all contributed to falling real wage rates. In Russia during the 1990s, unemployment was unattractive to workers compared to decreasing real wages, for several reasons: first, access to social services was largely determined by one's place of employment; second, there was an extremely underdeveloped labor market infrastructure, that is, a lack of institutions for redirecting employment, such as temporary employment and job placement agencies, classified advertising sections, and so forth; third, unemployment benefits from the

---

[43] Esther Duflo and Claudia Senik-Leygonie, "Industrial Restructuring in Russia: Early Reactions of Firms to the Shock of Liberalization," *Economics of Transition*, Vol. 5, No. 1 (1997), p. 48.

state were quite low; and finally, the lack of housing alternatives and political restrictions on moving between cities within the Russian Federation meant that even if workers found new jobs in other locations, they might be prevented from moving to live near their workplaces. From the perspective of managers, there were no short-term gains from laying off workers, because the cost of a layoff was equal to three months' salary.[44]

In addition to the lack of both investment and efficiency-improving employment mobility, restructuring was also hampered by a lack of expertise and skill among management. This was compounded by the lack of clarity in the legal basis for privatization, including the lack of shareholder rights. This meant that managers who became owners were not really subject to demands of shareholders and were free to do as they wished, incurring few costs for continued inefficiency. Reformers themselves recognized this problem, but still maintained that depoliticization – private ownership by nonstate actors – would in itself create enough incentives for restructuring and improved efficiency.

The second major reason why the neoliberal program did not improve efficiency was that it was not implemented under competitive conditions, and did not engender further rule-based competition. At the time of liberalization, the Russian economy was full of monopoly producers; these included actual single producers as well as de facto single producers. Considering the spatial arrangement of industry and the fact that transportation networks were in disarray during the early 1990s, many enterprises were able to exercise monopoly control over goods in particular regions. Moreover, due to the restructuring limitations discussed earlier, competitive enterprises were not created through privatization. Finally, the legal system did not protect or support the entry of new competitive firms.

Investment

In addition to the lack of gains in efficiency, the reform program did not result in strong levels of investment in Russia. There were two main causes of low investment in Russia. The first was the government's inability to handle macroeconomic policy in a way that would produce an investment climate attractive to capital. The second was the lack of legal infrastructure for protecting investment and property rights. I will discuss each of these issues in turn, but first will present some data on the level of investment in Russia. Figure 4.4 shows foreign direct investment for the 1994–98 period.

[44] Ibid.

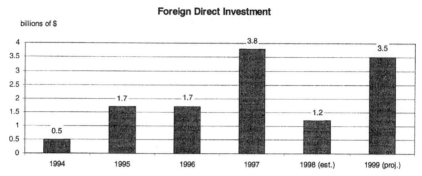

Figure 4.4. Foreign direct investment, 1994–1999. *Source*: EBRD, *Transition Report 1999* (London: EBRD, 1999), p. 261.

While there has been an increase in foreign direct investment since reforms began, for the 1989–97 period Russia's per capita foreign direct investment was a mere $63 per capita, which was below the CIS per capita average of $84 and well below the central and East European and Baltic state average of $439 per capita.[45]

Moreover, Russia's FDI in the 1990s was rather paltry when compared to the estimates for how much capital left the country during the same period. The estimates for capital flight vary enormously, but current estimates are in the range of $150 billion since the reform program began.[46] The argument against regulation of capital flight is that if capital is not free, then investment will suffer. In practice, through barter operations, fraudulent losses, and excess payments schemes, liberalization – in the absence of a legal infrastructure that would have protected capital entering the country – simply lined the pockets (and foreign bank accounts) of those involved in foreign trade, without providing incentives for increased investment. Insofar as it reflects a poor investment climate, capital flight is also a testament to the mismanagement of the macroeconomy.

Some reformers considered the period of relative macroeconomic stability beginning in 1995 as proof of the success of the neoliberal approach. However, although inflation and the deficit did begin to decrease, as discussed earlier, stabilization was achieved mainly by shifts in financing of the deficit. The shift to domestic debt was noninflationary, but that policy did not adequately deal with the problem of tax collection or the problem of persistently high deficits and accumulating

---

[45] *Transition Report 1998*, p. 81.
[46] "Robbing Russia," *The Nation*, October 4, 1999, p. 4.

debt. Moreover, the neoliberal approach to stabilization did not fundamentally improve the financial position of the state, because it did not begin to solve the political and institutional problems that were at the heart of fiscal instability. By not addressing these fundamental political problems, neoliberal Russian reformers missed an opportunity for a stabilization program that would have gone much further toward making Russia an attractive site for investment.

Another major and related impediment to investment was the deficient legal system. In the most general sense this referred to the lack of law and order, as well as to contract enforcement. In particular, there was also a lack of financial regulation. This impacted investment in several arenas, but especially dramatically in the scandals surrounding investment funds, where thousands of people lost their savings. Most of the thousands of investment funds that sprung up in 1992 and 1993, and which were supposed to be the vehicles that allowed average Russians to invest in the economy, simply turned out to be pyramid schemes or otherwise went bankrupt. Many of these funds opened in advance of privatization or other property form definition and therefore had nothing to invest in, even if there had been a desire to actually invest.

The reform program also failed to deliver clarity on the legal basis for privatization, including shareholder and investor rights. This substantially limited the attractiveness of privatized enterprises to investors. In essence, enterprise directors, as the "stakeholders," were given free reign over "their" enterprises. The Russian Federation's Chamber of Commerce and Industry estimated in 1995 that, in terms of shareholders' rights, "Russia today is the most unattractive market in the world."[47] Moreover, they claimed that "experts estimate that as yet not a single Russian registry and depository corresponds to international standards. The responsibility of depositories to investors for possible losses and for securing the necessary level of market liquidity remains an *open question.*"[48] Similarly, in November 1995, well after privatization of most enterprises had been completed, the Chamber of Commerce claimed that "there are still no reliable legal barriers to machinations with stock registries."[49]

In addition to creating problems with shareholders, the emphasis on stakeholders' rights, as opposed to property rights, also had a particularly negative effect on foreign participation in investment projects.

[47] "Russian Business – Priorities of the National Economy in 1995: Annual Report of the Russian Federation's Chamber of Commerce and Industry," *Problems of Economic Transition*, Vol. 38, No. 7 (1995), p. 22, reprinted from *Voprosi Ekonomiki*, No. 2 (1995), pp. 83–103.
[48] Ibid., p. 23 (emphasis added).   [49] Ibid., p. 22.

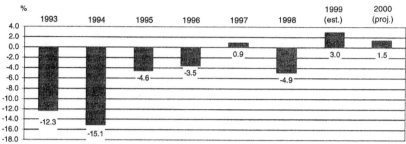

Figure 4.5. Percentage change in GDP, 1993–2000. *Source*: Calculated from "Monthly Update," *Russian Economic Trends*, April 1997, December 1997, and May 2000.

Industrial directors and regional governments, as the stakeholders, were allowed to exercise illegal authority in handling major investment projects. For example, in the oil and gas sectors there were several cases where Russian companies colluded with regional governments to block foreign projects. The privatization program clearly demonstrates that it was a mistake to think that legal institutions would spontaneously develop in response to "private ownership." In order to attract investment, state institutional development should have been an integral part of the economic reform process in general, and of the privatization process in particular.

Growth

The sharp fall in output since 1991 remains one of the strongest indicators of the failure of the reform program in Russia. As Figures 4.5 and 4.6 demonstrate, production has come nowhere close to recovery.

Even in the most favorable circumstances, with 5 percent growth every year starting from the year 2000, it will take Russia fifteen years to get back to its 1989 level of GDP.[50] For comparison, the American drop in GDP during the Great Depression was 30.5 percent for the 1929 to 1933 period.[51] Russia's GDP in 1998 was estimated at 55 percent of the 1989 level.[52] This figure is slightly above the average amongst CIS countries,

[50] Popov, "The Political Economy of Growth in Russia," p. 1.
[51] *Historical Statistics of the United States, Colonial Times to 1970* (Washington, D.C.: U.S. Department of Commerce, Bureau of the Census, 1975), pp. 224–225, as cited in Stefan Hedlund and Niclas Sundström, "The Russian Economy after Systemic Change," *Europe-Asia Studies*, Vol. 48, No. 6 (1996), p. 889.
[52] See *Transition Report 1999*, p. 73, for all subsequent growth figures cited in this paragraph.

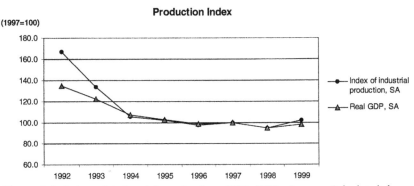

Figure 4.6. Index of industrial production, 1992–1999. *Source*: Calculated from "Monthly Update," *Russian Economic Trends*, April 1997, December 1997, and May 2000.

which was 53 percent, and it is well below the average for central and Eastern Europe and the Baltic states, which was 95 percent of the 1989 level. These figures show that the CIS on average has fared much worse than Eastern Europe and the Baltic states. Moreover, the results amongst CIS countries that have not taken the neoliberal path are varied. Some, such as Uzbekistan and Belarus, showed positive GDP growth from 1996 to 1998. Uzbekistan's GDP in 1998 was estimated at 90 percent of the 1989 level, and Belarus's 1998 level was 78 percent of the 1989 level. On the other hand, Ukraine has fared extremely poorly; its GDP in 1998 was estimated at only 37 percent of the 1989 level. The point, then, is not that low growth is an indictment of neoliberalism per se, but that low growth is one indicator that the Russian economic reform program has not been as successful as had been hoped at the beginning of the reform period.

Although growth has become positive since 1999, mainly as a result of the ruble devaluation in the fall of 1998, prospects for long-term economic recovery are not entirely favorable. Moreover, the reasons for pessimism regarding long-term sustainable growth have to do with the types of reforms that have been pursued thus far. To understand the long-term prospects for growth, it is necessary to explain the underlying causes of the fall in output during most of the 1990s, as well as the subsequent post-1998 rise.

Although economic reforms normally lead to a decrease in consumption (demand), the fall in output after 1991 was not a result of decreased demand, nor was it a result of decreased investment by the center. Decreases in state expenditures occurred only in 1992 and later. The economic collapse of 1991–92 was caused largely by the perestroika reforms

(1985–91), which cut back the central ministries but left state enterprise managers with more power. Following the breakdown of the
Communist Party, state enterprise directors were largely unaccountable
to anyone, and they were free to cut production and hoard inputs.[53]

Price liberalization in 1992 and the removal of protective barriers
made the price of inputs rise, while the breakup of the USSR, and the
subsequent breakdown of supply networks, resulted in a physical lack
of supplies. Numerous factory-level accounts of falling production point
to this physical lack of supplies, as well as to the rising cost of existent
supplies. As noted above, enterprises did not react to these price shocks
with significant cost cutting or restructuring. Rather, they just stopped
paying each other and delivering supplies. This supply deficiency caused
a negative chain reaction in economic production throughout the
country.

During this period of weakness due to massive supply problems
among Russian producers, trade liberalization allowed imports to fill
the stores. This was good for consumers, but these imports obviously
lowered the demand for lesser-quality, more expensive, Russian-
produced light industry and consumer goods. At the same time, slashing
of the military budget and declining state orders lowered demand for
heavy industry. Export trade was mainly driven by exports of raw mate-
rials, including, gas, oil, and metals, and hence did not result in increases
in domestic productivity or manufactured-goods exports. In liberalizing
trade, Russian manufacturers lost protected markets and got competition at home from cheaper, better made, better designed products. In this
way, trade liberalization hurt farmers, food producers, light industries,
and consumer goods manufacturers most.

Neoliberals would argue that short-term declines in growth might
simply be the hard reality of liberalization and market-oriented reforms.
However, as Przeworski and his colleagues have noted, "the argument
that 'the worse, the better' cannot be maintained indefinitely; at some
time things must get better."[54] Some analysts have claimed that the
positive growth beginning in 1999 signaled the long-awaited fruition
of Russian economic reforms; that is, things were finally getting better.
However, a closer look at the nature of recent trends in growth shows
that Russia's macroeconomic situation remains precarious.

The post-1998 growth can mainly be attributed to devaluation of the
ruble. Ruble devaluation limited imports, by making them much more

[53] Henry Bienen and Mansur Sunyaev, "Adjustment and Reform in Russia," *SAIS Review*,
Vol. 13, No. 1 (1993), p. 36.
[54] Adam Przeworski (ed.), *Sustainable Democracy* (Cambridge: Cambridge University
Press, 1995), p. 69.

costly, and in turn boosted exports and domestic industrial production. International experience would predict gains in growth following a devaluation, but it also suggests that post-devaluation growth will be short-lived due to inflationary pressures.[55] In the short term, Russia's continued growth depends on the government's handling of the ruble, that is, its slow appreciation in real terms. Too much appreciation of the ruble will erode the fragile gains in industrial productivity. However, if export prices decline too much, weakening Russia's current account and spurring further capital flight, the ruble could again sharply fall, producing negative consequences for Russia's foreign currency debt and inflation. In addition, any optimistic scenario for even short-term growth in Russia crucially assumes that, at a minimum, the government's budget deficit will be kept in check and that the government will not borrow from the Central Bank. However, the more important prerequisite for long-term sustained growth is investment.

Adam Przeworski's East-West group argued that liberalization and stabilization, even if they were carried out according to plan and did improve efficiency, would be insufficient for generating growth.[56] The factors crucial for growth, such as improved technology, education, and skills, are often undersupplied by firms in competitive markets. For this reason, Przeworski and colleagues suggest that successful economic reform requires, in addition to liberalization and stabilization, an explicit program that targets those factors necessary for growth.

In assessing the longer-term prospects for growth and economic recovery in Russia, we should consider what Russia's neoliberal reform program over the past ten years has contributed to future prospects for growth. Liberalization, stabilization, and privatization were undertaken with the idea that efficiency gains would lead to growth. The Russian reform program did not compensate for the fall in output with any type of restructuring, retraining, or investment policy. Rather than focusing on these tangible and intangible inputs, neoliberalism relied solely on increasing efficiency to promote growth. Moreover, the ideology of neoliberalism championed, at least in the short-term, inattention to the active development of Russian state institutions and other market-supporting institutions necessary for successful market-oriented reform and, in particular, for creating the conditions for investment. For example, reducing and indeed remaking the bureaucracy, which served to stifle investment throughout the 1990s, and seriously developing the legal infrastructure needed to protect investors were just two areas where progress was extremely limited. It also became clear that during the

[55] *Russian Economic Trends*, monthly update, May 2000, p. 5.
[56] Przeworski (ed.), *Sustainable Democracy*, p. 74.

reform process, certain actors developed a material interest in keeping institutions underdeveloped, but little was done to combat these real incentives for stalled institutional reform.

Recently, mainly in the aftermath of the 1998 financial crisis, criticism of the Russian economic reform program, which was specifically focused on the lack of institutional development, began to surface. World Bank Senior Vice President and Chief Economist Joseph Stiglitz remarked,

> ... most economists said the problem in the former Soviet Union was that they had central planning, no property rights and therefore inefficiencies, distorted prices. You were going to change all that and it was supposed to release a burst of energy of entrepreneurship and output was supposed to increase. Instead output has fallen markedly and poverty has increased markedly and I think the lesson we've learned is that market economies are far more complicated than text book models often describe them. And that issues of governance, issues of legal infrastructures, issues of institutions are absolutely central.[57]

Rather than considering the lack of institutional development as simply a lack of will or oversight on the part of economic reformers, I argue that we should consider the absence of institutional development in light of two ideas: first, reformers' understanding of the nature of institutional development, a view which held that institutions would develop endogenously as a result of demand, and which gave minimal credence to the possibility that certain actors might develop interests in thwarting institutional development; and second, reformers' unwillingness to appreciate the necessity of working with one's political enemies in order to find politically feasible solutions to economic problems – here the recurring problems with the budget deficit and reform of state institutions come to mind. Both of these ideas – endogenous institutional development and avoidance of difficult politics – were unfortunately part of the neoliberal consensus that contributed to the lack of institutional development in Russia, a deficiency that has and will continue to negatively impact sustainable growth.

Crime and Corruption

The growth of crime in Russia is obviously important in terms of social welfare, but it is also important to the evaluation of economic reform, because criminalization negatively affects investment, and increases transaction costs and inefficiency. All too often, the position on criminality of many of those involved in the reforms in Russia was first to deny the existence of a serious problem, and then to argue that if there

---

[57] Robert Lyle, "The East: World Bank Asks If Economic Transition Has Failed Former USSR," *RFE/RL*, April 27, 1999.

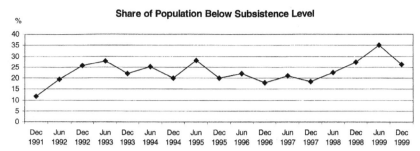

Figure 4.7. Share of the population below the subsistence level, 1991–1999. *Source*: "Excel Database," *Russian Economic Trends*, May 2000.

was a problem, it was a temporary condition of adjustment to the market, and further, that criminalization was one of the necessary costs of reform.[58]

It is obvious now that there was inadequate attention given to the development of efficient state regulation of the economy. On the one hand, a plethora of unfair predatory state practices went unchecked. On the other hand, liberalization entailed not only the freeing of prices and trade, but also the dismantling of certain state institutions that were necessary for the monitoring of economic transactions. By not giving the state the tools to monitor the market – in the form of active development of state regulatory institutions concomitant with economic reform – the liberalization of prices and the legalization of any kind of trade activity contributed to criminalization. The experience in Russia teaches us that state *size* is not the only variable that matters for corruption. For it was not simply state largesse that caused the criminalization of Russia. Rather, corruption was largely the result of the lack of appropriate regulations and institutions that could have given the state information about the economy and made illegal economic activity more costly.

Social Welfare Consequences: Poverty and Income Inequality

One can no longer escape the conclusion that Russia's experience with economic reform has resulted in extremely negative social welfare consequences.

Figure 4.7 shows that the percentage of the population living below the subsistence (not poverty, but subsistence!) level has more than

---

[58] See especially Åslund, "Economic Causes of Crime in Russia," and Andrei Shleifer, "Round Table on Russia: Agenda for Russian Reforms," *Economics of Transition*, Vol. 5, No. 1 (1997).

doubled since 1991. The Russian government defined the subsistence
level at 436 rubles per month as of June 1998 (before the currency collapse), and at 963 rubles per month as of December 1999.[59] Before the
currency collapse, the subsistence level in June 1998 was approximately
$70 per month, at the rate of 6.2 rubles to the dollar; it had fallen by
about one-half, to just $36 per month (at the rate of 27.0 rubles to the
dollar), by December 1999. In addition to increases in absolute poverty,
Figure 4.3 (page 152) showed that real wages are more than four times
lower than their 1990 levels, while the nonpayment of wages continues
to grow.

Moreover, the overall income inequality that resulted from the neoliberal reform program far surpassed the differential effects of inflation and
subsidy decreases. According to the UN Human Development Report of
1997, the per capita income of the highest quintile of the population in
Russia was fourteen times that of the lowest quintile. This rate is double
the 1997 average rate among industrialized countries and Eastern European countries, both of which average seven times difference between
the highest and lowest quintiles.[60] This extreme income inequality is not
the result of entrepreneurship or gains in efficiency or production;
rather, it is the result of the insider profiteering that was accepted by reformers as a necessary step toward marketization. The negative effects
of the neoliberal program were also unevenly distributed among Russia's
regions. Hedlund and Sundström reported that from 1992 to 1994, the
gap in per capita income between the richest and poorest regions of the
federation increased from eight to forty-two times.[61] This implies that
there is a serious regional element to income inequality.

The problem with income inequality is that when it is the result of
illegal activity, it is inefficient. And when it is legal, it becomes like pol-
lution or environmental degradation, a public bad. A public bad represents a collective action problem in which individual actors stand to
gain from action that makes everyone collectively worse off. A public
bad increases the profits of firms, and perhaps the wages of workers, but
at the same time decreases the overall welfare of the population.[62] Income
inequality in Russia can be considered a public bad insofar as it des-
troys a sense of fairness in shared costs and responsibilities for economic
reform, which is vital to the development of democratic institutions. In

[59] "Excel Database," *Russian Economic Trends*, June 1999.
[60] UNDP, "General Trends and Statistics on Income Disparity," *Human Development Report 1997*.
[61] Hedlund and Sundström, "The Russian Economy after Systemic Change," p. 899.
[62] John E. Roemer, "A Future for Socialism," *Politics and Society*, Vol. 22, No. 4 (1994), p. 461.

the conclusion of this volume, Steven Fish discusses in greater detail the effects of income inequality on democratic development in Russia. What is notable about public bads is that, as collective action problems, their solution is not to be found in the freedom of individuals to maximize their interests but in the ability of the political process to negotiate the interests of different groups in society. This implies the need for government action and state institutions, as opposed to the invisible hand of the market.

DISCUSSION: WHAT HAVE WE LEARNED?

By examining Russia's negative experience with economic reform, we have learned important lessons about the appropriateness of certain economic models, and we have also learned that *politics* matters for economic reform. The economic lessons are mainly related to the apparent inadequacy of the neoclassical model for handling information problems and the unsettled debate over the gains of private ownership. On the political side, Russia's experience teaches us, first, that state capacity and the building of state institutions are crucial for successful marketization. Second, the political *process* of economic reform – in the Russian case, this meant reliance on executive decrees and the unfair privileging of certain groups in society – has important consequences for the growth of corruption and the development of democratic governance institutions.

Inadequacy of the Neoclassical Model

Leaving aside ideological arguments, the economic logic behind creating markets in Russia was that markets are supposed to handle several economic problems better than central planning; primary among these quandaries are informational problems, entry and exit problems, and lack of product variation. That markets handle such issues better than central planning is not so controversial. However, the question of precisely how markets work (or sometimes fail) is less well understood. The Russian case suggests that the neoclassical model of the market is not the only obvious basis for creating markets.

The program of liberalization in Russia was largely based on neoclassical economic models, where price was the main conveyor of information to consumers and producers. However, as economist Peter Murrell has pointed out, the last two decades of work in economics have produced ample evidence that important informational problems are not solved by price.[63] The Hayekian assumption of symmetrically dispersed

---

[63] See K. J. Arrow, "Rationality of Self and Others in an Economic System," in Robin M. Hogarth and Melvin W. Reder (eds.), *Rational Choice: The Contrast between Economics*

knowledge often does not hold, and when there is asymmetric and/or incomplete information, competitive prices are not sufficient statistics.[64] The implications of this work are extremely important to the theoretical possibilities for efficiency gains from simple liberalization. Murrell argued that because in reality the ways in which markets solve economic problems are quite complex, the theoretical basis for market-oriented economic reforms must be far more nuanced than the "simple free-market paradigm."[65] Murrell noted that "if one attaches significance to the informational problems now at the center of theoretical inquiry, then the clear-cut prescriptions of the invisible hand theorems no longer hold."[66]

Because the goal was to replicate the benefits of Western market economies in post-socialist contexts, it was necessary to think seriously about how markets in capitalist countries actually work. The superior ability of markets in handling economic problems was not replicated in the post-socialist Russian context simply by the quick transfer of outdated, but ideologically appealing, metaphors. To argue for complexity in market design is to appreciate the major theoretical currents in economics; it is not an argument against markets. By offering a very simple market model, the neoliberal reform program in Russia failed to deliver the necessary expertise and understanding of complexity in market institutional design that was necessary for the transition to a functioning market economy.

Debate over Private Ownership

Another aspect of the oversimplification of a functioning market economy by Russian reformers concerned the privatization program. Several proponents of privatization explained the necessity for the privatization program by asserting the superiority of markets.[67] In their

and Psychology (Chicago: University of Chicago Press, 1987), pp. 201–16; S. J. Grossman and J. E. Stiglitz, "Information and Competitive Price Systems," *American Economic Review*, Vol. 66 (1976), pp. 246–53; F. Hahn, "General Equilibrium Theory," *Public Interest* (1980), pp. 123–38; B. Holmstrom, "Differential Information and the Market: Comment," in K. J. Arrow and S. Honkapohja (eds.), *Frontiers of Economics* (Oxford: Basil Blackwell, 1985), pp. 200–212; and L. Hurwicz, "Incentive Aspects of Decentralization," in K. J. Arrow and M. D. Intrilligator (eds.), *Handbook of Mathematical Economics: III* (Amsterdam: North-Holland, 1986), pp. 1441–82, as cited in Peter Murrell, "Can Neoclassical Economics Underpin the Reform of Centrally Planned Economies?", *Journal of Economic Perspectives*, Vol. 5, No. 4 (1991), pp. 59–76.

[64] For a discussion of work on this issue see Murrell, "Can Neoclassical Economics Underpin the Reform of Centrally Planned Economies?", pp. 61–64.

[65] Ibid.

[66] Ibid., p. 72.

[67] Boycko, Shleifer, and Vishny, *Privatizing Russia*, p. 9.

analysis, they repeatedly conflated arguments for markets in general with arguments for privatization in particular. It is telling that the IMF (and also the World Bank), along with several other Western advisors, chose to focus almost exclusively on stabilization and liberalization first, reserving consideration of privatization for later. This may have reflected an understanding among IMF and World Bank officials that quick and immediate privatization was not necessarily a requirement for building a market economy (especially when it meant immediate distribution of assets according to political rather than economic goals).

The Russian experience confirms the skepticism toward privatization, and it reaffirms that the case for privatization requires evidence beyond the case for markets. While scholars may agree with market-oriented reform, private ownership is a separate issue. Moreover, in contrast to the assertions of reformers and officials in the Russian government, there is not one path to privatization. There is inadequate theoretical support for the Russian reform team's persistent conflation of private ownership with property rights, and it was plainly inaccurate to consider private ownership the only possible property form available under capitalism. John Roemer pointed out that under capitalism there is "the widest variety of property forms." These include nonprofit firms, not-for-profit firms, limited liability corporations, partnerships, sole proprietorships, labor-managed firms, property that is subject to various types of taxation and regulation, as well as a variety of forms of public ownership at the national, regional, and municipal levels.[68]

Moreover, the efficiency gains of private ownership are not self-evident. Roemer wrote that "property relations should engender competition and innovation and should shelter firms from certain kinds of inefficient government interference. Private ownership of firms *sometimes* accomplishes these objectives."[69] The point here is that private ownership is not the only way to reap the benefits of property rights, because private ownership in itself does not enhance efficiency. Rather, private ownership "engenders competition," which may improve efficiency, but only when there is not too high a concentration of ownership within an industry – that is, in the absence of monopolies. In addition, private ownership may increase efficiency by reducing inefficient state interference, but only when there is a legal system in place that would allow owners to demand enforcement of their rights. By simply creating private owners with uncertain property rights, privatization in Russia did not lead to gains in efficiency or restructuring. Regulation of monopolies and active development of the legal system

[68] Roemer, "A Future for Socialism," p. 456. [69] Ibid.

were needed in order to create the competitive conditions under which efficiency-enhancing property rights could be enforced.

State Capacity and Institutions

Because liberalization entails structural reforms (including the introduction of markets by freeing prices and trade and cutting government subsidies), liberalization is necessarily concerned with establishing some kind of role, be it limited or expansive, for the state in the economy. However, rather than understanding the introduction of markets as being fundamentally related to simultaneously establishing the parameters of state institutions, the neoliberal reform program in Russia considered the introduction of markets to be a substitute for reform of state institutions. Moreover, by denying institutional complexity, reformers reduced "the market" to an extremely simplistic model nearly devoid of supporting institutions. For example, in response to scholars who objected to "instant trade liberalization" because Russia "lacked market infrastructure," Anders Åslund explained that this criticism overstated the complexity of markets. He wrote, "The market was perceived as a centralized computer system, which reflected a failure to understand the decentralized and simple nature of the market: if two people meet to exchange anything, a market exists."[70]

This simplistic formulation of markets fails to consider the well-recognized collective action problems among rational actors and the idea that institutions, both formal and informal, are crucial in shaping incentives. If Russians are subject to universal economic rationality, then we should expect that, as in the rest of the world, in the absence of institutions, individually rational action will not *necessarily* lead to the most efficient or collectively beneficial outcome.

This gap between scholarly acknowledgement of the complexity of markets and states, on the one hand, and the Russian reform program, on the other, was highlighted by the fact that in both 1991 and 1993 the Nobel laureate lectures in economics specifically mentioned the necessity for the development of institutions in the economic transformations of Eastern Europe. Coase argued in his 1991 Nobel lecture that "the value of including institutional factors in the corpus of mainstream economics is made clear by recent events in Eastern Europe. The ex-communist countries are advised to move to a market economy, and their leaders wish to do so, but without the appropriate institutions no market economy of any significance is possible."[71] In 1993, North emphasized

---

[70] Åslund, "The Russian Road to the Market," p. 314.
[71] Ronald H. Coase, "The Institutional Structure of Production," *American Economic Review*, Vol. 82, No. 4 (1992), p. 714, as cited in Hedlund and Sundström, "The Russian Economy after Systemic Change," p. 888.

the important distinction between informal and formal institutions and argued that simply importing the latter to the third world and Eastern Europe "is not a sufficient condition for good economic performance."[72]

Similarly, in 1996, a joint statement by five Russian economists and seven leading American economists (including five Nobel laureates – K. Arrow, L. Klein, W. Leontief, R. Solow, and J. Tobin) made a plea for an expanded role for state institutions in the Russian economic reform process.[73] They directly argued that the government in Russia should have a role in the economy similar to the role of government in the United States, Germany, or Sweden. They wrote, "The government must play a central coordinating role in establishing the public and private institutions required for a market economy to function."[74] They argued that this role would involve government support for restructuring and the establishment of market institutions such as property rights, a stable currency, a legal system that could enforce laws and regulate newly privatized enterprises, and an enforceable, simplified tax system. The authors also stated that many of Russia's present economic troubles stem "directly or indirectly from the fact that the government has not assumed its proper role in a market economy."[75]

It is important to underline that the call for attention to institutions and a reformulated role for the state in the economy is not a retreat from marketization. Nor is it a call for simply a "bigger" state. Rather, as these prominent economists have emphasized, the Russian experience with marketization teaches us that the development of state capacity and institutions must be an integral part of any successful market-oriented reform program.

---

[72] Douglass North, "Economic Performance through Time," *American Economic Review*, Vol. 84, No. 3 (1994), p. 366, as cited in Hedlund and Sundström, "The Russian Economy after Systemic Change," p. 888.

[73] Michael D. Intriligator (ed.), "Round Table on Russia: A New Economic Policy for Russia," *Economics of Transition*, Vol. 5, No. 1 (1997), pp. 225–231. The authors included on the Russian side were Leonid Abalkin, Oleg T. Bogomolov, Valery L. Makarov, Stanislav Shatalin, and Yuri V. Yaryomenko. On the American side the authors included Kenneth J. Arrow, Nobel laureate and professor of economics, Stanford University; Michael D. Intriligator, professor of economics, political science, and policy studies, UCLA; Lawrence R. Klein, Nobel laureate and professor of economics, University of Pennsylvania; Wassily W. Leontief, Nobel laureate and professor of economics, New York University; Marshal Pomer, U.S. coordinator, Economic Transition Group; Robert M. Solow, Nobel laureate and professor of economics, MIT; James Tobin, Nobel laureate and professor of economics, Yale University.

[74] Intriligator (ed.), "Round Table on Russia: A New Economic Policy for Russia," p. 226.

[75] Ibid.

Political Process

A second lesson of the Russian marketization experience is that the political process of reform has important economic consequences. Unfortunately, the reform program began in Russia with the presentation of overly sharp distinctions in the characterization of reform possibilities. Reformers such as Anders Åslund and Richard Layard characterized the choice facing Russia as a choice between two paths: to the neo-liberal market, or to Gehenna.[76] The rhetoric of reform consisted of a rather stark dichotomy between a fully regulated, centralized, state-run economy on the one side, and an idealized laissez-faire market on the other. With such a dichotomy, any suggestion of government regulation, much less support for production, was characterized as necessarily a move against the stabilization and liberalization efforts.[77] This kind of analysis was based on simplistic models of both the state and the market, and it supported the reductionist claim that there was only one path possible for successful economic reform in Russia.

The confidence that reformers had identified an undeniable, single path toward economic reform made the use of technically legal, but generally undemocratic, means – specifically, rule by executive decree – not only palatable, but preferable. Reformers applauded the behind-the-scenes approach to policy making taken by a small group of officials selected by the president, because they claimed that so few people in Russia understood what should be done. Those outside of the government were considered either intellectually ill-prepared or ideologically tainted.[78] For example, Anders Åslund wrote, "Stabilization is enjoying neither intellectual nor political support, since this presupposes some familiarity with macroeconomic theory, which barely seems to be found outside of the government in Russia today."[79] Because of the prevalence of such critics within the parliament, reformers denounced the sovereignty of parliament and expressed disappointment that new elections were not held and that parties that would have supported the govern-

[76] Åslund and Layard open their introduction to *Changing the Economic System in Russia* with the following sentences: "At the end of 1991, Russia faced a horrendous economic crisis. The imminence of Gehenna hung in the air." Åslund and Layard, *Changing the Economic System in Russia*, p. xi.

[77] See, for example, Anders Åslund, "The Gradual Nature of Economic Change in Russia," in Anders Åslund and Richard Layard (eds.), *Changing the Economic System in Russia*, p. 29, and David Lipton, "Reform Endangered," *Foreign Policy*, No. 90 (1993), p. 57.

[78] See, for example, Åslund, "The Gradual Nature of Economic Change in Russia," p. 30.

[79] Ibid., p. 35.

ment were not formed.[80] However, the appeal to "the people," who would support the government as opposed to parliamentarians, belies the reformers' commitment to democracy. Most of the reformers were not committed to the democratic *process*, but rather saw elections as a way of strengthening the power of the government's undemocratically selected group of policy-making reformers. For the reformers, the parliament was an institution that should have supported the government's neoliberal program; it was not the deliberative institution where policy was to be decided.[81]

The use of executive decrees and the sidestepping of parliament in policy making bolstered reformers' sense that they possessed a monopoly on good economic advice, but it also fueled a fear that the ignorant masses or the communists might organize to stop the reforms. Because of this threat of organized opposition, reformers reasoned that they needed to make strategic alliances with certain groups in society. Conveniently, this logic allowed reformers to present their seemingly corrupt support for certain groups as being the only way to secure the passage of the reform program. For example, in a well known account of privatization, Maxim Boycko, Andrei Shleifer, and Robert Vishny explained that it was acceptable for free-market reformers to pursue policies that enriched themselves personally, because "the policies that reformers pursue to serve their personal political goals are much closer to the public interest than the policies of the anti-reformers interested in a powerful state."[82] The reformers used the same argument to justify making insider deals with industrial elites. In praise of their co-optation of stakeholders, Boycko and his colleagues argued that unless the reformer has "absolute political power," he has no chance of defeating stakeholders as well as "traditional politicians."[83] By denying the possibility of alternative programs, this argument implies that reformers cannot be criticized for selling out to insiders.

As evidenced in debates in political science and economics over the relationship between democratization and economic reform, the concept of supporting authoritarian means in order to pursue economic reform is not new. Maxim Boycko, Robert Vishney, and Andrei Shleifer are not the first economists to praise brutal dictators such as Augusto Pinochet for their economic policies.[84] However, in analyzing the relationship between the neoliberal economic reform program and democratization

---

[80] Åslund, *How Russia Built a Market Economy*, p. 100.
[81] For more on the value of democratic deliberation to economic reform, see Przeworski (ed.), *Sustainable Democracy*.
[82] Boycko, Shleifer, and Vishny, *Privatizing Russia*, p. 49.
[83] Ibid., p. 69.   [84] Ibid., pp. 47–48.

in Russia, we have to be clear about the fact that the political means used in the economic reform process had consequences. In the Russian experience, the presentation of a single path for marketization, the use of executive decrees, and the granting of unfair concessions to groups progressed rather quickly toward support for corruption as a means of achieving the goals of economic reform. Despite pronouncements by reformers, corruption has increased rather than decreased as the "reforms" have continued. This development strongly suggests that the political means used in carrying out economic reform are important, and that the idea of "marketization by any means necessary" should be looked upon with great skepticism.

Comparisons to Other Post-Socialist States

Although we don't have space for a systematic comparative analysis of the post-socialist states, in evaluating the efficacy of neoliberalism as a general economic reform strategy, and as a particular strategy for Russia, we need to have a sense of the relationship between the choice of neoliberalism and the success of economic reforms in other post-socialist countries. A consideration of regional patterns of reform suggests that economic reform programs have been much more successful, according to a variety of indicators, in central and Eastern Europe and the Baltic States, as opposed to in the countries of the CIS.

At first glance, because neoliberal reform programs were more prevalent in central and Eastern Europe and the Baltics, there appears to be a correlation between neoliberalism and stronger economic performance. However, if we consider the pre-reform configuration of the state and market institutions in each country, we find that economic reform in general, and neoliberalism in particular, has been most successful where state institutional capacity was high. Poland, Hungary, and the Czech Republic are often cited as evidence of neoliberalism's efficacy, but those states were also among the strongest in the region. In the weak states of the CIS – despite great differences in the types of policy programs, including in some cases the choice of neoliberalism – economic reform has been relatively unsuccessful.

This finding suggests that weak state institutional capacity may be a limiting condition for the success of neoliberal economic reforms. And it suggests that neoliberalism – with its emphasis on stabilization, liberalization, and privatization, *instead of* state institutional development – was inappropriate for Russia, because, by neglecting state institution building, it did not address one of Russia's primary economic needs. Neoliberal Russian reformers did consider the question of state capacity in developing the economic reform program in Russia; however, the consensus was that legal reforms, along with all other necessary state institutions, would *spontaneously* develop in response to the demands of the newly marketized economy. Moreover, the assumption that nearly any state activity constituted negative interference in the economy led reformers to the resolution that if a state functions poorly, greater curtailment of any state activity, rather than rebuilding of state institutions, was the answer. For example, after concluding that the problem in Russia, as opposed to Poland, was Russia's dysfunctional state, Åslund wrote, "The obvious conclusion is that the more messy the situation is, the more important it is to go for a rigorous solution with a maximum of liberalization and stabilization."[85] This belief was consistent with the idea that institutional change is driven by economic efficiency, but, unfortunately for Russia, efficiency-driven institutional development did not spontaneously materialize.

It is important to reiterate that the argument being presented is not that initial conditions determine all outcomes, but rather that given its weak institutional starting conditions, Russia, and other weak states, could not have benefited from an economic program that explicitly neglected institutional development – that is, neoliberalism. Moreover, it must be emphasized that neoliberalism is not the unique cause of every undesirable outcome in Russia. There was a mixture of bad advice, bad policies, bad timing, and bad luck. But, by directing attention away from the crucial variable in political and economic reform, namely, state institutional development, neoliberalism greatly contributed to most of Russia's current political and economic problems.

Nevertheless, in making the claim that neoliberalism is inappropriate where state institutions are underdeveloped, we also have to consider the experiences of weak states that did not adopt neoliberal programs. Ukraine is often cited as an example of a country that is worse off than Russia because it did not adopt a neoliberal economic reform program. However, Ukraine's experience is not the only alternative to neoliberalism, or even the antithesis of neoliberalism – the antithesis of neoliberalism would be a program that clearly emphasized the importance of state capacity and institutional development for economic reform. While it is true that Ukraine did not implement shock therapy, Ukraine also did not seriously address the problem of reconfiguring state institutions to support market reforms. I argue that Ukraine has not achieved successful economic reform because, like Russia, the content of the reforms did not address state institutional weakness. Ukraine's experience is, however, an important reminder that the adoption of a neoliberal program is not the only way to neglect state institutional development.

---

[85] Åslund, "Has Poland Been Useful as a Model for Russia?", p. 169.

However, as the discussion of neoliberalism has shown, because it explicitly directs attention away from the question of state institutional development, it is unlikely that neoliberalism would have improved Ukraine's economic performance.

Finally, if the lack of state capacity or a weak institutional context renders neoliberalism an inappropriate option for economic reform, we must address the question of what type of economic reform program is best suited for weak states. The analysis in this chapter suggests that weak states, like Russia and Ukraine, should explicitly concentrate on building state institutions as market-supporting infrastructure in the process of economic reforms. Again, we must emphasize that the old dichotomies of "institution-building versus market reforms," "fast versus slow reform," and "big versus small government" are not helpful. By recognizing the important differences in the configurations of states and markets at the time of reform – which include the level of direct state involvement in the economy through government organizations, as well as the level of involvement through the oversight of nonstate or informal institutions and organizations – we can better specify and understand the needs of particular countries during periods of economic reform.

CONCLUSION

After considering the neoliberal economic reform program in Russia in terms of its theoretical basis and in terms of the actual results – which consisted of negative gains in efficiency, investment, and growth, as well as burgeoning criminalization, income inequality, and poverty – it is not possible to produce a positive assessment of the neoliberal approach in Russia, on either theoretical or empirical grounds. The principal reason for the lack of success of the neoliberal program in Russia was the mistaken belief that economic reform would produce state institutional reform, and the consequent neglect of the development of institutions necessary for supporting a market economy. This argument suggests that with regard to economic reform, the distinction between the state and the market must be relaxed, so as to accommodate the extensive and complex state institutional development necessary for transitional markets.

One implication of this argument is that if market-oriented reforms require attention to the building of state institutions, then successful economic reform must proceed with respect to the political institutional context. In light of this implication, the analysis of the Russian reform experience informs the debate over political versus economic reform by revealing that the assumed dichotomy in the question, of economic reform versus political reform, is misleading. By confirming that successful economic reform cannot follow from a hard distinction between the market and the state (or politics), we can move beyond questions such as "Should political *or* economic reforms be undertaken first?" or "Can political and economic reforms be undertaken simultaneously?" This analysis suggests that the answer to these questions does not lie in choosing the market *or* the state, economics *or* politics. Rather, the answer to the question of what type of reform should be undertaken will depend on the starting material and institutional conditions (as well as understandings regarding those conditions). It is only with an accurate and specific understanding of the context in which reform is to take place that an appropriate set of policies can be conceived. Again, this is no call to exceptionalism; rather, it is a call to greater specificity in the comparative analysis that informs policy choices.

5

Politics and the Russian Armed Forces

Zoltan Barany

> The Russian armed forces are out of control. The threat is
> not Bonapartism but, rather, civilians or officials who might
> similarly use the politicized armed forces.[1]

> Not since June 1941 has the Russian military stood as per-
> ilously close to ruin as it does now.[2]

Analyses of established democracies rarely include sections examining
the political involvement of their armed forces, for the simple reason that
it is inconsequential. General studies on Eastern European democratic
transitions are usually attentive to the armed forces only to the extent
that, by virtue of their control of the tools of coercion, the military's
political stance could potentially determine whether the transfer of
power was peaceful or violent. By contrast, the military had assumed a
key political role in Latin American and Iberian democratic transitions,
because prior to democratization these were praetorian systems ruled by
the armed forces, and therefore the most important concern of transition was the manner in which generals left politics.

What about Russia? The Soviet Union was not a praetorian state, and
the Russian/Soviet military has essentially no modern tradition of political involvement. Why are civil-military relations a portentous component of Russian politics? The reason is that the depoliticization of the
military and the extension of solid civilian oversight authority to all
armed forces are imperatives of successful democratization, yet Russia
has not accomplished them. In fact, its political elites have done little to

---

[1] Stephen J. Blank, "Who's Minding the State: The Failure of Russian Security Policy,"
Problems of Post-Communism, Vol. 45, No. 2 (1998), p. 4.

[2] Alexei G. Arbatov, "Military Reform in Russia: Dilemmas, Obstacles, and Prospects,"
International Security, Vol. 22, No. 4 (1998), p. 83. The author is deputy chairman of
the Russian Duma's Defense Committee.

develop democratic civil-military relations. With all the political, social, and economic problems affecting it, the post-Soviet Russian military has become a weak, disorganized institution marked by low morale and pitiful material conditions. Champions of diverse political interests have time and again sought to enroll the armed forces' active assistance. Still, the large majority of the Russian officer corps has managed to preserve its professional outlook and its traditional aversion to political involvement in spite of many temptations. This is a remarkable outcome worthy of scrutiny.

The objectives of this chapter are to analyze the development of Russian civil-military relations and to explain the reasons behind the absence of autonomous and overt political interference by the military. Section I offers a summary background discussion of the party-military relationship in the Soviet Union and briefly outlines the fundamental criteria for democratic civil-military relations. Section II examines the relationship between the Russian state and its armed forces following the Soviet Union's collapse. Section III focuses on the armed forces' political participation since 1991 and the reasons for the absence of overt military interference in politics. Finally, in Section IV, the attention shifts to the Russian army's everyday challenges generated by its institutional crisis. Military politics is closely connected to a number of areas like strategy, international regimes, arms control, and weapon systems. This chapter is not concerned with them. It focuses, instead, on domestic politics, more precisely on the relations between the Russian state, society, and the armed forces.

I. PARTY CONTROL OVER THE SOVIET MILITARY AND THE CRITERIA FOR DEMOCRATIC CIVIL–MILITARY RELATIONS

In communist states, the Communist Party's self-perceived vanguard role created a system in which the party was sovereign, and in practice its hegemony depended upon how successfully it was able to exert its control over nonparty political institutions.[3] The Soviet armed forces were the partners of the Communist Party of the Soviet Union (CPSU) in an interdependent alliance in which the party was firmly in control. On the one hand, the CPSU needed an armed force that was loyal to the regime and could reliably discharge its missions, which included the protection of not only the country but also the Communist Party–state. Besides this role, the military was the guardian of the party's revolutionary-ideological heritage, acted as an agent of political social-

---

[3] Amos Perlmutter and William M. LeoGrande, "The Party in Uniform: Toward a Theory of Civil-Military Relations in Communist Political Systems," *American Political Science Review*, Vol. 76, No. 4 (1982), p. 779.

ization, offered assistance following natural disasters, and aided the economy with the labor of armed forces personnel. On the other hand, the army needed the party to provide a stable political environment and to preserve and improve its material status, armaments, and social prestige.

The army was the only institution capable of forcibly ousting the party. In other words, the party's survival hinged on the army's loyalty. Consequently, the CPSU did its best to control the armed forces. The Soviet regime countered its fear of Bonapartism with violence (e.g., the decimation of the high command in the 1930s), appeasement (e.g., Marshal Georgii Zhukov's appointment to the Presidium of the CPSU in 1957), and the reassignment of generals perceived to be political threats (e.g., Zhukov's ouster from the Presidium a few months later). More important was the party's penetration of the armed forces by means of a variety of political control mechanisms, the cooptation of armed forces personnel in political affairs, and extending privileges to the officer corps. From its inception, the Soviet army had been watched over by the Main Political Administration (MPA), a large intramilitary organization of political officers whose main function was to bolster ideological purity within the armed forces. The hierarchy of political officers extended from the highest echelons of military leadership down to the battalion and (during World War II) company levels.

To further assure the armed forces' fidelity, the CPSU also utilized regular and military intelligence organizations. At times when the CPSU leadership lacked confidence in the political reliability of the military, the system of dual command was introduced, which meant that orders given by a line officer had to be countersigned by a political officer to be valid. Another method of party control was the creation of dual elites, the cooptation of senior military officers into the party leadership. Members of the armed forces were represented in every tier of the CPSU hierarchy, although they seldom advanced beyond the level of the Party's Central Committee. The CPSU granted seats in its various organizations to military leaders to reward their loyalty and to build yet another bond between the party and army elites.

Weakening Civilian Control under Gorbachev

The "golden age" for the Soviet armed forces coincided with the rule of CPSU leader Leonid Brezhnev (1964–1982). Brezhnev reestablished the stability in party-military relations that had been threatened by the mercurial policies of his predecessor, Nikita Khrushchev. Under Brezhnev, the military had received resources on an unprecedented scale, its societal prestige had increased, and the high command had become a trusted power base for the Kremlin leadership. The Soviet invasion of Afghanistan, unlike the first Chechnya campaign a decade and a half later, did not elicit much criticism in the armed forces, although, like the war in Chechnya, there was only minimal military involvement in its planning. The war in Afghanistan (1979–89) induced political processes within the Soviet armed forces and society, however, that were to have long-term effects.

Mikhail Gorbachev (1985–91) inherited a state beset by major economic and political problems. The army leadership had mixed feelings about the new general secretary, owing to his inexperience with military and security affairs and the policies he was expected to pursue: improved relations with the West, arms limitation treaties, and a variety of economic reforms that implied reductions in defense outlays.[4] The few generals who were genuinely supportive of Gorbachev's initiatives were unable to control the ranks, however, especially the army's opinion makers: senior officers at military institutes and academies. To make matters worse, not only were Gorbachev's military policies inconsistent, ambiguous, and poorly (if at all) implemented, but he also failed to establish the party's primacy in setting national security policy. Although the generals rarely risked open defiance of Gorbachev's military reform initiatives, they successfully stonewalled their execution.

The rank and file had never really understood what was expected of them in the era of glasnost' and perestroika, primarily because no one clearly explained it to them. The Kremlin charged the MPA with conveying its policies to the armed forces, but opposition to Gorbachev's policies within the MPA elite made that group unlikely to advocate and spearhead military reform. Much to the MPA's dismay, Gorbachev actually gave military officers a voice in politics, encouraging semidemocratic governance mechanisms to take root in the army. By the late 1980s, a variety of officers' groups and assemblies had sprung to life, such as the "Fatherland" Military-Patriotic Union, frankly discussing domestic and international political developments for the first time. The armed forces' political voice had been emboldened by the establishment of these formal and informal organizations, most of which propagated conservative communist messages, criticized Gorbachev's policies, and undermined civilian control.[5] Many discharged veterans of the Afghan war,

---

[4] See Thomas M. Nichols, *The Sacred Cause: Civil–Military Conflict over Soviet National Security, 1917–1992* (Ithaca, N.Y.: Cornell University Press, 1993), pp. 130–237 and William E. Odom, *The Collapse of the Soviet Military* (New Haven: Yale University Press, 1998), for accounts of Gorbachev's military policies and how they helped destroy the Soviet armed forces.

[5] See, for instance, John B. Dunlop, *The Rise of Russia and the Fall of the Soviet Empire* (Princeton: Princeton University Press, 1993), pp. 132–133.

the *Afgantsy*, became influential in these political activities. In fact, most of the military leaders who were to play important roles in the 1990s were members of this Afghan "brotherhood."[6]

With the passing of time, the military leadership's support for Gorbachev had become increasingly tenuous. After 1985, the armed forces' circumstances had deteriorated in virtually every dimension: domestic and international prestige, political clout, privileges, armaments, and living conditions. Still, the army was sufficiently subdued to shy away from actively resisting civilian policies, and some of the generals continued to believe that Gorbachev's economic reform proposals could actually create a solid economic base from which the armed forces, too, might eventually benefit. As the Soviet leader increasingly lost control of the political and economic situation, so disappeared the remnants of the armed forces' support for him.

A critical need of militaries everywhere is a stable political environment. The Soviet high command perceived the Gorbachevian threat not so much in his bold disarmament initiatives and murky military reform proposals but in his waning ability to control political developments. In desperate attempts to reassert his control, Gorbachev thrice deployed the Soviet army against civilians (Tbilisi, April 1989; Baku, January 1990; and Vilnius, January 1991), resulting in nearly 300 casualties altogether. These events further eroded the military's confidence in the abilities of its civilian masters. They also produced an outburst of public outrage and debate about the appropriate links between state, society, and armed forces.[7]

Criteria of Democratic Civil–Military Relations

In order to properly gauge Russia's record of civil–military relations, one ought to understand the essential requirements of the state–armed forces nexus in democracies. One of the objectives of democratization is to bring the armed forces under institutionally balanced, constitutionally regulated, and nonpartisan civilian control.[8] In democracies, civilian supervision of the military has several indispensable components: (1) the armed forces must be subordinated to institutionalized control, balanced

---

[6] See Mark Galeotti, *Afghanistan: The Soviet Union's Last War* (London: Frank Cass, 1995), pp. 171–189.

[7] See Robert V. Barylski, *The Soldier in Russian Politics: Duty, Dictatorship, and Democracy under Gorbachev and Yeltsin* (New Brunswick, N.J.: Transaction Publishers, 1998), p. 61.

[8] See Larry Diamond and Marc F. Plattner, "Introduction," in Larry Diamond and Marc F. Plattner (eds.), *Civil-Military Relations and Democracy* (Baltimore: Johns Hopkins University Press, 1996), pp. xxviii–xxxiv and Richard H. Kohn, "How Democracies Control the Military," *Journal of Democracy*, Vol. 8, No. 4 (1997), pp. 140–153.

between the executive and legislative branches; (2) the military chain of command and the political institutions' areas of responsibility over the armed forces must be codified for all potential scenarios (peacetime, emergencies, war); (3) the conditions that warrant the military's utilization in peacetime must be constitutionally regulated; (4) the executive and legislative branches must share fiscal responsibility over defense expenditures; (5) the armed forces must be depoliticized, and its members must not be permitted to play any political role other than exercising their civic right to vote; (6) the military establishment itself must be democratized; and (7) civilian experts must be trained to provide objective advice to politicians on defense-related issues and to staff pertinent state institutions (including the ministry of defense).

Several additional conditions facilitating the development of democratic civil–military relations are worth exploring. A weighty decision facing democratizers is the manner in which political institutions exercise their control over the military. Dividing civilian oversight responsibility between the president, government, and legislature strengthens the prospects for effective civilian control and reduces the likelihood of abuses of power (i.e., utilizing the armed forces for partisan purposes) by any one of these institutions. Appointing an authoritative civilian defense minister reduces the danger of the formation of military opposition to the democratizing state.

A proper balance must be found between civilian oversight, on the one hand, and granting the armed forces a significant amount of autonomy to exercise their professional judgment within the broad policy parameters set by civilian institutions of the state (promotions, training methods, tactics, etc.), on the other.[9] The democratizing state should consolidate its authority over military affairs decisively, while acting with restraint to avoid unnecessary conflict with the armed forces. To prevent civil-military strife, the state should follow the principle of incrementalism, particularly in matters of personnel (i.e., when pruning the armed forces of elements suspected of potential disloyalty to the new democratic state), force restructuring, and the implementation of new military doctrine. Optimal military democratization processes are marked by negotiations and consensus building between civilian and military elites. Civilian authorities should assure the armed forces that national security will not be compromised and ensure, as far as circumstances allow, the officers' continued high social status and remuneration.

Like democracy itself, civilian control is not a fact, but a process that must be continually developed and perfected.[10] The best guarantee

[9] Diamond and Plattner, "Introduction," p. xxviii.
[10] See Kohn, "How Democracies Control the Military," p. 143.

against military interference in politics is a smoothly functioning democratic government and strong political institutions supported by the
public that are able to withstand the challenges of antidemocratic political forces. In Iberia and Latin America, where generals were the de facto
rulers of the state, the requisite process was the *demilitarization of politics*. In Russia and Eastern Europe, where the military was an institutional servant of the Communist Party, the critical goal has been the
depoliticization of the military.[11]

II. THE RUSSIAN STATE AND THE ARMED FORCES

Although the failed coup attempt of August 1991 actually took place a
few months prior to the collapse of the USSR, it had a major impact on
the development of Russian civil-military relations.[12] The coup was conceived and supported by a group of politicians opposed to democratization and committed to the preservation of the Soviet Union. Their ranks
included most of the USSR's leading politicians as well as Soviet Defense
Minister Dimitrii Yazov. The coup failed partly because of the active
resistance of the Russian government and thousands of ordinary
Muscovites, who were courageously rallied by Russian President Boris
Yeltsin and the militia's (police) refusal to assume a political role by
supporting the coup.

Most importantly, however, the armed forces' decision not to support
the overthrow of Russian political elites effectively prevented a successful coup. A number of top military leaders vigorously opposed the coup
and were able to carry the day by convincing their subordinates of its
folly. General Yevgenii Shaposhnikov, commander-in-chief of the USSR
air force and deputy minister of defense, played a key role in uniting the
anti-coup opposition in the Ministry of Defense (MoD). Even some of
the army leaders who supported the coup were uncertain plotters. Yazov
revealed that he might have made a mistake after the first day, and
throughout the coup attempt tried to prevent his soldiers from fighting
with the protesters.[13] The coup attempt reflected the polarization

---

[11] Zoltan Barany, "Democratic Consolidation and the Military: The East European Experience," *Comparative Politics*, Vol. 30, No. 1 (1997), pp. 26–31.

[12] For insightful articles on the coup and its aftermath, see Stephen M. Meyer, "How the
Threat (and the Coup) Collapsed: The Politicization of the Soviet Military," *International
Security*, Vol. 16, No. 3 (1991/92), pp. 5–38 and John W. R. Lepingwell, "Soviet Civil-
Military Relations and the August Coup," *World Politics*, Vol. 44, No. 4 (1992), pp.
70–92.

[13] Mark Galeotti, *The Age of Anxiety: Security and Politics in Soviet and Post-Soviet
Russia* (London: Longman, 1995), p. 142. The dilemmas of military leaders, especially
of Shaposhnikov, are lucidly presented in Jerry F. Hough, *Democratization and Revolution in the USSR, 1985–1991* (Washington, D.C.: Brookings Institution Press, 1997),
pp. 483–488.

between the reformist and conservative wings of the army's elite. Ironically, as Dale Herspring has noted, "it was the Soviet Army that saved the reform process, and it was the Soviet Army that in the end was destroyed by the events of August 1991."[14]

The President and the Military: Control and Appeasement

The military's part in the political upheaval underscored the dilution of civilian control over the armed forces that had begun under Gorbachev. Since the inception of the sovereign Russian Federation in 1992, the country's leaders have failed to institute a system of strong civilian authority over the army. They have succeeded in "departifying," but not in depoliticizing, the military establishment. Immediately after the August coup attempt, President Yeltsin issued a decree that abolished CPSU organizations in the KGB, the Ministry of Internal Affairs (MVD), and the armed forces. A considerable proportion of the military elite, led by Marshal Shaposhnikov, strongly endorsed the party's banishment from the armed forces and the abolition of the MPA. The crucial defect of Russian civil-military relations is that the vacuum created by the elimination of the party-based control system has not been filled by a balanced institutional structure of civilian supervision. Instead, the president, the legislature, and a variety of political forces have time and again attempted to recruit the military to do their bidding. Russian politics has been marked by an ongoing power struggle between the president and the legislature. The outcome of this confrontation has been the evolution of dramatically increased presidential powers – in effect, a form of super-presidentialism.[15] President Yeltsin's (1991–2000) growing prerogatives were exemplified by his gradual acquisition of ever more civilian authority pertaining to military matters. Although his approach toward the military may be different, President Vladimir Putin (2000–) has shown no inclination to relinquish the authority he inherited from his predecessor.

Until the Armed Forces of the Russian Federation were officially created by a May 1992 presidential decree, the Russian military existed in an organizational limbo within the framework of the USSR's super-

---

[14] Dale R. Herspring, *Russian Civil-Military Relations* (Bloomington: Indiana University Press, 1996), pp. 153–154.

[15] On this notion, see Timothy J. Colton, "Superpresidentialism and Russia's Backward State," *Post-Soviet Affairs*, Vol. 11, No. 2 (April–June 1995), pp. 144–149; M. Steven Fish, "The Pitfalls of Russian Superpresidentialism," *Current History*, Vol. 96, No. 612 (1997), pp. 326–330; and Scott Parrish, "Presidential Decree Authority in Russia, 1991–1995," in John M. Carey and Matthew Soberg Shugart (eds.), *Executive Decree Authority* (New York: Cambridge University Press, 1998), pp. 62–103.

seded structures. The September 1992 Defense Law prepared by the Supreme Soviet prescribed firm state control of the military establishment, despite the last-minute withdrawal of the stipulation that the defense minister had to be a civilian.[16] Although the law required the president to obtain parliamentary consent for top military appointments, in practice Yeltsin did not abide by this rule. Though amended hundreds of times between 1991 and 1993, the Constitution was nonetheless clear in denying the president the right to dissolve parliament, yet that is precisely what Yeltsin did on September 21, 1993. The September–October 1993 conflict between the Supreme Soviet (parliament) and the president was conclusively won by the latter, who proceeded to expand his authority over the armed forces. The new Constitution (adopted in December 1993) removed controls over the armed forces once possessed by the legislature, shifted responsibilities over the army to the president, and generally endowed the executive with near-dictatorial powers. The legislature, for instance, no longer had the authority to appoint military leaders. A January 1994 presidential decree subordinated all "force organs" to the president.

In December 1994, when Russian troops invaded Chechnya, the president again violated the Constitution (Articles 8 and 88) by not informing either the Duma or the Federation Council (the legislature's lower and upper house, respectively) prior to taking action. In August 1995, the Constitutional Court created a troubling precedent by refusing to rule against the president, concluding that the use of armed forces in Chechnya was legal. The 1996 Law on Defense denied the legislature virtually any checks and balances over national defense policy, and, due to its ambiguities and loopholes, the president could conceivably commit Russian forces without consulting with the Duma. The law gave Yeltsin some twenty powers relevant to military matters and reserved only two, albeit crucially important ones, to the legislature (to pass the defense budget and to write pertinent laws).[17] Although the president was required by the law to report to the Federation Council, he was not, in fact, accountable to it.

By all appearances, Yeltsin equated civilian oversight of the armed forces with presidential control. He repeatedly courted the army leadership at times critical to his own political fortunes and failed to deliver on his promises once the military agreed to support him. Just before his final showdown with Gorbachev in December 1991, Yeltsin announced a 90 percent pay raise to all military personnel, proving once again that

---

[16] Pavel K. Baev, *The Russian Army in a Time of Troubles* (London: Sage Publications, 1996), p. 55.
[17] Barylski, *The Soldiers in Russian Politics*, p. 416.

he was far more astute in enrolling the generals' backing than his rival. Until his October 1993 clash with the legislature, the president was relatively effective in gaining the armed forces' support with assurances of pay increases, the disbursement of overdue salaries and benefits, and increased military prerogatives in armed forces reform. Prior to the September–October 1993 events, the president transferred extensive bonuses to selected units and, after a reluctant military came to his rescue, rewarded loyal generals with medals, promotions, and a 40 percent salary increase to all armed forces personnel. On the eve of the 1996 presidential elections, Yeltsin once again found it expedient to appease the armed forces leadership by ordering payment of overdue wages, increasing salaries, and promoting all five senior commanders to the rank of army general. In mid-1997, around the time that retired general and Duma Defense Committee Chairman Lev Rokhlin started to organize his All-Russia Movement to Support the Army, which openly called for the legal removal of the president, Yeltsin once again began to entice the armed forces with promises of quick financial relief and other perquisites.

The political and economic turmoil in late summer 1998 signified another major challenge to Russian democratization and economic reform processes. Yeltsin's approach to the army had not changed: in August 1998 he announced that he would take direct control over military policy in order to ensure that officers and soldiers were paid.[18] Throughout the crisis, the president met on several occasions with Defense Minister Igor Sergeev, who assured his boss of the armed forces' loyalty. A proponent of military reform, Sergeev was one of Yeltsin's few superior personnel choices and was duly rewarded for his allegiance with a promotion to the rank of marshal in November 1997.

These political upheavals weakened a president beset by a sharp decline in popular and elite support and poor health. Still, his erratic dismissals of several prime ministers, starting with the firing of Viktor Chernomyrdin in 1998, actually had a positive overall effect on the armed forces. The reason is that no Russian government paid less attention to the military than Chernomyrdin's.[19] Not surprisingly, the armed forces leadership endorsed all of the prime ministers following him. In turn, Prime Ministers Sergei Kirienko, Yevgeny Primakov, Sergei Stepashin, and Vladimir Putin (prime minister, August–December 1999; acting president, January–May 2000; president, May 2000–) all confirmed Sergeev in his post.[20] During his short tenure, Primakov quickly took

---

[18] Itar-Tass (Murmansk), August 21, 1998.
[19] Reuters (Moscow), September 18, 1998, and *Financial Times*, October 7, 1998.
[20] See *Kommersant-Daily*, March 29, 2000.

charge of financial levers and indicated that the army would not have to go for months without pay in the future. After a career spent entirely in the internal police and security apparatus, Stepashin elevated national security on his cabinet's list of priorities, especially owing to NATO's 1999 spring war against Yugoslavia, which reawakened the Russian political elites' concerns about defense.[21]

In June 1999 Yeltsin gave the order to Russian army units serving as peacekeepers in Bosnia to enter Kosovo and thereby present NATO leaders, who envisioned no Russian security zone there, with a fait accompli. Military leaders went over the heads of the prime minister and cabinet members, sharing their proposal only with Yeltsin. The president was eager to share the political rewards of a successful unilateral military deployment, particularly after several weeks of humiliation at the hands of Western leaders who had ignored his appeals for a halt to NATO's air strikes against Serbia, Russia's historic ally.[22]

Putin, whose resume includes many years in the KGB's employ, has kept security high on the government's agenda, as shown by his determined handling of Russia's second war in Chechnya (August 1999–). In a February 2000 speech in Volgograd, he rejected "all talk of the collapse of the army" as "an open lie" and insisted that a new army was in the making, in which the well-being of officers and soldiers would receive special regard.[23] As acting president, Putin repeatedly urged the Duma to give priority to defense and security matters.[24] The Russian armed forces' second campaign in Chechnya has been exceedingly popular, both with the general population and with the military. Putin's triumph in the March 2000 presidential elections and his popularity among ordinary Russians and in the military are inextricably linked to this war. In the first few months of 2000, the new president also managed to improve the strained relations between Russia and NATO, although his suggestion in a March 5 interview with the BBC that Russia, too, might some day become a NATO member drew mixed responses in Brussels.[25]

---

[21] For a profile of Stepashin, see Amy Knight, "Updating the Russian Who's Who," *The New York Times*, May 13, 1999. For an account of the effect of the war in Kosovo on the Russian political and military establishment, see Deborah Yarsike Ball, "How Kosovo Empowers the Russian Military," Program on New Approaches to Russian Security (hereinafter PONARS) memo no. 61 (Harvard University, May 1999).

[22] AFP (Moscow), June 13, 1999, in Johnson's Russia List (hereafter JRL), No. 3340 (June 14, 1999).

[23] *RFE/RL Newsline*, Part I, February 23, 2000.

[24] Interfax (Moscow), May 11, 2000.

[25] See AFP (Brussels), March 7, 2000; *RFE/RL Newsline*, March 8, 2000; and Reuters (Moscow), May 9, 2000.

Presidential Counterweights: Councils, Commissions, and the "Multiple Militaries"

Civilian control over the Russian armed forces amounts to an unregulated arrangement of checks and balances largely created by President Yeltsin, who occasionally played off individuals and institutions against each other. Yeltsin established several institutions to aid him in controlling the armed forces. Some of these, most importantly the Security Council (SC), have endured, while others – such as the Defense Council (DC) and the Ministry for Defense Industries – were abolished as suddenly as they were called to life, highlighting his erratic leadership style and the specific political contingencies by which their very creation was justified.

The SC was originally formed by Gorbachev and has been retained by Presidents Yeltsin and Putin. The members of the SC – the relevant power ministers (defense, foreign affairs, finance, etc.) and other high ranking defense/security officials – are appointed by the president, who not only chairs the SC but also selects its secretary. The SC has enjoyed a significant but shadowy role in deciding defense, foreign, and security policy.[26] Although bureaucratic infighting has often reduced the council's effectiveness in controlling the armed forces, it has been the most important pillar of support for the president in his conflicts over defense and security issues with the legislature. The SC has been a loyal presidential institution that has traditionally sustained the executive's decisions no matter how ill-considered they may have been. For instance, in its November 27, 1994, session the council voted unanimously to invade Chechnya before discussing the issue.[27]

Yeltsin established the DC in July 1996 to serve as a counterweight to retired general Aleksandr Lebed, whom he had appointed as SC secretary in June 1996 as part of a political bargain. The DC was fundamentally a powerless intradepartmental consultative body. It was entirely up to the president to adopt the DC recommendations by issuing decrees, which were to be implemented by the relevant ministries.[28] The president had no further use for the DC after Lebed's forced resignation (October 1996), and he unceremoniously abolished it in March 1998 and incorporated its personnel into the SC bureaucracy. In May 1998, Yeltsin established another organization of potential future significance,

---

[26] Galeotti, *The Age of Anxiety*, p. 159.

[27] Richard F. Staar, *The New Military in Russia: Ten Myths that Shape the Image* (Annapolis, Md.: Naval Institute Press, 1996), p. 17.

[28] Eva Busza, "Hard Times for the Russian State: State Dysfunctionality and the Russian Military," APSA convention paper, Boston, September 1998, p. 23.

the so-called government presidium. It consists of eleven ministers (including ministers of the defense and interior), but its functions have yet to be clearly defined.

Although, strictly speaking, the Ministry for Defense Industries was not a presidential institution, in practice it was created in 1996 and disbanded a year later by Yeltsin for short-term political reasons. As a result of the relentless pressure and lobbying of the military-industrial complex, the president agreed to form a ministry in 1996 that increased the defense industries' access to the state and, more specifically, eased the licensing of arms exports and allowed more effective lobbying for military contracts. Yeltsin's key response to the unfolding military crisis was the forming of "extra-legal and extra-constitutional commissions to usurp existing state functions of the MoD."[29] In May 1997, Yeltsin organized two new commissions on military affairs, although in retrospect this appears to have been a mere public relations maneuver to satisfy certain constituencies rather than a substantive policy decision. In February 1998, Prime Minister Viktor Chernomyrdin appointed First Deputy Prime Minister Anatolii Chubais to chair a new commission created to hasten the financial recovery of the defense industry. There have been separate commissions for military construction, finance, and reform, but in practice they have done little. Like many Russian institutions, they were created with some fanfare only to be forgotten six months later.

The myriad of organizational shifts and changes betray not only the president's informal "checks and balances" scheme but also the unpredictability and disorientation of presidential policy toward military affairs. At the same time, Yeltsin was quite consistent in his attempts to gain control over the "multiple militaries," the dozen or more organizations spawned by the KGB, MVD, and other Soviet-era paramilitary formations, which include the troops of the MVD, border guards, presidential guards, the Federal Security Service, the Foreign Intelligence Service, the Federal Agency for Government Communications and Information, and numerous other bodies. Some of these organizations are quite large, although none of them come near to the Ministry of Interior, which currently employs just under two million people.[30] Under Yeltsin, these troops were fortified, removed from parliamentary supervision, and subordinated to the president, who selected their comman-

---

[29] Stephen J. Blank, *Russia's Armed Forces on the Brink of Reform* (Carlisle, Pa.: U.S. Army War College, 1998), p. 8.

[30] Itar-Tass (Moscow), March 25, 1999, as cited in *RFE/RL Newsline*, March 26, 1999. According to *Vremya MN*, June 17, 1999, as cited in *RFE/RL Newsline*, June 18, 1999, the MVD's active forces represent only one-eighth of Russia's security forces.

ders according to their personal fealty to him in order to build an effectual counterbalance to the regular armed forces. He followed the political maxim *divide et impera* with remarkable skill, as illustrated by the growing enmity between the Russian army and the multiple militaries.

The increasing rivalry between the armed forces, the MVD, and other uniformed services has become one of the most important and troubling factors in Russian military politics. In this new situation, the armed forces services (army, air force, navy, and the strategic rocket forces [SRF]) compete for resources and conscripts not only with each other but also with the multiple militaries. Following the Soviet army's withdrawal from Eastern Europe, the other uniformed organizations, particularly the MVD, successfully recruited thousands of former army officers by offering them better pay and living conditions. In general, the regular armed forces have been on the losing side of this contest. Since October 1993 the multiple militaries have been dramatically strengthened in terms of personnel and equipment.[31] For instance, in 1994 the army received five helicopters in contrast to the fifty obtained by the MVD troops.[32] The army only became involved in the first war in Chechnya (December 1994–July 1996) after the Federal Counterintelligence Service had failed to overthrow Chechen President Dzokhar Dudaiev and capture the capital city of Grozny.[33] Naval units fighting in Chechnya were outfitted with obsolete gear and weaponry, such as thirty-pound bulletproof vests and combat helmets manufactured during World War II, while MVD troops received the latest equipment.[34]

In the sphere of high politics, the competition between the leaders of the various uniformed services for political favors has constituted another problem that is impermissible in a democracy. The multiple militaries pose a special threat to Russian democratization, not only because of the disunity that has developed between them and the regular armed forces, but also because they are under the personal authority of the president (*not* the government), their use in domestic contingencies is not clearly regulated, and politicians have not established anything resem-

---

[31] *Komsomolskaya Pravda*, August 29, 1998, as cited in JRL, No. 2339 (September 1, 1998).

[32] Stephen M. Meyer, "The Devolution of Russian Military Power," *Current History*, Vol. 94 (1995), p. 324.

[33] See Lilia Shevtsova, "Russia's Fragmented Armed Forces," in Diamond and Plattner (eds.), *Civil-Military Relations and Democracy*, p. 119.

[34] Staar, *The New Military in Russia*, p. 70. For the conditions of Russian units in Chechnya, see also Anatol Lieven, *Chechnya: Tombstone of Russian Power* (New Haven: Yale University Press, 1998).

bling balanced and firm civilian control to oversee them. The ease with which units of the multiple militaries may be deployed in domestic contingencies was demonstrated in the fall of 1994, when presidential guards raided the offices of MOST Bank and when the head of the Federal Security Service extended his authority over arms exports and technology transfers.[35]

During the 1998 crisis, Yeltsin once again turned to the multiple militaries by instructing then–interior minister Sergei Stepashin to put MVD units on alert around Moscow. According to Russian sources, 250,000 internal troops and 36,000 airborne forces were the only coercive power on which authorities could count to protect them and maintain order in October 1998.[36] The political resolution of the crisis fortunately did not require the deployment of these units. In contemporary Russia, forces are rewarded according to the Kremlin's perception of their usefulness for its own political designs. The privileged situation of the multiple militaries vis-à-vis the Russian army is reminiscent of the preferential position of the Securitate in Nicolae Ceausescu's Romania, or of the Republican Guards in Saddam Hussein's Iraq.

The Legislature, the Army, and Its Budget

Since 1991, the Russian legislature has seen its authority over the country's military establishment considerably erode. Prior to the September–October 1993 crisis, the president and parliament had been locked in a political battle for power over the armed forces. Following the crisis, the 450-member Duma – created in late 1993 – has been able to exercise its control over the conventional armed forces and the multiple militaries only through the two important licenses it has retained: to write laws and to determine the armed forces budget. Through the years, the military leadership has repeatedly managed to evade legislative supervision by siding with a president who has refused to allow the Duma to encroach on his authority. Parliamentary oversight is also thwarted by the fact that no law prohibits military officers from serving as Duma representatives *and* in government (i.e., in both the legislative and executive branches) simultaneously.

The Duma has time and again attempted to curb the widespread corruption in the armed forces but has been ineffectual. In response to a deadly bomb attack on a journalist investigating fraudulent generals, in mid-1994 the Duma formed a committee investigating military

---

[35] Baev, *The Russian Army in a Time of Troubles*, p. 58. See also Sergei Parkhomenko, "Merlin's Tower," *Moscow News*, April 28–May 4, 1995.

[36] *Moskovskii Komsomolets*, September 5, 1998, as cited in JRL, No. 2375 (September 15, 1998).

corruption, which resulted in several high-level resignations. Whatever goodwill may have existed in the army leadership toward the legislature prior to the October 1993 events quickly evaporated when rebellious deputies led by Supreme Soviet Speaker Ruslan Khasbulatov and Vice President Aleksandr Rutskoi "appointed" their own defense minister and openly encouraged armed forces units to split from the MoD and support their putsch. The officer corps has also found that politicians who endorsed increased military spending on the campaign trail in order to obtain the soldiers' electoral support tended to vote against it. Since the 1995 Duma elections, three distinctive approaches have emerged in the legislature regarding defense policy in general and military reform in particular.[37] The first view is emblematized by former generals who argue that Russia's economic, social, and foreign policies should be adjusted to accommodate the needs of the military establishment. The second group is represented by the ruling elite, the party of power (Russia's Choice [1993–95], Our Home Is Russia [OHR, 1995–99], and the Unity Party [1999–]), as well as supporters of the Yeltsin and Putin Administrations who perceive military reform as reconciling the army to meager defense budgets and tend to underestimate the armed forces crisis. The third group is comprised of members of the parliamentary opposition who advocate a balanced and consistent defense policy, including higher defense outlays to support military reform. Given the post-1995 dynamics of Russian politics, it is not surprising that the second approach has been dominant. Prior to the 1995 Duma elections, the OHR enticed the popular military hero General Lev Rokhlin to join its ranks, assigning him the third place on its electoral list. After the election, the OHR nominated Rokhlin to the chairmanship of the Duma's Defense Committee, its most important organ on military affairs. Rokhlin turned out to be an uncompromising critic of the administration's defense policy, however, and was pushed out of his chairmanship in May 1998.

Determining defense expenditures has been a critically important area in which the legislative branch has been able to exercise some control over the armed forces. Even in this realm, however, the Duma's authority has been thwarted by the incomplete or false information provided by the MoD. Deliberations over the military budgets have become extremely heated affairs, with the MoD requesting figures higher than its actual needs, knowing that the amount the Duma will eventually agree to will be significantly smaller. The Duma's frustration over its diminished prerogatives vis-à-vis the armed forces has been manifested by continuous budget cuts, at least until the late 1990s, partially justified by its

[37] This discussion draws on Arbatov, "Military Reform in Russia," pp. 113–115.

lack of authority in determining how the MoD spends funds and the absence of the ministry's accountability to the legislature.

To make matters worse, owing to financial problems, plummeting state revenues, and plain power politics, the Ministry of Finance has repeatedly failed to transfer approved funds to the MoD.[38]

In 1997, for example, defense spending amounted to just 55.6 percent of budget targets, causing long delays in payments to personnel and plunging expenditures on military services, clothing, and equipment.[39] In the first ten months of 1998, the armed forces had received only 31 billion of the 80.4 billion rubles allocated for defense in 1998, and the MoD's wage arrears totalled 9 billion rubles.[40] This state of affairs improved during the deliberations over the 1999 defense budget only to the extent that the Duma seemed to have acknowledged the magnitude of the armed forces' impoverishment. As a result, the amount earmarked for defense in 1999 was increased by 17 billion rubles ($744 million), to 107 billion rubles ($4.68 billion) or 18.6 percent of the government's budget.

In April 1999, in part due to the war in Kosovo and rapidly deteriorating relations between NATO and Russia, the Duma adopted a non-binding resolution urging the government to transfer all approved funds to the MoD.[41] In the summer of 1999 the government, alarmed by the state of the military and its deteriorating relations with NATO, promised to increase spending on security to $6.7 billion or 28.5 percent of its budget.[42] Nonetheless, owing to the substantial devaluation of the ruble in the fall of 1998, the actual value of these funds had diminished. These increased defense outlays amount to approximately 2.4 percent of the U.S., 19 percent of the British, and 46 percent of Brazilian annual defense expenditures.[43] And yet, 1999 might be the year the Russian army turned the corner to more sufficient funding. For the first time in many years, the government actually spent 124.1 percent (or 116.3 billion rubles) of the sum stipulated by the annual budget on national defense (officially, the operation in Chechnya cost 5 billion rubles in 1999).[44] In January 2000, the government announced that defense spending for the year will

---

[38] See, for instance, Reuters (Moscow), August 12, 1998, as cited in JRL, No. 2396 (August 13, 1998).

[39] Itar-Tass, January 12, 1998, as cited in *RFE/RL Newsline*, Vol. 1, No. 194 (January 13, 1998).

[40] *Jamestown Foundation Monitor*, November 2, 1998.

[41] See *RFE/RL Newsline*, February 22, 1999; *Kommersant-Daily*, April 7, 1999; and *Vremya MN*, April 20, 1999, as cited in *RFE/RL Newsline*, April 21, 1999.

[42] AP (Moscow), July 2, 1999.

[43] *World Factbook* (Langley, Va.: CIA, 1999); AP (Moscow), July 2, 1999.

[44] "Growth through Cuts," *Novaya Gazeta*, No. 18 (May 2000).

increase by 50 percent, though it did not elaborate on where the additional funds will come from.[45] According to official figures, in the first quarter of 2000 Moscow spent 6 billion rubles on its military campaign in Chechnya, although independent observers suggest that the real amount may be twice as high.[46]

Eroding State Authority and Elusive Military Reform

The deficiencies of Russia's military reform reflect both the shortcomings of the country's democratization process and the lack of available funds for the implementation of defense programs. The pattern of diminishing state control over defense issues that started under Gorbachev has not been halted, much less reversed. This notion is underscored by virtually every aspect of military reform. In a political environment where neither the legislature nor the executive effectively controls the armed forces, it is no wonder that ambitious plans and high-minded intentions are hampered by top-brass inertia. General Alexander Piskunov, a Duma deputy, recently admitted that essentially no military reform took place from 1992 to 1996.[47] The other side of this coin is that, in any event, the envisioned reforms could scarcely have been adopted due to the lack of financial resources.

In the wake of the cold war, the post-Soviet military establishment had lost not only its traditional external mission but also a significant portion of its most sophisticated arsenal, located in the non-Russian countries of what became the Commonwealth of Independent States. The presence of nearly 25 million ethnic Russians outside the Russian Federation's borders has been an additional stimulus in the adoption of a new military doctrine. The debate centered on potential threats to Russian security that military elites were determined to exaggerate in order to secure large defense outlays. Most politicians, citing declining international tensions, insisted that only regional security challenges existed, which required modest military budgets sustaining a much smaller armed force than Russia had inherited from the Soviet Union.[48] The loss of state control over military affairs was demonstrated by the fact that, as a reward for rescuing him in October 1993, Yeltsin allowed the armed forces to adopt a military doctrine of their own design

---

[45] *New York Times*, February 29, 2000.
[46] See *RFE/RL Newsline*, March 4, 2000; *RFE/RL Newsline*, April 21, 2000; and *Kommersant-Daily*, April 22, 2000.
[47] *Segodnya*, March 10, 2000, as cited in JRL, No. 4160 (March 10, 2000).
[48] See Stephen Foye, "Updating Russian Civil-Military Relations," *RFE/RL Research Report*, Vol. 2, No. 46 (November 19, 1993), pp. 44–50, and Karen Dawisha and Bruce Parrott, *Russia and the New States of Eurasia: The Politics of Upheaval* (New York: Cambridge University Press, 1994), pp. 233–238.

(though, to be sure, they did not receive the funds for its implementation), despite the fact that it sharply contradicted Yeltsin's personal blueprint.

The erosion of state authority has also been observable with regard to the conscription system.[49] Since the beginning of the 1990s, nationwide conscription rates have fallen precipitously as a result of draft evasion, particularly in large urban areas. According to Defense Minister Pavel Grachev, in 1992 as many as 75–80 percent of draftees evaded military service in Russia.[50] In the first half of 1993, 95 percent of young men evaded the draft in the Moscow military district. Declining state authority is exposed by the fact that only 11 percent of draft dodgers were prosecuted, and only 0.18 percent were convicted.[51] The MoD was able to win important concessions in the framing of the February 1993 Law on Conscription, which contributed to decreases in draft evasion to 25–30 percent in 1993 and even further thereafter, though it continues to be a serious problem. After August 1999, when the second war in Chechnya began, the number of draft dodgers increased by 50 percent, according to the head of the Operation and Mobilization Department of the Armed Forces General Staff.[52] Draft-related corruption is so widespread that in May 1999 former first deputy prime minister Boris Nemtsov suggested that by allowing draftees to buy their way out of military service rather than bribing military officials (bribes run between $5,000 to $10,000 for a "medically unacceptable" classification), the defense budget could be replenished by 40 percent.[53]

Regional authorities have increased their power vis-à-vis the central state in many respects, and the military is no exception. At the heart of the draft evasion problem itself is the local and regional officials' obstruction of state policy – granting deferments easily and refusing to charge those who break the law, thereby encouraging further infractions. Primarily as a result of the financial problems experienced by military installations in the regions, their commanders have often been compelled to enter into illegal arrangements with regional governors. In recent years, regional governors have assumed an important position in the lives of military units based in their bailiwicks. Many commanders who are

---

[49] An excellent examination of this issue is Chapter 6 in Steven L. Solnick's *Stealing the State: Control and Collapse in Soviet Institutions* (Cambridge: Harvard University Press, 1998), pp. 175–217.

[50] *RFE/RL Daily Report*, No. 78 (April 26, 1993).

[51] *The Economist*, August 28, 1993.

[52] Itar-Tass (Moscow), April 11, 2000; *RFE/RL Newsline*, April 12, 2000; and *Christian Science Monitor*, April 28, 2000.

[53] See Itar-Tass (St. Petersburg), May 16, 1999.

unable to provide for their troops have become dependent on the bene-volence of provincial officials or on their willingness to enter into arrange-ments like bartering soldiers' labor for food, fuel, and other necessities. The interference of local authorities in military affairs has at times also taken more ominous forms, such as in July 1998, when the governor of the Krasnoyarsk region, Alexander Lebed, threatened to take control of a Siberian nuclear missile battery if the MoD failed to send wages for officers who had been unpaid for five months.[54]

A similar weakness in state authority has been evident in the army's downsizing, which has advanced in spite of strong opposition from the high command during the early 1990s. In 1985, there were 4.25 million authorized positions in the Soviet armed forces, which was to be reduced to 3 million by the year 2000. It is impossible to know precisely how many men are under arms in contemporary Russia, because MoD leaders have obfuscated the issue by using various methods of calculating force levels and by manipulating the armed forces' authorized versus actual strength and the number of their civilian employees. Clearly, though, since 1991 the size of the armed forces has been drastically reduced and currently stands around 1.2 million. Russian analysts contend that in the foreseeable future the country can only adequately finance an army that is reduced by a further 50 percent, to 550,000–600,000 military personnel.[55]

An important caveat, however, is that the size of the multiple mili-taries has grown substantially in the meantime. Although their numbers are difficult to estimate, according to experts they employ close to 1.2 million people.[56] The key reason that significant progress has been made in downsizing the Russian military has been the tight budgets that have made force cutting imperative. Although the MoD and most politicians concur that an all-volunteer army would be desirable – indeed, in his 1996 reelection campaign President Yeltsin identified ending conscrip-tion by 2000 as a major objective – its introduction is not expected in the near future, due to the lack of funds.

Russia's massive defense-industrial sector, another legacy of the Soviet period, has also been in dire need of, but resistant to, reform. As a number of penetrating recent studies have argued, little has been done

[54] Reuters (Moscow), August 12, 1998, as cited in JRL, No. 2306 (August 13, 1998).

[55] *Nezavisimaya gazeta*, February 4, 1999; and see the report by the independent military weekly *Nazavisimoye Voyennoye Obozreniye*, as cited in Reuters (Moscow), February 9, 1999.

[56] Arbatov, "Military Reform in Russia," p. 98. According to Stephen J. Blank, all mili-tary organizations currently comprise as many as three to four million men. See his "Who's Minding the State?", p. 5.

to transform, convert, and streamline the weapons industry.[57] Defense-related enterprises have been devastated by sharply reduced military expenditures that allow minimal new procurement by the MoD. Defense contracts between 1990 and 1997 fell by nearly 95 percent. Very few of the 1,300 companies lost to defense cuts have been able to successfully convert to civilian production. The government has formed commission after commission to oversee the restructuring of defense industries, but owing to institutional apathy, lack of change on the enterprise level, and the persistent lobbying of industry groups for reduced state control, remedies have been slow in coming. In July 1998, Sergei Kirienko's short-lived government unveiled a new plan to restructure defense industries by reducing the number of arms-producing firms from the current 1,700 to no more than 600–700.[58] In May 1999, after less than two weeks in office, Prime Minister Stepashin – with high hopes for a revitalized defense industry as a motor of Russian economic recovery – appointed a special deputy prime minister, Ilya Klebanov, and agreed to establish a special state commission, both responsible for the armaments industries.[59]

Just days before the unfolding of the August–September 1998 crisis, SC Secretary Andrei Kokoshin presented to the armed forces a new "foundations concept" for military development. This document, signed by Yeltsin, reflected the MoD's view that large-scale wars involving Russia were unlikely in the future, and that therefore the long-delayed military development and restructuring should concentrate on potential local wars and regional conflicts.[60] NATO's war against Yugoslavia in the spring of 1999 provoked a great deal of anxiety in Russia's military and political circles and prompted a rethinking of defense and security priorities and a revisiting of reform imperatives. In April 1999, Sergeev announced that Russia would change its military doctrine to emphasize keeping nuclear deterrence forces at maximum combat readiness, developing air defense troops, and generally minimizing security risks.[61] The new military doctrine, approved by the SC in February 2000, is much more up-to-date than its predecessor. While it does not contain a list of

[57] See Clifford G. Gaddy, *The Price of the Past: Russia's Struggle with the Legacy of a Militarized Economy* (Washington, D.C.: Brookings Institution Press, 1996) and Kimberly Marten Zisk, *Weapons, Culture, and Self-Interest: Soviet Defense Managers in the New Russia* (New York: Columbia University Press, 1997).
[58] *Russkii telegraf*, June 30, 1998, as cited in *RFE/RL Newsline*, July 1, 1998.
[59] See *Segodnya*, May 27, 1999; *RFE/RL Newsline*, May 28, 1999; and Itar-Tass (St. Petersburg), May 31, 1999.
[60] *Nezavisimaya gazeta*, August 4, 1998.
[61] See the interview with Sergeev in *Krasnaya Zvezda*, April 27, 1999, and *RFE/RL Newsline*, June 25, 1999.

Russia's potential enemies, it conceives of the possibility of using all forces and means at Russia's disposal, including nuclear weapons, if diplomacy fails. NATO leaders have contended that the new doctrine represents a turning away from the previous policy of increased openness and cooperation with the West, while most Russian experts have given it an approving nod.[62]

In the Putin era, military reform is expected to be pursued with renewed vigor. The second war in Chechnya highlighted only modest improvements in the performance of the Russian military, particularly in combat readiness, internal organization, communications, and fighting effectiveness. According to independent experts, the overall pattern of Russian military disasters is essentially the same:

The rebels isolate or ambush a Russian unit of less than 100 men; the battle continues for hours, but Russian reinforcements are unable to break through to the surrounded men and reach the battlefield until sometimes days after the beginning of the engagement; the rebels continue their attacks with vigor until they achieve full victory and they successfully withdraw.[63]

Many challenges remain. These include unifying the separate components of Russia's extensive nuclear arsenal (currently missiles based on land, on submarines, and on long-range aircraft are under separate command) and streamlining the armed forces command structure, which includes reducing the number of generals and admirals from 1,500 to 1,200, and of colonels from 37,000 to 20,000, between January and December 1999.[64]

An even more important initiative from the perspective of democratization is the ongoing effort to establish the legal basis for firm civilian control over the armed forces. A draft bill prepared by Prime Minister Primakov's government would ensure the constitutional use of the armed forces, guarantee the transfer of all approved funds to the military and the generals' accountability for them, protect servicemen's rights and interests, and set up separate civilian control commissions for all legislative bodies of the Federation.[65] The future of the law is in question, however, because its only strong supporter in the cabinet has been Sergeev. Though the defense minister seems intent on pursuing substan-

[62] See, for instance, *RIA Novosti – Moscow Diary*, February 21, 2000, as cited in JRL, No. 4127 (February 22, 2000); *RFE/RL Newsline*, March 4, 2000; JRL, No. 4273 (April 27, 2000).
[63] Pavel Felgenhauer, "Top Brass Fails to Learn from Chechen Disasters," *Moscow Times*, April 5, 2000.
[64] Interfax (Moscow), October 1, 1999.
[65] *Segodnya*, November 16, 1999, and *RFE/RL Newsline*, November 18, 1998.

tive military reform and a "new cost-cutting drive," financial problems and institutional opposition have thwarted speedy implementation.

III. THE MILITARY'S POLITICAL ACTIVISM

Despite the occasional warnings of Russian and Western experts, the Russian military has not interfered in political battles, either between the August 1991 coup attempt and the October 1993 revolution or since then. Russian generals first and foremost need political stability and economic prosperity. They are opposed to doing the politicians' bidding by intervening on their behalf; they are far more concerned with securing a steady flow of financial resources than with political matters. At the same time, the Russian military has corporate interests that have remained unsatisfied. Armed forces elites have often and openly voiced their concerns, yet they have been fundamentally unsuccessful in improving their situation because of the relatively low priority assigned to national defense by political elites until recently, because of poor funding, and because they are affected by numerous internal cleavages that weaken their political influence.

It is difficult to concisely define the size of military elites, but one acceptable measure is based on rank. One can appreciate the potential influence of this cohort by considering that at the end of 1996 there were still 2,865 generals in the Russian armed forces, 1,925 in the army alone. This number might sound modest compared to the 5,660 generals of the Soviet military in 1987, but more germane is the fact that in 1996 there were only 1,700 positions for generals in the army.[66] Furthermore, generals have been notoriously stingy with their support for MoD leaders and defense ministers. In 1994, for instance, less than 20 percent of mid- and senior-ranking officers had expressed trust in Defense Minister Grachev (General Lebed, for instance, had rated much higher).[67]

By failing to establish firm and balanced civilian oversight, political elites have contributed to the politicization of the military. Dozens of generals and officers have taken advantage of the law that permits soldiers to run for and hold political office. Armed forces officers habitually criticize the president, the government, the legislature, and other political actors in television and radio broadcasts and in the print media. Even foreign researchers and journalists have little difficulty securing interviews with high-ranking Russian military personnel, who can be relied on to castigate civilian leaders and their policies in harsh terms. Such behavior on the part of serving officers would have been scarcely

[66] *Kommersant-Daily*, July 22, 1997, as translated in *Current Digest of the Post-Soviet Press*, Vol. 49, No. 29 (August 20, 1997), pp. 5–6.
[67] Herspring, *Russian Civil-Military Relations*, p. 169.

imaginable in Soviet times; indeed, it is strictly prohibited in established democracies. Moreover, although a large institutional entity like the armed forces represents all kinds of political orientations, conservatism has always been a dominant political value among officers everywhere. Not surprisingly, since the October 1993 events, reformers have seemed to disappear from the forefront of Russian military activism as generals have become increasingly radicalized.[68] It must be emphasized that although the officer corps is highly politicized (to the extent that it has strong political opinions that it is not shy about publicly expressing), it has never gotten involved in political conflicts voluntarily.

The Military in Russia's Political Conflicts

During September–October 1993, the conflict between the president and the parliament drew the military into the emerging political crisis. The military was an extremely reluctant participant; the MoD leadership decided to intervene on the side of the president only after parliamentary elites attempted to undercut its authority by backing a group of rebellious officers. Following Yeltsin's dissolution of parliament, it was not the armed forces but MVD troops that stormed the White House (then the seat of the Supreme Soviet). Defense Minister Grachev insisted on a written presidential order before he agreed to commit MoD troops to action. In sum, the armed forces were not only slow to come to the Yeltsin regime's defense but also did their utmost to avoid playing any role in the conflict.[69]

The first war in Chechnya was the creation of the president's close circle of advisors, who did not involve the military leadership in their planning. Its main supporter in the MoD was Defense Minister Grachev, who expected that a brief victorious war would raise his political stock.[70] As late as August 1994, Yeltsin contended that "forcible intervention in Chechnya was impermissible." Two years later, he called the war the greatest mistake of his first term in office.[71] The astonishing lack of preparedness (commanders were sent to take Grozny without maps, clear

[68] Dale R. Herspring, "The Russian Military: Three Years On," *Communist and Post-Communist Studies*, Vol. 28, No. 2 (1995), p. 176.

[69] See, for instance, Brian D. Taylor, "Russian Civil-Military Relations after the October Uprising," *Survival*, Vol. 36, No. 1 (1994), pp. 3–29 and Brian D. Taylor, *The Russian Military in Politics: Civilian Supremacy in Comparative and Historical Perspective*, Ph.D. dissertation, Massachusetts Institute of Technology, 1997, pp. 582–605.

[70] Former U.S. national security advisor Zbigniew Brzezinski had called Grachev a "war criminal" for his role in the Chechen war. See Brzezinski, "Russian Defense Minister Is a War Criminal," *New Perspectives Quarterly*, Vol. 12, No. 2 (1995), pp. 60–61.

[71] Robert Cottrell, "Chechnya: How Russia Lost," *The New York Review of Books*, Vol. 45, No. 14 (September 24, 1998), pp. 45–46.

orders, or trained soldiers!),[72] the incompetent command, the low morale
of the troops, and the embarrassing outcome all revealed the humiliat-
ing depths of Russia's military decline.[73] Participating high-ranking
officers publicly called the resolution to invade a "criminal decision."
Colonel General Eduard Vorobyov, deputy head of Russia's ground
forces, refused command of the entire Chechen military operation in
December 1994, not wanting "to stain his honor."[74] General Rokhlin,
who managed to overpower the Chechen capital's defenses a month later,
refused to be heroized, spurned the medals Yeltsin offered him, and subsequently became an aggressive defender of the armed forces' interests
in the Duma.

Military opposition to the war was not limited to the battlefield. In
Moscow, about 500 officers resigned rather than be responsible for the
bloodshed. Numerous generals, including three deputy defense ministers
(Boris Gromov, Valerii Mironov, and Georgii Kondratiev), fervently criticized the political leadership for ignoring the lessons of Afghanistan and
for cutting the MoD's highest advisory body, the Defense Collegium, out
of deliberations. Such high-level protest against the war, however, gave
a president a perfect excuse to dismiss a number of outspoken generals
and to reorganize the MoD hierarchy in early 1995. Aleksandr Lebed,
the Yeltsin Administration's national security czar, managed to negotiate
an inconclusive end to the conflict in mid-1996.

In many ways the Russian army may be viewed as a victim of the war,
which contributed to the deterioration of their morale, increased their
politicization, and accelerated their institutional disintegration. The campaign in Chechnya magnified splits within the military establishment,
particularly between the units of the regular armed forces and the MVD
troops. The conflict also demonstrated that the military's influence was
not strong enough to avoid getting into the war. The fact that the armed
forces participated in a war they had no stomach for showed that most
generals had maintained a sense of professionalism and subordination to
civilians.

Although 66 percent of Russians believed that force was going to be
used to resolve the September 1998 political and economic crisis, the soldiers played no role in it.[75] This is all the more important because in
1998 Russian officers and soldiers had experienced further deterioration
of their conditions. Sergeev had dismissed rumors of possible use of

[72] *The Washington Post*, January 19, 1995.
[73] See Anatol Lieven, "Russia's Military Nadir: The Meaning of the Chechen Debate," *The National Interest*, Vol. 44 (1996), pp. 24–33.
[74] *The Washington Post*, January 17, 1995.
[75] Interfax (Moscow), September 4, 1998, as cited in JRL, No. 2364 (September 10, 1998).

military force but urged the president to quickly select a compromise prime minister. The retired General Lebed, with presidential and prime ministerial ambitions of his own, was far more skeptical of the army's quiescence throughout the crisis. He and Communist Party leader Gennadii Zyuganov had repeatedly warned that the army was in a "revolutionary mood" and sketched dark scenarios of its imminent political involvement.[76]

The renewed military conflict between the Russian armed forces and Chechen rebels in 1999 has been less controversial, in part owing to popular support (especially after alleged terrorists detonated bombs in Moscow), better supplies, and better equipment. Most members of the armed forces have been as much in favor of the war as the general population, whose support has ranged between 52 percent in February 2000 to 73 percent a month later (a similar 1996 poll showed that only 6 percent of respondents approved of then-president Yeltsin's Chechnya policy).[77] According to U.S. Deputy Secretary of State Strobe Talbott, the second Chechen war brought out one of the worst habits of the Russian and Soviet past, "the tendency to treat an entire category of people, indeed, of its own citizens, as an enemy."[78] In contrast to the first conflict, however, in the second Chechen war the Russian military has enjoyed the full support of state and society. Though in Moscow politicians may debate about strategy, they seem to agree that Russia's territorial integrity must be protected at all costs.

The Armed Forces' Electoral Participation

Military officers had served as members of the legislature throughout the Soviet period. In the 1990 Russian Republic Congress of People's Deputies elections, forty-four of them were successful in gaining seats. By October 1992, three of these officers had chaired parliamentary commissions. After the August 1991 coup attempt, Defense Minister Grachev had tried to keep the military out of politics in general, and in particular had discouraged armed forces personnel from running in the December 1993 Duma elections. Nearly all political parties had courted the military vote during the electoral campaign, promising more resources and higher prestige. Despite Grachev's counsel, officers actively participated in the elections; nine managed to secure seats in the legislature. Many officers voted for a right-wing nationalist party, Vladimir Zhiri-

---

[76] See *International Herald Tribune*, September 1, 1998; Reuters (Moscow), September 3, 1998; AFP (Moscow), September 6, 1998; *The Times* (London), September 15, 1998; Reuters (Strasbourg), September 21, 1998; AFP (Moscow), November 10, 1998.

[77] Interfax (Moscow), February 23, 2000; *RFE/RL Newsline*, March 20, 2000.

[78] Reuters (Washington), April 4, 2000.

novsky's Liberal Democratic Party of Russia (LDPR). The LDPR garnered 72 percent of the vote in the SRF, and in the important Taman and
Kantemir divisions, based near Moscow, 87.4 percent and 74.3 percent
respectively.[79] Such military support for the LDPR should be explained
not so much by the pitiful material conditions and low morale of the
armed forces, but by Zhirinovsky's absurd plans for imperial revival,
which appealed to many officers because of their nostalgia for the USSR,
their resentment over Yeltsin's inclusion of the armed forces in his political battles, and the relatively large number (nine) of military candidates
running under the LDPR's banner.

Owing to the continued deterioration of the army's overall situation
and its yearning for a more defense-friendly environment in the Duma,
the MoD's view of the electoral participation of its personnel had radically shifted by the December 1995 Duma elections. This time around,
Grachev had actually encouraged officers to stand for election, granting
candidates temporary leave with pay during their campaigns. He realized that, at least in theory, the armed forces should be nonpartisan;
therefore, he urged military candidates to run as independents. Although
123 officers answered Grachev's call, merely a handful succeeded, and
only two of them were independents. There were two main reasons for
the lackluster performance of military candidates: the officers' uniform
had apparently lost some of its luster after the October 1993 events and
the ongoing embarrassment of the war in Chechnya, and the MoD was
prohibited by law from using its resources to support its candidates.[80] In
addition, independent candidates faced the built-in handicap of not
receiving campaign support from either parties or coalitions. In order to
discourage officers from running in future elections, a May 1997 presidential decree denied salary and benefits to officers seeking elective office
from the time of registering their candidacy until election day.

During his 1996 campaign for reelection, President Yeltsin once again
pursued the support of active and retired armed forces personnel through
promises of increased funding, payment of salary arrears, better training
conditions, and various decrees (calling for an end to conscription by the
year 2000, prohibiting the deployment of conscripts in crisis zones)
desired by most officers. Yeltsin's most important challenge, however,
was to neutralize Lebed, who came in third in the first round of elections (June 18, 1996) with 15 percent of the vote. The retired general
was quite popular, not only in the armed forces but also with the general
public, owing to his integrity, honesty, and demonstrated willingness to

[79] Thomas M. Nichols, "'An Electoral Mutiny?' Zhirinovsky and the Russian Armed
Forces," *Armed Forces and Society*, Vol. 21, No. 3 (1995), pp. 328–329.
[80] Barylski, *The Soldiers in Russian Politics*, p. 343.

resist politicians and MoD bureaucrats. As a result of a political compromise, he agreed to terminate his campaign in Yeltsin's favor in return for being named the administration's point man on national security. Lebed's leadership style – marked by abrasive statements, provocative meddling in bureaucratic politics, and the capricious sacking of top generals – quickly used up Yeltsin's patience, however. No longer having a compelling reason to appease him, the president fired the general in October 1996.[81]

From the perspective of much of the armed forces – and that of the general population – the 2000 presidential election was hardly a serious contest. Army leaders did not need to campaign for Putin, who received the votes of more than 80 percent of military personnel (and 52.94 percent of the electorate).[82]

In the 1990s, active-duty generals at times defied civilians and openly questioned politicians' competence. Partly as a result of the momentary escalation in Lebed's political influence, his political ally General Sergei Rodionov was appointed as defense minister by Yeltsin in July 1996. Rodionov became Russia's first – and, thus far, only – civilian defense minister in December 1996, when the president transferred him to the reserves in order to "reflect the progress of Russian democracy." Actually, it was an empty gesture, as demonstrated by the active-duty status of Rodionov's successor, General Igor Sergeev, and by the fact that the MoD has continued to be staffed entirely by military men. Rodionov was apparently unpersuaded by his changed status and proceeded to openly criticize the Yeltsin Administration's national security policy and condemn its slew of broken promises to the army.

Rodionov was one of the key supporters of General Rokhlin and his All-Russia Movement to Support the Army. The organization's membership as well as its defiance of civilian authorities had continued to increase throughout the 1990s. Its founding statement called not only for the improvement of life in the armed forces but also for the removal of President Yeltsin.[83] In June 1997, as Duma Defense Committee chairman, Rokhlin publicly castigated the president's criminal neglect of, and

[81] Lebed's autobiography is worthwhile reading not only for what it says about the man but also for its insightful reflections on the Soviet/Russian officer corps. See Alexander Lebed, *General Alexander Lebed: My Life and My Country* (Washington, D.C.: Regnery, 1997). For a critical examination of his record, see Wayne Allensworth, "Derzhavnost: Aleksandr Lebed's Vision for Russia," *Problems of Post-Communism*, Vol. 45, No. 2 (1998), pp. 51–58.
[82] AFP (Moscow), March 17, 2000, as cited in JRL, No. 4176 (March 17, 2000); Itar-Tass (Moscow), March 26, 2000; and *RFE/RL Newsline*, March 27, 2000.
[83] See Sarah Mendelson, "Current Russian Views on US-Russian Security Relations and Military Reform," PONARS memo no. 25 (Harvard University, January 1998).

"rash and ill-considered decisions" regarding, the armed forces. Rokhlin also appealed to officers and servicemen to unite, to organize, and to send their "legitimate demands" to the Kremlin in order to "preserve" the army.[84] Although Rokhlin died in July 1998 (he was allegedly murdered by his wife), his movement – staffed primarily by retired officers and veterans – remains influential in the armed forces.[85]

The Army's Opposition to State Policy

Aside from overt political conflicts, throughout the 1990s the army leadership repeatedly interfered with actual or expected state policy. In foreign affairs – a policy area in which the military had traditionally considered declaring its interests to be its prerogative – generals had publicly countered Yeltsin's anticipated readiness to reach a compromise with Japan on the issue of the Kuril Islands, and with NATO regarding the Yugoslav crisis. The MoD has also been aggressive in promoting its interests in the "near abroad" (the Newly Independent States [NIS]), for example, by delaying the division of the Black Sea fleet with Ukraine and the withdrawal of its troops from the NIS. The Foreign Ministry has not been the MoD's only nemesis in the government. The high command has also clashed with the Ministry of Finance on numerous occasions over the latter's ongoing call for decreased military expenditures and repeated refusals to disburse approved funds to the MoD. Partly as a result of this situation, and in order to increase his support, in 1995 Grachev granted a 25 percent salary increase to military personnel, a measure that well exceeded his authority.

Military elites had publicly opposed Yeltsin's defense doctrine concept prior to winning the president's concession in 1993 allowing them to keep their own, a defense concept that was neither clearly external nor distinctly military.[86] The MoD leadership has impeded military reform, unsuccessfully resisted budget cuts, and managed to marginalize military leaders, like General Vladimir Lobov, who were in favor of the army's restructuring. As a result of the top brass's defiance of state policy, throughout 1990s the Russian military has remained fundamentally immune to the sweeping reforms envisioned by the political elites during 1991–92. The weakness of Russian political institutions has allowed the army to become more politicized. For a number of reasons, though, the military has not openly interfered in political processes (and was

---

[84] *Pravda*, June 26, 1997. See commentaries in *Segodnya*, June 25, 1997; July 1, 1997; and *Krasnaya Zvezda*, June 27, 1997.

[85] *The Vancouver Sun*, July 4, 1998.

[86] Michael C. Desch, "Threat Environments and Military Missions," in Diamond and Plattner (eds.), *Civil-Military Relations*, p. 25.

extremely reluctant to do so when it did, in 1991 and 1993). This is an important conclusion that needs further scrutiny.

Explaining Military Quiescence

The lack of firm civilian control, the weakness of political institutions, the recurring political and economic crises, the attempts of various political organizations to court the military, the inflammatory rhetoric of popular army leaders, and the extraordinarily difficult conditions in the armed forces would all seem to support the inference that violent political intervention by the military – or even an outright military coup – is to be expected in Russia.[87] Yet this has not happened. There are three main reasons that explain this puzzling phenomenon.

The most important reason for the absence of violent and autonomous military interference in Russia is the lack of institutional cohesion within the armed forces. The oft-repeated assertion of commentators and politicians that the generals are about to revolt should not be taken at face value, because they never specify which group of the nearly 3,000 generals or which segment of the officer corps might constitute a threat to political order. The thousands of generals and the tens of thousands of officers are sharply divided on a number of substantive issues, and these cleavages effectively preclude concerted action. Some officers are supportive of Yeltsin and his regime; others prefer the opposition. Some generals are proponents of military reform; others favor the status quo. Some, particularly older officers, view the Soviet period with nostalgia; others endorse Russia's nascent democracy. Geographic position often serves to split officers; those close to the center may be more inclined to support the status quo than those in faraway regions. The economic interests of officers who have profited from relaxed supervision are different from the those of their colleagues who enjoy no opportunity to enrich themselves. These fissures have developed within the last decade, and they are complemented by more traditional cleavages, such as interservice rivalries, divisions between officers on the general staff or the MoD and their colleagues in the field, competition between elite and regular units, and the split between senior and junior officers. Furthermore, the interests of the Russian army – in terms of its budget, institutional prestige, and political clout – are diametrically opposed to those of the multiple militaries.

Some of these cleavages were clearly observable in the crises outlined earlier. The 1991 coup attempt was partially prepared and backed by a group of high-ranking officers, but their endeavor was effectively resisted

---

[87] For more elaboration on these points, see Zoltan Barany, "Controlling the Military: A Partial Success," *Journal of Democracy*, Vol. 10, No. 2 (1999), pp. 65–66.

by their colleagues. In October 1993, too, rebellious parliamentarians could win the participation of only a small segment of the military elites for their cause: the MoD leadership and its troops lined up behind the president. In a like vein, the first war on Chechnya was actively supported by a small group of the top brass (primarily Grachev and his entourage); the majority of the officer corps obeyed orders grudgingly; while a minority publicly opposed the campaign and even resigned their commissions rather than participate in it. Not surprisingly, in each case "the military was hesitant and indecisive in its deliberations on what to do and in the actual implementation of orders."[88]

It also bears remembering that hundreds of thousands of officers with better career prospects elsewhere have left the armed forces, and it is not unreasonable to suggest that those still wearing uniforms might have no better place to go – for the time being, at least, the armed forces offer the best employment alternative for them. Russian conscripts are also split along traditional lines, such as the length of service, socioeconomic and ethnic background (about 25 percent of conscripts are non-Slavs),[89] regional loyalties, and more recent fissures between volunteers (contract soldiers) and draftees. In sum, these divisions not only preclude the development of a unified political stance by the army, but also frustrate efforts to ascertain the corporate interests of the military establishment.

The second reason is that the Russian officer corps has apparently developed a firm allegiance to democratic values and principles. A wide array of survey data suggests that officers are committed to an apolitical stance. A poll of 600 field-grade officers (majors through colonels) conducted in the mid-1990s found that: (1) the majority supports democracy and opposes the creation of an authoritarian government; (2) they do not desire the forcible restoration of the Soviet Union; and (3) they are not equally dissatisfied with all facets of military life.[90] Considering the poverty of a large proportion of their countrymen and the appalling material circumstances that dominate the lives of Russian officers, it is easy to appreciate why, as survey results also convincingly show, the majority of officers reject free-market capitalism.

Finally, unlike the militaries of Iberia, Latin America, and of some Eastern European states like Poland, the Russian armed forces have no tradition of political interference. Notwithstanding the numerous wars, revolutions, and mutinies in its history, Russia has never been ruled by

---

[88] Meyer, "The Devolution of Russian Military Power," p. 326.
[89] *Segodnya*, December 4, 1998.
[90] Deborah Yarsike Ball and Theodore P. Gerber, "The Political Views of Russian Field Grade Officers," *Post-Soviet Affairs*, Vol. 12, No. 2 (1996), pp. 155–180, especially pp. 155–156.

military men. This strong legacy of eschewing autonomous political involvement has become an integral part of the Russian army's organizational culture.

IV. CONDITIONS IN THE ARMED FORCES

The absence of military coups and other forms of violent interference in Russian politics is all the more surprising because conditions in the post-Soviet armed forces have deteriorated almost beyond belief. In less than a decade, the once proud and mighty Soviet army has become a demoralized, impoverished, and enfeebled institution. In fact, Pavel Felgenhauer, one of the most perceptive Russian military analysts, has argued that although Russia has a credible nuclear deterrent, it is vulnerable to attack by a force of 1,000 well-trained guerrillas because of its weakened conventional forces.[91]

The Poverty of the Armed Forces and Its Personnel

A large part of the Russian officer corps, not so long ago a privileged stratum of Soviet society, has become destitute. In a 1994 testimony to the Duma, Defense Minister Grachev lamented that "no army in the world is in as wretched a state as Russia's."[92] The only source of income for the vast majority of officers is a salary that is – when it is being paid – inadequate to meet even modest needs. Since the MoD often does not get the money allocated in the state budget from the Ministry of Finance, commanders have been compelled to use payroll funds to pay local suppliers for food, electricity, and other indispensable services. The erosion of military salaries compared to other occupations has contributed to plummeting morale. In 1991, regimental commanders earned half as much as city bus drivers.[93] In July 1994, after a 40 percent pay increase, army officers still made only two-thirds as much as comparable MVD employees, and half as much as those working for the Federal Counterintelligence Service.[94] Not surprisingly, by 1998 over 30 percent of the MVD's professional corps were former army officers.[95] Many army officers are forced to give blood, drive taxis, or work as parking attendants in order to feed their families.

---

[91] *Austin American-Statesman*, May 28, 1999.
[92] Benjamin S. Lambeth, "Russia's Wounded Military," *Foreign Affairs*, Vol. 74, No. 2 (1995), p. 88.
[93] Galeotti, *Afghanistan*, p. 186.
[94] Lilia Shevtsova, "Russia's Fragmented Armed Forces," in Diamond and Plattner (eds.), *Civil-Military Relations*, p. 113.
[95] *Moskovskii Komsomolets*, September 5, 1998.

The poverty of personnel is reflected in the overall destitution of the armed forces. In September 1994, the Moscow regional electricity authority cut all power to the federal Strategic Nuclear Missile Command Center for nonpayment of bills.[96] Repeated occurrences of power stoppage forced the Federation Council in 1997 to pass an amendment to the criminal code that introduced fines and prison sentences for officials responsible for terminating service to military installations. The MoD has encountered major difficulties in feeding the troops as well. The army's food budget was cut by 50 percent in 1995, and by December of that year widespread reports were circulating about hungry Russian soldiers in Chechnya who occasionally raised cash for food by selling their weapons and supplies to the enemy. In 1997, army privates were allotted 5,000 rubles (about 70 cents) a day for nourishment, in contrast to prisoners, who received 7,750 rubles' worth of food each day.[97] In July 1998, an inspection found 1,000 tons of dog food and large quantities of food products purchased after their expiration dates in a military food depot near Moscow; two months later, newspapers reported that budgetary allocations covered provision of a three-meal diet for only the first 290 days of the year.[98]

The housing situation of active and retired military personnel shows parallel patterns. The problem has been exacerbated by the hundreds of thousands of officers and soldiers returning from Eastern Europe during the early 1990s and by the retirement or dismissal of even more people for whom the army was obligated to provide housing. Notwithstanding lofty plans for apartment construction that had been periodically announced with great fanfare, in 1997 there were over 100,000 homeless officers.[99]

Declining Morale and Professionalism

The sinking morale of the Russian armed forces in the post-communist period has been caused by the deepening divisions within its ranks, the inadequacy of funding for the military in general and the increasing poverty of its personnel in particular, and the massive and poorly planned troop reduction process. A 1994 poll of midcareer officers found that 80

---

[96] See *The New York Times*, September 23, 1994.

[97] *The New York Times*, July 28, 1997.

[98] *Kommersant-Daily*, July 10, 1998 and Itar-Tass (Moscow), September 26, 1998.

[99] In June 1998, for instance, Deputy Prime Minister Boris Nemtsov promised that 50,000 officers who were leaving the armed forces would be able to acquire apartments. Given the shortage of funds, one must be skeptical about the program's implementation. See *RFE/RL Newsline*, Part I, June 16, 1998.

percent were pessimistic about their futures, 87 percent were concerned about the decline in the prestige of military service, 40 percent wanted to leave their profession, and only 3 percent indicated a strong desire to remain.[100]

As a result of deficient remuneration, qualified officers had started to resign in droves as early as the late 1980s, a time that also marked the beginning of the MoD's growing recruitment difficulties. From 1990 to 1993, nearly 100,000 young officers left the service. By the mid-1990s, midcareer officers (captains to lieutenant colonels) who should have comprised the army's backbone had begun to leave as well. In a February 1998 article, Felgenhauer noted that although military schools graduated more than 20,000 lieutenants annually, they had been quitting the army as soon as they could. To alleviate the problem, the MoD had been drafting nearly 15,000 graduates of civilian high schools each year, turning them into "two-year lieutenants" who were no better trained than conscripted sergeants. As a result, Felgenhauer went on, the Russian armed forces had virtually no professional military personnel at the squad and platoon level.[101] Today 90 percent of sergeants are draftees under twenty-one who are totally unqualified to supervise conscripts. Their lack of competence has contributed to the rising incidence of accidents and criminal behavior among soldiers.

The Chechnya campaigns and the general political quiescence of the armed forces have demonstrated that most Russian officers remain sufficiently professional to carry out unpopular orders. At the same time, insubordination has been on the rise. In 1993, 73 percent of polled officers declared that resisting the coup plotters in August 1991 was a mistake.[102] By the tense days of mid-May 1999, when the Duma deliberated whether or not to impeach President Yeltsin, Felgenhauer remarked that the broke, poorly prepared, and splintered military had "no loyalty to anyone," and even Yeltsin's "bodyguard won't even fight for him."[103] Military leaders, Dale Herspring has noted, cannot be certain that their orders will be obeyed, for the average Russian soldier has trouble deciding whom to follow in a crisis situation. Results of a 1995 survey showed that 39 percent would not follow orders in an unpopular scenario.[104] This finding was echoed by a more recent poll, in

[100] Lambeth, "Russia's Wounded Military," p. 92.
[101] *Segodnya*, February 2, 1998.
[102] *Kuranty*, February 17, 1993, as cited in Dawisha and Parrott, *Russia and the New States of Eurasia*, p. 243.
[103] Quoted in Angela Charlton's AP dispatch (Moscow), May 15, 1999.
[104] Herspring, *Russian Civil-Military Relations*, p. 178.

which 20–40 percent of officers said that they would be reluctant to carry out "dubious orders."[105] Although this professed reluctance would likely doom attempts at military intervention, most military leaders would find the attitudes of these officers toward their superiors and their commands alarming.

A parallel development has been the decline of military professionalism, emblematized by poor training, insufficient maintenance of aging equipment, and the overall deterioration of the quality of armed forces personnel. Not only has the military lost many of its best weapons after the collapse of the USSR, but declining budgetary outlays have had a negative impact on the procurement of new and the maintenance of old armaments, including nuclear weapons. In 1988 the Soviet army possessed 53,300 tanks; ten years later the Russian military had 14,000, of which only 6,000 were said to be battle-ready.[106] In the mid-1980s, the MoD purchased 300–400 new aircraft annually; this figure had been reduced to 10 a decade later and, in 1996–1997, to zero, while the commissioning of combat ships was cut from fifteen to one and that of submarines from twenty to two.[107] Due to low maintenance budgets and lax discipline, much of the MoD's equipment is not in working order. Thousands of tanks are out of action, hundreds of aircraft are entombed in hangars, and dozens of navy vessels are rusting away at port. According to the air force's commander, Colonel-General Anatolii Kornukov, the combat fitness of aviation equipment was only 45–55 percent in March 1998.[108] Given Russia's financial woes, matters should not be expected to improve soon, even with the recent deployment of Topol-M (classified by NATO as SS-27) ballistic missiles at some SRF bases. In February 1999, Marshal Sergeev announced that the armed forces would begin to receive new weapons and hardware only after the year 2005.[109]

Not surprisingly, training has suffered greatly. Owing to the absence of substantive force restructuring and the concomitant reduction of personnel, many units are filled only to 50 percent or less of capacity. Training maneuvers and exercises for all armed forces services have been drastically reduced due to ammunition and fuel shortages. According to air force officials, combat pilots in 1995 spent only ten hours in the air, which is not sufficient to maintain skill levels, much less to improve

---

[105] Cited by Brian D. Taylor, "The Russian Military outside Politics," PONARS memo no. 2 (Harvard University, October 1997).
[106] *The New York Times*, September 6, 1998.
[107] Arbatov, "Military Reform in Russia," p. 108.
[108] Interfax (Moscow), March 13, 1998.
[109] Itar-Tass (Tver), February 8, 1999, as cited in JRL, No. 3048 (February 8, 1999).

them.[110] The army's daily reported that in 1998 some navy ships fulfilled only 50 percent of their required quota for time at sea, while navy aviation pilots had flown only 18 percent of the targeted time.[111] If anything, the fact that public support for the military as an institution remains comparatively high is a reflection not of the armed forces' performance but of the overwhelming lack of trust and confidence in other Russian institutions.

Notwithstanding the fact that a military career is no longer considered prestigious by most Russians, they place a great deal of trust in the armed forces. After years of mixed opinions regarding the military, a February 2000 poll found that 45 percent of respondents had positive attitudes toward the armed forces, and the proportion of those harboring negative feelings had fallen to 29 percent.[112] According to another spring 2000 survey, the army is by far the most trusted Russian institution (72 percent of respondents indicated that they "trust" or "totally trust" it), far ahead of the church (57 percent), the federal and local governments (34 percent), the judiciary (34 percent), and the police (28 percent).[113]

Growing Crime and Corruption

One key reason for politicians' reluctance to increase defense expenditures is their assumption that corrupt generals misuse MoD's resources. Much evidence supports their impression. The withdrawal of Soviet troops from Eastern Europe had been accompanied by the wholesale squandering of the army's equipment and supplies. In 1992, Yeltsin declared that "[t]he embezzlement of weapons and military hardware with the view to their sale has acquired menacing proportions."[114] Five years later, Defense Minister Rodionov harshly criticized the Soviet's "disorderly flight" from the region. "The troops, the equipment and the combat potential vanished. Where did it all go?" he asked.[115] During 1990–93, serving Soviet soldiers and officers openly sold uniforms, memorabilia, medals, and, a bit more surreptitiously, a wide range of weapons, from Kalashnikov submachine guns to tanks and heavy artillery pieces, in Eastern European markets. According to reliable

[110] Lieven, "Russia's Military Nadir," p. 27. See also Benjamin S. Lambeth, *Russia's Air Power in Crisis* (Washington, D.C.: Smithsonian Institution Press, 1999), pp. 168–172.
[111] *Krasnaya Zvezda*, October 6, 1998.
[112] RIA Novosti (Moscow), February 17, 2000, as cited in JRL, No. 4119 (February 18, 2000).
[113] Itar-Tass (Moscow), March 18, 2000, as cited in JRL, No. 4180 (March 18, 2000).
[114] Herspring, *Russian Civil-Military Relations*, p. 175.
[115] *Nezavisimaya gazeta*, February 8, 1997.

estimates, during 1993–94 alone Russian generals pocketed as much as
$65 million.[116] In 1994, Deputy Defense Minister Matvei Burlakov –
who oversaw the Soviet withdrawal from both Hungary and East
Germany – was forced to resign as a result of persistent allegations that
he had accumulated a fortune from the sale of army property.[117] Since
then, army storage facilities have continued to be plundered. In fact,
every third illegally owned firearm in the country – currently one out
of every nine Russian men owns a firearm – was stolen from Defense
Ministry stocks.[118]

The seemingly endemic corruption among the top brass is often difficult to prove, although prosecutors have managed to hold some generals accountable. In mid-1997, twenty-one generals, among them army
general and former deputy defense minister Konstantin Kobets, were
charged with bribe taking, illegal sale of arms, and a number of other
crimes.[119] Military prosecutors convicted seventeen army generals and
navy admirals on corruption charges in 1998 and noted that the incidence of such crimes among the military elite had been on the increase.[120]
These offenses often involve multimillion-dollar damages to Russia's
armed forces. Admiral Igor Khmelnov, commander of the Pacific Fleet
from 1992 to 1995, received a comparatively light sentence in 1997
because prosecutors could not conclusively prove that he had sold
sixty-four ships from his fleet to India and South Korea.[121] His colleague
Rear Admiral Vladimir Morev was found guilty of embezzlement
and abuse of office – he and two subordinates sold parts of a radar
system to a Vladivostok businessman – and sentenced to eight years in
prison in 2000.[122] Not surprisingly, generals do look out for each other,
and many disgraced and convicted military leaders sooner or later find
lucrative jobs with the MoD. In 1998, the MoD – partly to preempt
opposition to its policies – rehired former defense ministers Grachev
and Yazov, former general staff of chief Mikhail Kolesnikov, and a
number of other high-ranking army officers as "advisors" to the MoD
or to the state-owned arms exporter Rosvooruzhenie, an organization Stephen Blank has described as resembling a system of "common
racketeering."[123]

[116] Lambeth, "Russia's Wounded Military," p. 93.
[117] See, for instance, *The New York Times*, November 2, 1994.
[118] *Trud*, June 19, 1999, as cited in *RFE/RL Newsline*, June 22, 1999.
[119] Interfax (Moscow), November 13, 1997, as reported in *RFE/RL Newsline*, November 15, 1997.
[120] Interfax (Moscow), July 1, 1999, as reported in *RFE/RL Newsline*, Part I, July 2, 1999.
[121] *Russkii telegraf*, December 9, 1997.
[122] Interfax (Vladivostok), April 28, 2000, as cited in *RFE/RL Newsline*, May 2, 2000.
[123] Blank, "Who's Minding the State?", p. 5.

Crime and disciplinary problems are rampant in the lower ranks as well. In the first eight months of 1992, 854 criminal acts were recorded in the Moscow area alone, and 3,711 military personnel were disciplined.[124] In the first eight months of 1998 alone, crimes in the armed forces were up 12 percent compared to the number registered in all of 1997.[125] It is particularly troubling that the proportion of violent crimes, such as soldiers killing fellow soldiers (fifty cases in 1997), is on the increase. In September 1998, a nineteen-year old sailor murdered eight crew members and locked himself into the torpedo bay of a nuclear submarine in Murmansk, eventually committing suicide.[126] A growing number of spontaneous strikes have broken out in protest of the dreadful living conditions and nonpayment of officers' salaries. Desperate times call for desperate measures: in one recent case, a colonel – the chief financial officer of the Moscow military district headquarters – committed suicide by immolating himself to protest his family's grave poverty; in another, an army major, unpaid for five months, took a tank from his base and drove it into downtown Nizhnii Novgorod to call attention to his regiment's tribulations.[127]

Conscripts and Their Mothers

The circumstances of conscripted soldiers are even more desperate than those of professional armed forces personnel. The main concern of an increasing number of draftees is to find enough to eat. In mid-1998, the MoD encouraged commanders to take their troops berry picking, mushrooming, and harvesting because no funds could be found to feed them. The only soldiers reporters could identify around Moscow during the September 1998 crisis were not the commandos many feared would intervene in affairs of the state but the 12,000 conscripts drafted to harvest potatoes on farms around the capital.[128] In addition, hundreds of thousands of soldiers must serve without proper uniforms, boots, and basic equipment because the army cannot outfit them. In terms of spending per serviceman, Russia ($4,000 each year) lags far behind not only leading NATO members like the U.S. ($180,000) and Germany ($100,000) but also Turkey ($15,000) and India.[129]

[124] Herspring, *Russian Civil-Military Relations*, p. 175.
[125] See *Trud*, September 25, 1998; *Nezavisimaya gazeta*, September 25, 1998; and *Segodnya*, September 24, 1998.
[126] *Los Angeles Times*, October 5, 1998.
[127] *The Sunday Times* (London), September 5, 1998, as cited in JRL, No. 2350 (September 5, 1998), and *The New York Times*, July 28, 1997.
[128] AFP (Moscow), September 13, 1998, as cited in JRL, No. 2370 (September 13, 1998).
[129] No figure is provided for India. *Nezavisimoe voennoe obozrenie*, No. 8 (March 2000), as cited in *RFE/RL Newsline*, March 8, 2000.

The brutal hazing of fresh conscripts (*dedovshchina*) has become commonplace. It is said to be the most frequent cause of the rising incidence of suicide among soldiers. MoD sources have revealed that in 1995 there were 459 suicides and 1,017 noncombat deaths in the armed forces; 430 out of a total of 1,046 in 1996; 487 out of 1,103 in 1997; while suicides were responsible for 22.7 percent of all deaths in 1998.[130] Human rights organizations insist that the real figures are much higher; they estimate that approximately 5,000 army recruits die or commit suicide annually.[131] The number of major accidents resulting from negligence or human error has risen precipitously. Stories of sailors dying of starvation because their commanders "forgot" them in remote areas, explosions in ammunition depots caused by criminal negligence, and soldiers begging for food in urban areas have been published in the Russian press, further wearing away whatever popular confidence remains in the armed forces. Not surprisingly, in addition to the still large number of draft dodgers (the MoD registered 49,000 in 2000), a rapidly increasing number of soldiers have become deserters.

Mothers of conscripted soldiers have long been outraged by the deployment of their untrained and unprepared sons in crisis zones as well as by the abysmal conditions in which they have been forced to serve. In the summer of 1989, after resistance to the draft had increased dramatically, they formed the Committee of Soldiers' Mothers (KSM) to represent their sons' interests and to publicize their predicament. According to KSM leaders, in recent years 40,000 soldiers have fled the army, most motivated by ruthless hazing.[132] In March 1998, the chief military prosecutor's office and the KSM organized a joint program promising amnesty for deserters who turn themselves in.[133] The second war in Chechnya reenergized KSM. Mothers urged citizens to vote for peace and against Putin in the March 2000 presidential elections; they have faked divorce, illness, and bribed officials to keep their sons out of the hands of the draft board; and they have loudly and publicly insisted that the MoD's figures on the number of servicemen killed and injured in Chechnya (2,284 and 6,645, respectively, between August 2, 1999, and May 18, 2000) cover only a fraction of the actual casualties.[134]

[130] *RFE/RL Newsline*, January 23, 1998, based on *Nezavisimaya gazeta*, January 23, 1998, and *RFE/RL Newsline*, April 21, 1999, citing Colonel-General Ivan Chizh, head of the armed forces medical service. See also the report in *Kommersant vlast*, December 8, 1998, summarized in *RFE/RL Newsline*, December 15, 1998.
[131] *The Times* (London), September 30, 1998.
[132] *RFE/RL Newsline*, March 5, 1998 and *Austin-American Statesman*, March 28, 1999.
[133] See *Novye izvestiya*, March 24, 1998 and *Nezavisimaya gazeta*, March 26, 1998.
[134] *New York Times*, January 30, 2000; AP (Moscow), March 22, 2000, as cited in JRL, No. 4192 (March 23, 2000); and *RFE/RL Newsline*, May 19, 2000.

CONCLUSION

Since 1989, the former Soviet army has lost an empire, an alliance, a country, a war, its identity, mission, funding, a large part of its personnel, weapons, social prestige, and cohesion. It may, in fact, be the former Soviet institution that has been the most devastated by the political and economic systemic changes.

With the fall of the Soviet Union, the institutionalized civilian control over the army had also begun to disintegrate. To be sure, civil-military relations have become far more transparent since 1991 than they were during the Soviet period, but the new Russia's political elites have not developed strong political institutions and have failed to establish firm and balanced control over the armed forces. The void created by the abolition of the Soviet era's civilian control mechanisms has not been filled by the structurally balanced and firm political supervision of the defense establishment, which is a prerequisite of democratic states. The Russian president's prerogatives concerning defense matters are excessive, even in a political system where the president enjoys extensive powers.

The lack of structural balance in civilian control is shown by the Russian Duma's limited influence over the armed forces, which has been only somewhat offset by its power to pass the budget and to write pertinent laws. Only somewhat, because the Duma's trump cards have often been effectively countered by the executive branch through its refusal to transfer funds to the MoD, and by military elites, whose implementation of the already insufficient laws governing civil-military relations has been decidedly lenient.

The growing authority of governors over the troops based in their regions has further impeded the central state's control over the armed forces. At the same time, lack of financial resources and commitment of the top brass to much-needed military reforms have effectively thwarted their introduction. In many ways, writes Blank, Russian conditions invoke sub-Saharan designs of civil-military nexus where, in states like Nigeria, there is no established, institutionalized framework for the subordination of the armed forces to civilians.[135] Alexei Arbatov, the thoughtful deputy chairman of the Duma's Defense Committee, has noted that the failure of civilian supervision has "left the armed forces virtually on their own during a period of profound political, social, economic, and strategic change."[136] In sum, as a result of an incomplete process of state-building and the weakness of political institutions, the situation in contemporary Russia does not approximate the elementary

---

[135] Blank, "Who's Minding the State?", p. 4.
[136] Arbatov, "Military Reform in Russia," p. 112.

conditions of democratic civil-military relations. A particularly distressing aspect of the weakening of central authority vis-à-vis the military is its implications for the safeguarding and maintenance of the country's nuclear weapons, which have become more vulnerable to sabotage.

The Russian military has been departified but not depoliticized. Its generals and officers run for and hold political office, publicly condemn elected politicians with impunity, and occasionally stonewall their policies. There is no legal instrument requiring the military's exclusion from political life. The accountability of the military to state authorities is not above suspicion, given its abysmal material situation, widespread distrust of politicians, and its particularly troubling rivalry with other uniformed services. In the meantime, crime and corruption are rampant in the armed forces, while their training, discipline, and social prestige have vastly deteriorated.

On the surface, these conclusions would justify fears of impending autonomous military involvement in political affairs. Still, the Russian army has not posed a serious threat to the country's nascent democratization process, primarily due to intra-institutional cleavages that preclude unified action, the officer corps' apparent allegiance to certain democratic principles, and the absence of political intervention from its institutional culture. "The [Russian] soldiers have long proved their great capacity for suffering," was former German defense minister Volker Ruehe's apt response to a question about the threat of a military coup in Moscow.[137]

In many ways the strengths and weaknesses of Russia's army reflect the characteristics of Russian society at large. Many of its generals are corrupt and have accumulated considerable wealth, even while line officers and ordinary soldiers frequently lack basic necessities. In the first decade of the post-communist era, the Russian armed forces have become an impoverished, demoralized, and humiliated institution in dire need of dynamic, reform-driven, and democratic leadership. The complete depoliticization of the military and the establishment of solid, balanced, and constitutionally codified civilian control over the entire armed forces are fundamental imperatives of democratic consolidation. Russia's political elites must accomplish these tasks if their professed desire to join the community of democratic states is to be taken seriously.

---

[137] German Defense Minister Volker Ruehe as cited in *Bild* (Hamburg), September 2, 1998.

Conclusion: Democracy and Russian Politics

M. Steven Fish

Russian democracy, as it passes the anniversary of its first decade, is in tatters. Russia cannot be depicted as a fully authoritarian polity. It has many of the components of democracy, including regular elections and a considerable degree of political openness and free competition. Unlike Belarus and Kazakstan, Russia did not slide into the abyss of dictatorship after an initial opening. Unlike Serbia and Uzbekistan, Russia did not drift from one form of harsh authoritarianism to another. Unlike many of its other neighbors, however, such as Poland, Bulgaria, the Baltic states, and Mongolia, Russia fails even to approximate an authentic democracy. The quality of Russian democracy is not only mediocre; it has actually declined since the advent of the new regime in 1991–92.

The first section of this chapter discusses the Russian experience in light of several theories and conceptions of democracy. It establishes criteria for evaluating the quality and character of the post-Soviet political regime in Russia and considers how the Russian experience might speak to issues in democratic theory. The second section offers a causal explanation for the emergence and persistence of what is characterized as "low-caliber democracy." The quality of popular rule in Russia is traced to a single critical institutional choice and a small set of momentous decisions taken by the chief executive. The third and concluding section of the chapter considers current obstacles to democratization in Russia and makes explicit the prescriptions for change that follow logically from the causal analysis.

THE RUSSIAN EXPERIENCE AND THEORIES OF DEMOCRACY

Scholars bring a host of conceptual frameworks to cross-national analysis of democracy and debates over the extent of democratic achievement in given countries. One widely used conception, explicated originally by Joseph Schumpeter, defines democracy in terms of free elections.

Schumpeter casts democracy as a regime in which a bare majority hold the right to change the ruler. Schumpeter conceived of the operation of democratic rule as the exchange of government policies for votes.[1] Such a notion may be dubbed a "Schumpeterian" or "electoralist" definition.

Another important definition is offered by Robert Dahl. Dahl's definition, which he labeled "polyarchy," since he regarded genuine "democracy" as an unachievable ideal type, is somewhat more demanding and restrictive than Schumpeter's. Dahl's conception amounts to a list of the "procedural minimal" conditions that include not only elections, but also provisions that ensure that major policy decisions are constitutionally vested in elected officials and that practically all adults have the right to run for elective office. The definition also demands the presence of the communicative and associational rights that Dahl regarded as necessary for the electors to be organized and well informed and for elections faithfully to represent public opinion.[2] Dahl's definition enjoys wide celebrity and influence. Many scholars have embraced it, even as some have offered their own elaborations or modifications. The criteria used by Freedom House, the leading agency in the world that regularly assesses countries' extent of political openness, are based essentially on Dahl's framework.[3] In the present discussion, this notion is called a "Dahlian" or "procedural" definition of democracy.

A third conception of democracy is far more demanding and restrictive than Dahl's. Advocates of this conception, which may be dubbed the "radical" alternative, criticize Dahl's definition for excessive "formalism" or "proceduralism," and they add to Dahl's criteria conditions that relate to equalities of many types, especially in the distribution of wealth and income. This notion is deeply rooted in the socialist tradition and is popular among Marxist scholars. It emphasizes democracy's "substantive," as opposed to strictly "formal" properties, and regards democratization as necessarily entailing the extension of citizenship rights from political to economic and social relationships.[4] Not all scholars who

---

[1] Joseph A. Schumpeter, *Capitalism, Socialism, and Democracy* (New York: Harper, 1975), pp. 269–283.

[2] Robert A. Dahl, *Dilemmas of Pluralist Democracy* (New Haven: Yale University Press, 1982), p. 11. See also Philippe C. Schmitter and Terry Lynn Karl, "What Democracy Is . . . and Is Not," in Larry Diamond and Marc F. Plattner, eds., *The Global Resurgence of Democracy*, 2nd ed. (Baltimore: Johns Hopkins University Press, 1996), pp. 55–56.

[3] See the "Survey Methodology" section of any recent volume of *Freedom in the World: The Annual Survey of Political Rights and Civil Liberties* (New York: Freedom House, various years).

[4] For classical statements, see C. B. Macpherson, *Democratic Theory: Essays in Retrieval* (Oxford: Clarendon, 1973) and T. H. Marshall, *Class, Citizenship, and Social Development* (Garden City, N.Y.: Anchor, 1965). For more recent extensions and applications, see Dietrich Rueschemeyer, Evelyne Huber Stephens, and John D. Stephens, *Capitalist*

embrace a radical definition are necessarily Marxists. Some non-Marxist scholars have also offered conceptions that attempt to capture the "substantive" components of democracy and that eschew the "formalism" or "thinness" of a Dahlian notion.[5] Both Marxist and non-Marxist conceptions that fall under this rubric are referred to here as "radical" definitions.

A fourth conception of democracy does not focus on equalities in the distribution or enjoyment of material resources, but rather adds other criteria to Dahl's definition and consequently also yields a definition more restrictive and demanding than Dahl's. Some prominent contemporary theorists add the presence of "the rule of law" and/or of "civil society" to democracy's defining attributes.[6] This notion is dubbed here a "rich" definition of democracy.

Assessing whether and to what extent democracy exists in Russia, or in any other country, naturally depends in part on which definition one uses. According to a Schumpeterian/electoralist definition, Russia indubitably achieved the status of a democracy within the first several years of the post-Soviet period, or perhaps even as early as June 1991, when Boris Yeltsin was directly elected present of the then-RSFSR. In a Schumpeterian conception, moreover, the quality of Russian democracy cannot be regarded as having declined during the 1990s, since elections have gone forward at regular intervals as prescribed by law. In fact, from a Schumpeterian perspective, the continued holding of regular elections would suggest that democratization has advanced and deepened in Russia throughout the 1990s and the beginning of the current decade.

In a Dahlian/procedural conception, Russia would in some but not necessarily all respects qualify as a polyarchy. In light of Dahl's criteria, moreover, Russia may be regarded as having slid away from polyarchy since the inauguration of the post-Soviet regime. The presence of regular elections helps establish the regime's nonauthoritarian status. For offices on the regional and especially the republican levels, however, basic electoral freedoms are often denied by regional barons. What is more, heavy-handed electoral manipulation at the subnational level did not subside during the second half of the 1990s. On the contrary, the problem in some places grew more acute, as local strongmen consolidated their grip

---

Development and Democracy (Chicago: University of Chicago Press, 1992) and Kenneth M. Roberts, *Deepening Democracy? The Modern Left and Social Movements in Chile and Peru* (Stanford: Stanford University Press, 1998).

[5] For example, Benjamin Barber, *Strong Democracy: Participatory Politics for a New Age* (Berkeley: University of California Press, 1984).

[6] Richard Rose and Doh Chull Shin, "Democratization Backwards: The Problem of Third Wave Democracies" (unpublished ms., 1999).

on power.[7] The de facto restrictions on political expression found in some places (including Moscow), where some regional officials have established records of responding to challenge or criticism with violence or intimidation, as well as Yeltsin's high-handed use of the media to advance his candidacy in the 1996 presidential election, further compromised Russia's polyarchical status.[8] So too did the war in Chechnya, which effectively cut off a portion of the citizenry from many types of political participation, even if not from voting in national elections. These problems have indeed been reflected in the "freedom ratings" issued by Freedom House. Russia's score deteriorated by one-and-a-half points (from 3 to 4.5 on a seven-point scale, with 1 representing the most free) between 1991–92 and 1999–2000.[9]

According to the third conception of democracy outlined here, the radical conception, Russia probably would not qualify as a democracy. Its democratic stock would probably be judged to have fallen during the 1990s, moreover, due to the growth in income and wealth differentials and the pauperization of a substantial portion of the population. While acknowledging that Russia in "formal" terms has made strides toward democracy since the collapse of the Soviet regime, analysts who include "substantive" criteria in their definitions would very likely assess Russia as – at best – a partial democracy, and one that is becoming less democratic every year.

Through the lens of the fourth image set forward earlier, a "rich" definition of democracy, Russia may also fail as an established democracy, albeit for different reasons. In this view, the absence of a well-structured civil society, consisting of autonomous organizations and networks of organizations, as well as the tenuousness of the "rule of law," would seriously compromise Russia's democratic credentials. Indeed, in a recent article, two leading scholars have made such an argument.[10]

Thus, one's theoretical perspective, and particularly the criteria that constitute one's definition of democracy itself, shape one's assessment of

[7] See Michael McFaul and Nikolai Petrov (eds.), *Politicheskii al'manakh Rossii 1997, tom 2, kniga 1: Sotsial'no-politicheskie portrety regionov* (Moscow: Carnegie Center, 1998), pp. 229, 241–42 and Mikhail Myagkov, "The 1999 Duma Election in Russia: A Step toward Democracy or the Elites' Game?", paper prepared for the Shambaugh Conference on Russia's Parliamentary and Presidential Elections, University of Iowa, April 2000.

[8] See Sarah Oates, "Television, Voters and Democracy in Russia: The Development of the 'Broadcast Party,' 1993–2000," paper prepared for the Shambaugh Conference on Russia's Parliamentary and Presidential Elections, University of Iowa, April 2000, and "Kaliningrad's Open Season on Journalists," *The Moscow Times*, December 16, 1999.

[9] Freedom House, "Annual Survey of Freedom, Country Scores, 1972–73 to 1999–00," at www.freedomhouse.org.

[10] Rose and Shin, "Democratization Backwards."

the extent of democratization and whether one regards a given polity as having crossed the threshold necessary to achieve status as a democracy. It also influences how one interprets the trajectory of political change.

Brief consideration of the Russian experience in light of these notions of democracy actually sheds some light on the utility of the concepts themselves. The Schumpeterian definition enjoys the advantages of simplicity, elegance, and parsimony. Yet one may question the utility of a definition that would classify Russia as a full-blown democracy and that would be insensitive to possible changes in a country's democratic status as a result of a constriction of associational and communicative rights. Given its reduction of democracy to the momentary ability of voters to prevent the coming to or maintenance in power of that politician whom they view as the most unresponsive, the concept provides little basis for distinguishing between Lithuanian and Armenian democracy, between Polish and Ukrainian democracy – or, for that matter, between German and Russian democracy. In fact, the only gradations in the *quality* of democracy that a Schumpeterian definition detects relate to the proportion of the adult population that is enfranchised. In a Schumpeterian conception, Russia would have to rank far ahead of Latvia or Estonia in terms of democratic achievement, since all adults enjoy the right to vote in elections in Russia, while a portion of the population in the two Baltic countries is disqualified from voting by restrictive citizenship laws based on length of residence in the country.[11] Russia would also have to be counted as a more democratic polity than the United States, since the former, unlike the latter, universally extends the franchise to convicted felons, including prisoners.

It should be noted that fulfilling Schumpeter's criteria for democracy is not an inconsiderable task and should not be dismissed as such. Even if well over half the countries in the postcommunist world, including Russia, have already crossed the Schumpeterian threshold, roughly one-third of them have not. For majorities in Serbia or Turkmenistan to enjoy the ability peacefully to change their rulers at the ballot box would amount to (and require) a revolution.

Still, it is intuitively obvious to most students of democracy, as well as to most students and residents of the countries under discussion, that the quality of democracy is much higher in Lithuania, Poland, Germany, and the United States than it is in Armenia, Ukraine, and Russia. One could further argue – although this point would be controversial – that even the disenfranchised minorities in the Baltic states in practice enjoy

---

[11] Such a Schumpeterian assessment in found in Philip G. Roeder, "The Rejection of Authoritarianism in the Soviet Successor States" (unpublished ms., 1999).

as much control over their own political destinies and sway over elected officials as do the vast majority of Russia's universally enfranchised adult population. Latvia's vigorously open and competitive political system created conditions under which a majority of eligible voters endorsed in a referendum a reduction in the restrictiveness of citizenship requirements, though discrimination based on time of residence in the country, which is related to ethnicity, remains a serious problem. Lithuania never imposed the same onerous requirements that its two northern neighbors did. In all three Baltic states, inhabitants in general, regardless of ethnicity, enjoy protections of associational and communicative rights that are far superior to those afforded the citizens of Russia, a difference that is reflected in Freedom House ratings.[12] In sum, a Schumpeterian conception of democracy, while commonly used and worthy of close consideration, is too unidimensional and undemanding to serve as a firm basis for assessing either Russia's overall extent of democratization in comparative perspective or changes in its level of democratic attainment over time.

The third and fourth definitions of democracy sketched out here suffer from the opposite shortcoming: they are so demanding as to be overly restrictive. The radical definition, which emphasizes "substantive" criteria, is difficult to operationalize. It is exceedingly hard to evaluate whether a given country has achieved "democracy" or not, since proponents of the radical concept rarely if ever include in their definition any threshold levels of "equality." What is more, the radical definition is subject to the serious criticism that democracy, by its very terminological nature, must apply exclusively to the political regime, and that economic and social systems, structures, and outcomes per se cannot reasonably be subsumed under any form of "ocracy." The fourth definition of democracy, the "rich" definition, may also be regarded as overly restrictive and exceedingly difficult to apply in practice. What criteria does one use to assess whether or not a given polity has a "civil society"? The concept of civil society itself is highly contested and subject to a multitude of definitions. Insisting upon the presence of a civil society as an ingredient of democracy may render the notion of democracy itself unwieldy and amorphous.

Perhaps the most serious problem inherent in the "radical" and the "rich" conceptions of democracy is that both fail to distinguish clearly between *diagnostic features* and *sustaining conditions*. Both a high level

---

[12] In the survey for 1999–2000, all three Baltic states received "civil liberties" scores of 2, while Russia received a 5 (with 1 representing the greatest extent of liberty and 7 least). Freedom House, "Annual Survey of Freedom, Country Scores, 1972–73 to 1999–00."

of socioeconomic equality and a vigorous civil society may help sustain democratization and maintain established democracy. But to confuse what helps to sustain something with the essence of the object itself constitutes a real conceptual error, albeit one that is often encountered in social science theories. What is more, while both socioeconomic equality and civil society may be highly desirable in and of themselves, and while both may well flourish under democracy more readily than under a nondemocratic order, to include them as diagnostic features of democracy is to confuse a possible prerequisite for the thing, or a sought-after product of the thing, with the thing itself.

The Dahlian definition, the second considered earlier, avoids both these pitfalls and those of the overly permissive and unidimensional Schumpeterian concept. Dahl's conception, since it includes the conditions necessary to make elections meaningful (communicative and associational rights) rather than just elections themselves, is not subject to the "electoralist fallacy" for which Schumpeter's concept has been justifiably criticized.[13] Yet neither is Dahl's conception encumbered with criteria that are exceedingly difficult to observe or measure or to achieve in real-world political life. It includes the *conditions* necessary for the emergence of civil society (specifically, associational freedoms), but avoids counting civil society itself as a necessary *attribute* of democracy. It includes a crucial condition that promotes the rule of law – namely, that "control over government decisions about policy is constitutionally vested in elected officials." But it steers clear of adding "the rule of law" itself – a difficult entity to observe directly – to the definition of democracy. Dahl's procedural definition, thirty years after its formulation, continues to enjoy advantages over the alternatives. It is parsimonious and includes only attributes that may be more or less readily observed. It avoids the trap of confusing diagnostic features with either sustaining conditions or desirable outcomes. Yet, in contrast with the Schumpeterian definition, it is not overly spare and undemanding.

Still, despite its obvious merits, Dahl's concept is limited to a list of traits, what its author calls the "procedural minima." Dahl's definition can and does provide a useful standard for evaluating both cross-national variation and within-country cross-temporal change in the extent of democratic achievement. But it does not really capture the way democracy *operates* in practice. In fact, no rigorous definition of a concept can be expected to do so. For example, the "totalitarian model" has been excoriated for decades for not capturing or anticipating or explaining the "dynamics of change" in the post-Stalin Soviet Union. But the model,

[13] See Terry Lynn Karl, "Dilemmas of Democratization in Latin America," *Comparative Politics*, Vol. 23, No. 1 (1990), pp. 1–22.

at least its most widely cited and criticized version,[14] was not intended to capture or anticipate or explain dynamics; this is not what such concepts do. They may be deployed or embedded in theories that seek to account for change, but definitions themselves cannot be expected to fulfill such a task. The totalitarian model, in this respect, closely resembles Dahl's model of polyarchy. Both are rigorous definitions made up of a list of readily observable characteristics. Both are, by nature, "stagnant"; both characterize a state of being. Real-world change may by be gauged against the standards of the models. One may assess the extent to which this or that polity does or does not satisfy the criteria for classification as "totalitarian" or "polyarchical," and may fruitfully endeavor to demonstrate empirically that a given polity has begun to be or ceased to be characterized by the concept. But one cannot expect such concepts themselves to "explain change."

For the scholar who seeks not only to make effective use of concepts but also to understand dynamics and transcend the limitations of conventional definitions, it may be desirable to introduce one or a few operational features of the system under consideration. Doing so necessarily entails costs in terms of simplicity and perhaps even of clarity, but the trade-off may be worth making. Simply loading more conditions into a definition, as the third and fourth conceptions of democracy discussed earlier do, does not necessarily yield a firmer basis for understanding. It may overburden a concept without really enriching it, or produce blurry definitions and conceptual confusion.

Dahl's definition, by emphasizing citizenship and the rights needed to make it meaningful, properly casts democracy as a relationship between rulers and the ruled. The definition specifies the conditions that make possible the control of the former by the latter. Popular control over the state is, of course, a matter of state-society relations. Dahl's definition, in a parsimonious fashion, specifies a set of attributes that enables society to control the state. But it includes nothing about the actual interaction of state and society in practice. For a concept that does introduce the notion of interaction, and that does so in a pithy and efficient way and without merely piling more items onto a list of necessary conditions, Emile Durkheim's theory of democracy provides an extremely useful referent. Durkheim was not concerned with rigorously cataloguing the attributes of a democracy, nor with drawing up a list of necessary conditions. Rather, he sought to illuminate what he called democracy's "gist," "special feature," and "advantage" over other regime types, which he characterized as the "constant flow of communication"

---

[14] Carl J. Friedrich and Zbigniew K. Brzezinski, *Totalitarian Dictatorship and Autocracy* (Cambridge, Mass.: Harvard University Press, 1956).

between state and society.[15] Durkheim did not have in mind a "culture of discourse" or the constant chattering of every part of society with every other part, such as was later theorized and advocated by Jürgen Habermas.[16] Nor, unlike Habermas, did Durkheim cast his theory in ethereal and pretentious terms. Durkheim's conception was not rigorous or fully operationalizable in a contemporary social-scientific sense, but it had a lucid, simple thrust. Durkheim explicitly depicted the "constant flow of communication" as the continual – not merely episodic or sporadic – openness of state agencies to the concerns and demands of the citizenry as a whole, and the duty of the citizenry habitually to accept the state's laws.[17]

This notion of reciprocal accountability is consonant with Dahl's definition. Durkheim pinpoints the central feature of how a polity that satisfies Dahl's criteria for polyarchy operates in practice. Furthermore, to Dahl's notion a Durkheimian conception adds the idea that citizens, in addition to controlling the state, must also be accountable to it. Durkheim's definition assumed the electoral, associational, and communicative rights embodied in Dahl's definition, and expressed what the exercise of these rights amounted to in practice. Durkheim's concept, like Dahl's, viewed state-society interaction as the locus of democratic practice. Like Dahl's, it did not insist upon the existence of a full-blown "civil society," a particular configuration of economic distribution, the presence of "social justice," or any other such criteria as diagnostic features of democracy. Durkheim insists merely that citizens "accept the laws of the country," just as they themselves enjoy the power to shape those laws through their representatives. In contemporary parlance, Durkheim's notion centered on reciprocal accountability of society and the state, achieved through continuous communicative interaction.

The fruitful convergence of the compatible but not identical concepts of a leading contemporary democratic theorist and a founder of political sociology yields tools that aid in assessing the character of Russian democracy. As already mentioned, in a Dahlian conception, Russia would have to be viewed as an incomplete polyarchy, and one that moved away from rather than toward polyarchy during much of the 1990s. Russian democracy, when held up to the light of Dahl's definition, is shown to be deficient in some crucial areas, including the areas of

[15] Emile Durkheim, *Professional Ethics and Civic Morals* (London: Routledge, 1992), p. 91.

[16] Jürgen Habermas, "Discourse Ethics: Notes on a Program of Philosophical Justification," in Jürgen Habermas (ed.), *Moral Consciousness and Communicative Action* (Cambridge, Mass.: MIT Press, 1993), pp. 43–115 and Jürgen Habermas, *The Theory of Communicative Action* (Boston: Beacon, 1984).

[17] Durkheim, *Professional Ethics and Civic Morals*, pp. 85–97.

communicative and associational rights. When the dynamic component of Durkheim's theory is introduced to supplement Dahl's notion, further shortcomings in Russian democracy become apparent. First, Russian politics is manifestly short on what Durkheim regarded as the "gist" of democratic practice – that is, the constant two-way flow of communication between state and society. The institutions of popular rule are present in Russia. But reciprocal communication of the type that Durkheim theorized is striking by its weakness or even absence. Despite the holding of regular elections for the presidency, the legislature, and many provincial and local offices, Russian politics between elections is characterized by an enormous accountability deficit. Whether one relies on ethnographic investigation of the lives of Russian citizens, public opinion surveys, analysis of the press, or study of the ways in which officials execute their responsibilities, it is exceedingly difficult to conclude that Russian political elites interact closely with and behave responsibly toward the mass public.[18] In fact, one of the most striking features of Russian democracy is the enormous gap between the institutions that are supposed to guarantee accountability of the rulers to the ruled – most notably, elections and the control of government offices by elected officials – and citizens' actual capacity to control their representatives' behavior between elections. Symptoms of the accountability gap are found in the near-universality of corrupt practices among high elected officials and their appointees and other behaviors that blatantly contravene the preferences and interests of voters.[19]

Interestingly, representativeness, at least in the strict sense of the term, does not really present a major problem for Russian democracy. The entire range of public opinion is well represented in the national legislature, which includes sizable contingents of communists, social democrats, liberals, and nationalists. What is more, to borrow from Clinton-era American political speech, governments do more or less "look like" the people. Tatarstan is led by an ethnic Tatar, with the other major groups

---

[18] See Stephen White, Richard Rose, and Ian McAllister, *How Russia Votes* (Chatham, N.J.: Chatham House, 1997), pp. 45–56, 131–41, 219–39; Michael Urban, *The Rebirth of Politics in Russia* (Cambridge: Cambridge University Press, 1997), pp. 291–310; M. Steven Fish, "The Roots of and Remedies for Russia's Racket Economy," in Stephen S. Cohen, Andrew Schwartz, and John Zysman (eds.), *The Tunnel at the End of the Light: Privatization, Business Networks, and Economic Transformation in Russia* (Berkeley: University of California International and Area Studies, 1998), pp. 86–137; and M. Steven Fish, "The Predicament of Russian Liberalism: Evidence from the December 1995 Elections," *Europe-Asia Studies*, Vol. 49, No. 2 (1997), pp. 191–220.

[19] See Thomas F. Remington, *Politics in Russia* (New York: Longman, 1999), pp. 228–30; Fish, "The Roots of and Remedies for Russia's Racket Economy"; and Alexei Verizhnikov, "Uncivil Society and Lawlessness-Enforcing Agencies," *Geschichte und Gegenwart*, Vol. 1 (1997), pp. 43–54.

in the autonomous republic also well-represented in the government. The same may be said of Kalmykia and many other autonomous republics, as well as of representation in parliament and the executive branch on the national level. The problem is not "who's there"; it is rather what they do (and do not do) once they're there. In other words, representativeness does not present nearly as acute a problem as accountability.

When taking account of the second component of Durkheim's conception, which refers to citizens' accountability to the state or, in Durkheim's words, their willingness to "accept the laws of the country" and to do so "based on reflection [and] . . . with more intelligence and thus less passively" than when under a nondemocratic regime, Russian democracy appears in an even more unflattering light.[20] The legal code and legal institutions in Russia in many respects resemble their counterparts in well-functioning European democracies. But an overwhelming proportion of citizens do not regard subordinating themselves to the laws as obligatory or even desirable. Public opinion surveys, statistics on crime and tax-collection rates, ethnographic study, and simple residence in Russia all reveal a colossal problem of citizens' accountability to public authority.[21] The problem is narrower and more specific than the wider issues of "consent" and "legitimacy" sometimes discussed by democratic theorists.[22] The conundrum in the Russian context is found not so much in a mass, wholesale rejection of the regime, as in citizens' contempt for the mundane but crucial rules and laws that regulate daily life. Just as state officials ignore citizens' preferences, so too do citizens ignore the state's dictates.[23] Such mutual nonrecognition constitutes the very

[20] Durkheim, *Professional Ethics and Civic Morals*, p. 91. The philosophical roots of Durkheim's notion of reciprocal accountability may be traced to Kant's writings on freedom, duty, and subjection to the law. See Immanuel Kant, *Groundwork of the Metaphysic of Morals* (New York: Harper and Row, 1964), pp. 102–07, and Immanuel Kant, *Political Writings*, ed. Hans Reiss (Cambridge: Cambridge University Press, 1995), pp. 132–35.

[21] "Bud' proshche–i k tebe potianutsia liudi," *Kommersant*, July 18, 1995; "Finansovaia diktatura," *Nezavisimaia gazeta*, October 22, 1996; "Predvybornyi opros VTsIOM, 29 noiabria–5 dekabria 1995" (mimeo, January 1996, Moscow); and Vladimir Shlapentokh, "'Normal' Russia," *Current History*, Vol. 96, No. 612 (1997), pp. 331–335.

[22] See Larry Diamond, "Three Paradoxes of Democracy," in Diamond and Plattner (eds.), *The Global Resurgence of Democracy*, pp. 111–23.

[23] The causes of the near universality of sentiment in Russia that the law does not deserve to be observed, and the broader implications of this state of affairs for democratization, merit more extensive discussion than can be offered here. For a fuller analysis, see Fish, "The Roots of and Remedies for Russia's Racket Economy." See also Ken Jowitt, "Undemocratic Past, Unnamed Present, Undecided Future," *Demokratizatsiya: The Journal of Post-Soviet Democratization*, Vol. 4, No. 3 (1996), pp. 409–19, and Richard Rose, "Living in an Antimodern Society," *East European Constitutional Review*, Vol. 8, No. 1/2 (1999), pp. 68–75.

antithesis of Durkheim's "constant flow of communication" between citizens and the state.

The problem of low-accountability (or no-accountability) democracy is not unique to Russia. It is also found in some other countries in the post-communist region, though among those that have open or partially open regimes, the accountability crisis in Russia may be particularly acute. The predicament is also evident in countries such as Mexico, the Philippines, Brazil, and South Africa.[24]

Democracy without accountability is low-caliber democracy. Despite the presence of institutions to ensure popular control, there is little accountability of officialdom to society. Nor does the state hold societal actors accountable for their behavior. The gulf dividing state from society that Alexander Zinoviev dubbed "the yawning heights" during the Soviet period may not gape as widely as it did when the party that claimed status as "the reason, honor, and conscience of our epoch" lorded over Russia.[25] But the gulf still yawns, and much more widely than in most other democracies. How did Russian democracy reach the state of degradation in which it finds itself at the beginning of the twenty-first century?

THE SOURCES OF LOW-CALIBER DEMOCRACY

One of the most striking things about Russia's low-caliber democracy is what *cannot* be numbered as its causes. Many of the usual culprits of stalled democratization or degraded democracy are not at fault in Russia. A politically meddlesome military did not cause the problem. During the 1990s, the Russian armed forces, unlike their counterparts in many African countries and in many Latin American and East Asian countries in earlier decades, were politically quiescent.[26] Nor can democracy's quandary be blamed on "polarized pluralism" of the type that Giovanni Sartori theorized and held up as a cause of the demise of democracy in some European polities during the interwar period.[27] Michael McFaul is

---

[24] See Miguel Ángel Centeno, *Democracy within Reason* (University Park: Pennsylvania State University Press, 1994); Kurt Weyland, *Democracy without Equity* (Pittsburgh: University of Pittsburgh Press, 1996); and Gabriella R. Montinola, "Parties and Accountability in the Philippines," *Journal of Democracy*, Vol. 10, No. 1 (1999), pp. 126–40.
[25] Alexander Zinoviev, *The Yawning Heights* (New York: Random House, 1979).
[26] Zoltan Barany, Chapter 5, this volume.
[27] Giovanni Sartori, *Parties and Party Systems: A Framework for Analysis* (Cambridge: Cambridge University Press, 1976). See also Juan J. Linz, *The Breakdown of Democratic Regimes: Crisis, Breakdown, and Reequilibration* (Baltimore: Johns Hopkins University Press, 1978), and Youssef Cohen, *Radicals, Reformers, and Reactionaries: The Prisoner's Dilemma and the Collapse of Democracy in Latin America* (Chicago: University of Chicago Press, 1994).

certainly right to highlight the contentiousness of Russia's post-Soviet politics and the presence of "stable polarization" at least until the time of the 1996 presidential elections. Yet, as McFaul astutely notes, Russia's polarization revolved around contention within *elites*.[28] The spectacle of ideologically coherent political parties or other organizations battling one another on behalf of rival social groups was unknown in Russia's first post-Soviet decade. The phenomenon that McFaul theorizes, therefore, is not classical polarization; it involved practically no social mobilization. It was not the kind of occurrence, nor did it include the same types of actors, that reversed prior democratic gains in interwar Europe or Latin America in the 1960s and 1970s.[29] Nor can the poverty of Russian democracy be attributed to a social-structural inheritance characterized by gross inequalities in the distribution of wealth, since Russia did not start its post-Soviet existence with a powerful upper class and a large, marginalized lower class in place. Whether the results of the economic transformations that *succeeded* the birth of the new regime may have created new obstacles to democratization is a separate question, and one that will be addressed later.

The anemia of Russian democracy can actually be explained exclusively in terms of a single institutional choice and three momentous decisions taken by the chief executive in the early 1990s. All of these causes are *political* in nature. None need be, nor can be, explained in terms of structural, cultural, or deep historical conditions. While structure, culture, and historical legacies are not irrelevant to the quality of Russia's democracy, the latter was determined largely by the politics of the revolutionary period, which was not foreordained by prior conditions.

Institutional Choice

The main institutional cause of Russia's low-caliber democracy is the super-presidential system. The overweening presidency has steadfastly enervated Russian democracy. It lies at the heart of Russian democracy's accountability deficit.[30]

---

[28] Michael McFaul, Chapter 1, this volume.
[29] See Stephen E. Hanson and Jeffrey S. Kopstein, "The Weimar/Russia Comparison," *Post-Soviet Affairs*, Vol. 13, No. 3 (1997), pp. 252–283.
[30] On Russian super-presidentialism, see, among other works, Eugene Huskey, "The State-Legal Administration and the Politics of Redundancy," *Post-Soviet Affairs*, Vol. 11, No. 2 (1995), pp. 115–43; Timothy J. Colton, "Superpresidentialism and Russia's Backward State," *Post-Soviet Affairs*, Vol. 11, No. 2 (1995), pp. 144–48; Robert Sharlet, "The Politics of Constitutional Amendment in Russia," *Post-Soviet Affairs*, Vol. 13, No. 3 (1997), pp. 197–227; and M. Steven Fish, "The Executive Deception: Superpresidentialism and the Degradation of Russian Politics," in Valerie Sperling (ed.), *Building the Russian State: Institutional Crisis and the Quest for Democratic Governance* (Boulder, Colo.: Westview, 2000), pp. 177–192.

Russian super-presidentialism indeed has had all of pathological effects that the advocates of parliamentarism predict will haunt polities with presidential constitutions, including institutional rigidities arising from the chief executive's fixed term, the presence of a chief executive who regards himself as a tribune of the people, and winner-take-all politics that incites frustration in and even encourages anticonstitutional action by the losers in presidential elections.[31] But super-presidentialism has had further pernicious effects in Russia, including some not always anticipated or theorized by the institution's detractors. First, since the Russian president himself spent nearly the entire second half of the 1990s in seclusion, with his health and mental faculties in decline, Russia found itself with what Robert Moser calls a strong presidency without a strong president.[32] Indeed, a presidency invested with overwhelming authority and responsibility on paper but occupied by a custodian who rarely commanded it to work weakened the state itself. If the centerpiece of the state structure was missing, it is little wonder that the state and, as Kathryn Stoner-Weiss demonstrates, its central organs in particular, underwent a steady process of enfeeblement during the 1990s.[33] And as all of the contributors to this volume suggest, a disintegrating state apparatus scarcely provides a sturdy institutional basis for popular rule. Despite the "strength" and "decisiveness" that overweening executive power supposedly supplies, in practice it has undermined rather than bolstered state capacity.

Super-presidentialism's enervating effect on state capacity results in part from its tendency to promote personalism and obstruct institutionalization. By investing so much power in one person, it offers that individual enormous discretion as well as incentives to check institution building. Politicians who seek to control everything themselves – that is to say, almost all politicians – prefer dictating and ruling directly to governing through impersonal, established rules and agencies. But leaders in systems in which power is separated and dispersed often must build institutions in order to compete effectively with other leaders. Thus, competitive politics in polities in which power is divided often assumes the character of competitive institution building. But if a single agency holds

---

[31] Juan J. Linz and Arturo Valenzuela (eds.), *The Failure of Presidential Democracy* (Baltimore: Johns Hopkins University Press, 1994) and Alfred Stepan and Cindy Skach, "Constitutional Frameworks and Democratic Consolidation: Parliamentarism versus Presidentialism," *World Politics*, Vol. 46, No. 1 (1993), pp. 1–22.

[32] Robert Moser, Chapter 2, this volume. See also "El'tsin ukhodit, chtoby ostat'sia," *Izvestiya*, October 31, 1998.

[33] Kathryn Stoner-Weiss, Chapter 3, this volume. See also "Krizis daet regionam vozmozhnost' ukrepit' nezavisimost'," *Finansovye izvestiya*, August 18, 1998.

most of the power, its custodian may regard himself or herself as capable of unmediated control of political life, and will often view institutions more as irritations and obstacles than as necessities and potentially useful weapons. Yeltsin provides a study in how superpresidentialism encourages the president to envision all power as his own patrimony, and how he in turn may regard any attempt to regularize the exercise of power in the form of institutions as a threat to his prerogatives.[34] The phenomenon is not, of course, unique to Russia. It is also found in some other countries in the NIS as well as in Latin America, East Asia, and Africa. In short, super-presidentialism not only fails to enhance state capacity, it actively undermines it.

One might argue that the very birth of the super-presidential system was more a response to state weakness than a cause of it. In comparative perspective, however, this notion does not stand up to scrutiny. The state was no "stronger" during the period of regime change in Romania, Bulgaria, Lithuania, Latvia, or Mongolia – none of which adopted super-presidential constitutions – than it was in Russia. Indeed, state apparatuses virtually fell apart during transitions in the two southeast European countries, had to be built almost from scratch in the Baltic countries, and labored under a near-collapse induced by the sudden disappearance of financial resources in the Asian case. The Russian state, by contrast, still enjoyed the formidable organizational, bureaucratic, and personnel assets inherited from the Soviet period. The notion that super-presidentialism *resulted* from state weakness is also suspect in logical and theoretical terms. It is rooted in the idea that a political regime emerges in response to some abstract "need" or "requirement" in the polity at large. Such unvarnished functionalism, though it has resurfaced in new guises in some rational choice approaches, has largely – and justifiably – been discredited in the social sciences.

The super-presidency has also multiplied the opportunities for corruption. Massive official corruption is the generic hallmark of unaccountable government, since citizens everywhere and at all times oppose the consumption by officials of public resources that otherwise could be invested in the provision of public services. In post-Soviet Russia, to a far greater extent than in most other nonautocracies, corruption is the very essence of political life. Since the regime invests most the central government's powers of the purse in the executive branch, the latter has, to a far greater extent than in moderate presidential or semi-presidential systems, abundant opportunities to buy off legislators with patronage, a point raised by Moser in his discussion of Yeltsin's use of clientelism to

---

[34] George W. Breslauer, *Evaluating Gorbachev and Yeltsin as Leaders* (Berkeley: University of California Press, forthcoming).

secure support for his budgets in the Duma.[35] The executive's control over the purse, combined with the absence of mechanisms and agencies for parliamentary oversight, means that those who control the state's resources are answerable only to the president. The only real check on corruption and predation is the president himself. Were he deeply committed to and capable of monitoring his subordinates, perhaps Yeltsin could have controlled corruption. But Yeltsin's manifest incapacity in this respect turned the executive branch into a feeding trough.[36]

The weakness of interbranch checks might not so strongly conduce corruption were societal organizations equipped to monitor politicians' behavior. In many democracies, a plethora of nonstate political and social organizations continually inspect the political class. The American polity is thick with such organizations. Some fledgling democracies in Latin America, Africa, East Asia, and parts of the post-communist region also do not suffer a shortage of them. What is more, political parties, which have reason to be concerned with their standing with the electorate, often monitor and discipline their own members. Despite the absence of checks between executive and legislative powers in Britain, the British enjoy accountable government in part due to the strength of political parties, whose sensitivity to their reputations for probity leads them sometimes to deal sternly with their own members for behavior that might be regarded as corrupt.

But super-presidentialism diminishes incentives for the formation of autonomous societal organizations, including and especially political parties. The impetus to engage in party building usually depends on the power of the legislature. Parties normally supervise the nomination of candidates in legislative elections and structure competition within legislatures between elections. In Russia, parties do indeed perform such tasks in the Duma.[37] But the weakness of parliament compared to the executive branch provides ambitious politicians and societal actors who

[35] Moser, Chapter 2, this volume.

[36] In the survey for 1998 conducted by Transparency International, Russia ranked seventy-sixth out of the eighty-five countries surveyed, meaning that only nine countries were rated as more corrupt. Russia's rating was the worst of the twelve post-communist countries surveyed, which included Serbia, Belarus, Bulgaria, and Ukraine. Corruption was also judged to be more severe in Russia than in India, Kenya, Vietnam, and Pakistan. Transparency International, "The Corruption Perceptions Index," at www.transparency.de/documents/cpi/index.html. See also Timothy Frye and Andrei Shleifer, "The Invisible Hand and the Grabbing Hand," *American Economic Review*, Vol. 87, No. 2 (1997), pp. 354–58 and Andrei Shleifer and Daniel Treisman, *Without a Map: Political Tactics and Economic Reform in Russia* (Cambridge, Mass.: MIT Press, 2000), pp. 101–105.

[37] Thomas F. Remington and Steven S. Smith, "The Development of Parliamentary Parties in Russia," *Legislative Studies Quarterly*, Vol. 20, No. 4 (1995), pp. 457–489.

seek to influence policy with little incentive to seek their fortunes by building, joining, or lobbying political parties. Were parties at least responsible for nominating candidates for the presidency, their role would be enhanced. But Yeltsin, from the very beginning of his struggle during the late 1980s until the end of his tenure in office at the beginning of 2000, showed little but contempt for political parties. He refused ever to lead or join a party, favoring instead the vain pose of the popular tribune who transcends ordinary "politics" and therefore somehow better represents "the nation" as a whole. While President Vladimir Putin's orientation toward political parties is not clear as of this writing, to date he has followed his predecessor's policy of shunning close association with a party. While he endorsed the Unity party, a motley conglomeration of political unknowns, in the 1999 parliamentary elections, Putin has claimed to have little or nothing to do with the party's decisions and internal life. While he clearly holds great sway over the party, which relied on his endorsement for its strong showing the parliamentary elections, Putin owes the party nothing. He won the presidency in March 2000 by virtue of his personal popularity alone; he relied neither on Unity nor on any other party in his election. Presidentialism's "consolidating effect" on the party system, which Moser notes, is indeed evident in Russia, but only insofar as the presidential elections allow for the participation of candidates from fewer political parties to compete in parliamentary elections.[38] Given the marginal role of parties in presidential elections during Russia's first post-Soviet decade, the consolidating effect may be understood strictly as a reduction in the number of organizations, not as a spur to organizational maturation and growth via amalgamation and integration.

If the accountability deficit that superpresidentialism generates is manifest in the corruption that pervades politics and government, it is also evident in several disastrous governmental actions whose occurrence would have been far less likely in a system that divided power more evenly between the president and the legislature. Perhaps the most egregious and destructive of these was the first war in Chechnya, launched in late 1994. Plans for the ham-fisted attack were hatched by Yeltsin and a clutch of ministers and other officials in charge of the armed forces, without consultation with parliament and without public discussion. The war was wildly unpopular from its outset.[39] It was opposed by a large majority of parliamentarians, including not only Yeltsin's traditional communist foes but also major liberal figures as well. Had the

---

[38] Moser, Chapter 2, this volume.

[39] See Gail W. Lapidus, "Contested Sovereignty: The Tragedy of Chechnya," *International Security*, Vol. 23, No. 1 (1998), pp. 5–49.

legislature enjoyed more authority in the matter, the war probably never would have been launched. Had the legislature and public opinion been able to assert themselves and restrain the executive after the onset of the war, Russian forces would have withdrawn from Chechnya quickly, rather than engaging in a protracted, futile struggle that laid an entire territory to waste, took 40,000 civilian lives, and destroyed what was left of the Russian armed forces' fighting capacity and prestige in society.[40] The second attack on Chechnya, initiated in the fall of 1999, enjoyed far greater public support due to acts of terrorism committed in Russia and attributed by the Russian government to Chechen separatists or their agents. However, despite the second war's relative popularity and ceaseless government pronouncements at the time of this writing that Russian troops have mastered the military situation, this conflict will eventually only exacerbate the effects of the first war. What is more, even as Putin has declared that "even to speculate about" the possibility that the Federal Security Service (FSB) was behind the bombing "is immoral and in essence none other than an element of the information war against Russia," the government as of this writing has produced no evidence that the bombings were carried out by Chechen terrorists or their agents. Worst of all, but entirely typical of political life under the super-presidential system, even calls by skeptical parliamentary leaders for a fuller and more searching probe of the bombings have had little effect. In the absence of genuine oversight authority, even the parliament's most powerful members have not been able to launch effective independent investigations or to prod the executive into conducting a more transparent and thoroughgoing inquiry.[41]

The pernicious effects of super-presidentialism on Russian democracy are paradoxical, since a strong executive was touted by the revolutionaries of the late Soviet and early post-Soviet periods as a weapon of democratization. The origins of the institution may be traced to the pell-mell but ultimately successful effort by the insurgent democratic movement to find a way to destroy communist power by withdrawing Russia from the Soviet Union via a relentless drive for Russian "sovereignty," and the simultaneous effort to create an office for the politician who would lead the struggle for this cause. The spring 1991 referendum, in which a majority called for the creation of a directly elected presidency, amounted at the time to a vote for democracy and against the Soviet system. Virtually every voter in Russia then realized that Yeltsin's personal stature and popularity were unrivaled and that he, the de facto

[40] Barany, Chapter 5, this volume.
[41] "Hackers Attack Novaya Gazeta," *The Moscow Times*, March 16, 2000 and "No Proof Chechens Blew Up Buildings," *The Moscow Times*, March 17, 2000.

leader of the anticommunist movement, would win election to the new office. Indeed, the office was created for Yeltsin.[42] Furthermore, the complete failure of Yeltsin's antagonists, as well as of the opponents of an overweening presidency who did not necessarily oppose Yeltsin, to advance their plans for a parliamentary or semi-presidential system between 1991 and 1993 was rooted in a broad public consensus that Russia needed a strong executive to enhance governmental decisiveness and combat conservative opponents of democratization and economic reform, who enjoyed a stronghold in the national legislature. Even after the bloody showdown of October 1993 that severely tarnished Yeltsin's image and ruined his charisma, voters at the end of the year endorsed Yeltsin's draft constitution, which codified the super-presidential system. Thus, the super-presidency was born in the heat of political struggle; its emergence was not predetermined by any structural factors. What is more, its role in degrading democracy has an ironic character, since the super-presidency was earlier regarded by many of its architects and advocates as an instrument of democratization.

The *roots* of constitutional choice vary widely throughout the post-communist region, and can be understood only on a case-by-case basis. Romania adopted semi-presidentialism as an act of pure and transparent imitation of the French Constitution. Mongolia's leaders self-consciously opted for a semi-presidential constitution that dispersed power in order to protect the country against manipulation by a foreign hegemon, since they thought that multiple sources of power would be harder for Russia or China to buy off and control than would a single source of power. Czechoslovakia fell back on the parliamentary constitution it had known between the wars and before sovietization.

The *consequences* of constitutional choice, however, have been remarkably tractable to unqualified generalization. Throughout the post-communist region, the concentration of power has been a prescription for stalled and/or reversed democratization. In all countries that adopted constitutions that afforded presidents overwhelming power, even in countries that made initial strides toward polyarchy and that were headed by presidents who were regarded as democratizers, democratization was subsequently obstructed or reversed by presidential high-handedness. Armenia, Kyrgyzstan, Kazakhstan, and, more ambiguously, Ukraine, in addition to Russia, serve as examples. Belarus's switch from parliamentarism to super-presidentialism in 1994 was the beginning of the end of the experiment with open politics in that country. Super-presidentialism is not the only form of regime inimical to democratization. Super-prime-ministerialism, evident in Slovakia under Vladimir

---

[42] See Urban, *The Rebirth of Politics in Russia*, pp. 240–244.

Meciar during 1994–98, set the stage for degraded democracy and an accountability deficit. The concentration of power, best characterized as *super-executivism*, has been democracy's gravest foe. But for reasons that include the greater difficulty of removing the ruler from office and the weaker incentives for party building under super-presidentialism, this regime type has been a far more consistent bane to democratization than has prime-ministerial absolutism.[43]

In sum, the effect of super-presidentialism in Russia has been entirely typical. As in other countries, it has stymied democratization.

Presidential Decisions

The other source of anemia in Russian democracy is found in three decisions taken by Yeltsin during the early post-Soviet period. If the executive branch had not occupied such a large portion of the political field, in particular in the realm of the central government and the state, the president's decisions might not have had the defining impact that they did in fact. In the presence of an unchecked executive, however, the president's choices had momentous and lasting effects. Interestingly, none of these decisions can be understood in terms of simple self-interest. They therefore could not have been – and were not – predicted at the outset of the post-Soviet period. Nor can they easily be ascribed to structural, historical, or cultural conditions.

Yeltsin did not pursue democratization as an end during his crucial initial years in office. But his political decisions were by no means consistently antidemocratic. Unlike his counterparts in many other post-Soviet polities, Yeltsin did not muzzle independent media, eliminate his opponents, or engage in other blatantly democracy-destroying activities. Indeed, in the Russian political arena of the early 1990s, Yeltsin justifiably was regarded as a relative liberal. Still, he failed to embrace measures that could have set the trajectory of regime change on a course conducive to long-term democratization. One may isolate a number of important policies that did nothing to advance democratization and several that clearly set it back. Yeltsin's failure to undertake massive personnel replacements in the aftermath of the August 1991 coup attempt and his decision to eschew personal involvement in party building merit note. The general thrust of Yeltsin's policy, as noted by McFaul in a broad sense and as shown by Barany in the case of the management of the military in particular, had a certain anti-institutional cast.[44] When faced with

---

[43] M. Steven Fish, "The End of Meciarism," *East European Constitutional Review*, Vol. 8, No. 1 (1999), pp. 47–55.

[44] McFaul, Chapter 1, this volume, and Barany, Chapter 5, this volume. See also Timothy J. Colton, "Boris Yeltsin, Russia's All-Thumbs Democrat," in Timothy J. Colton and

the choice between managing a challenge by building an institution and managing by ad hoc and personalistic means, Yeltsin consistently chose the latter.

By far the most fateful of Yeltsin's political choices in terms of its effect on democratization, however, was his decision not to call new elections for parliament and to leave in place the old Supreme Soviet elected in the spring of 1990. In hindsight, this appears to be a peculiar decision, particularly given how the legislature subsequently turned against him and how the conflict between him and the legislature degenerated into violence and cost him his charismatic authority. But hindsight is not even required in this case. Even in the early months of the post-Soviet period it was a manifestly peculiar decision, and one that had starkly negative effects on both Russia's fledging democracy and on Yeltsin's political authority.

There are two main explanations for Yeltsin's decision not to organize new elections. The first holds that Yeltsin was well aware that fresh elections in the fall–winter of 1991–92 would yield a less conservative body, but Yeltsin nevertheless placed asserting full presidential dominance over the new regime above gaining a friendlier parliament. Yeltsin might have thought that an ineffective and/or unpopular legislature would be more docile than a reinvigorated one that enjoyed a fresh mandate, and Yeltsin may have calculated that a weak foe would be less vexing to his own exercise of power than a strong and independent ally.[45] The second possible explanation is that Yeltsin believed that new elections would have yielded a parliament that was more conservative and more hostile to his plans for reform than was the sitting Supreme Soviet. McFaul argues that Yeltsin may have made such a judgment.[46] In his memoirs, Yeltsin himself stated that he had held such a view, and intimated that even several years after the fact he still believed that elections held immediately after the failed putsch would not have produced a legislature more to his liking.[47]

Whichever hypothesis best explains Yeltsin's decision to forgo new elections, his calculations were deeply flawed. If the first hypothesis is valid, then Yeltsin grossly underestimated the potential hostility and

Robert C. Tucker (eds.), *Patterns of Post-Soviet Leadership* (Boulder, Colo.: Westview, 1995), pp. 49–74.

[45] M. Steven Fish, *Democracy from Scratch: Opposition and Regime in the New Russian Revolution* (Princeton: Princeton University Press, 1995), pp. 218–220.

[46] Michael McFaul, "The 'Human Factor' in State Dissolution: Economic Reform, Political Change, and State Effectiveness in the Soviet Union and Russia," paper presented at the conference Beyond State Crisis? The Quest for the Efficacious State in Africa and Eurasia, University of Wisconsin–Madison, March 11–13, 1999, pp. 15–16.

[47] Boris Yeltsin, *The Struggle for Russia* (New York: Random House, 1995), p. 126.

staying power of the old Supreme Soviet. He probably also exaggerated the disadvantages of dealing with a new legislature that would be both friendlier to his own program and infused with fresh legitimacy. If the second hypothesis is on target, then Yeltsin suffered from a colossal information problem. What the composition of a new legislature elected in the fall of 1991 "would have been" had new elections been held cannot be established with any certainty. But virtually all signs in the early weeks and months following the failed putsch of August 1991 indicated that new elections would have produced a far more progressive legislature. Yeltsin enjoyed astronomical popularity. As difficult as it might be to imagine from the vantage of the early post-Yeltsin period, most Russians regarded Yeltsin in the wake of the 1991 putsch not only as a hero, but as a doer of extraordinary deeds. At the time, he enjoyed charismatic authority in the strict, Weberian sense of the term. Whatever forces he endorsed in new parliamentary elections would have held tremendous advantages. What is more, the prestige of the forces arrayed behind him – then known in Russian parlance simply as "the democrats" – was enormous, and certainly as high as it could ever be expected to be. Elections held in the fall of 1991 would have produced a far less conservative body than the extant Supreme Soviet, and Yeltsin would have found the new legislature more congenial than the one that he left in place.[48]

Yeltsin compounded his error in 1993. In April, as conflict between himself and the Supreme Soviet mounted, he held a referendum on his policies and on public support for himself and for the legislature. Yeltsin won on every one of the four questions on the ballot. Majorities supported him personally, endorsed his policies, opposed fresh elections for president, and called for new elections for parliament. But again Yeltsin failed to act. His constitutional right to dissolve the legislature was murky at best. But this moment, like the time immediately following the August 1991 putsch attempt, provided him with a precious opportunity to strike. Instead, in a stunning case of inaction, he did nothing. Finally, fully six months later, after the legislature had grown even more intransigent and the glow of legitimacy lent by the referendum had dissipated, Yeltsin abruptly announced the dissolution of the parliament, initiating an ill-timed test of wills that would cover Moscow's streets with blood, bury the Yeltsin mystique, and degrade the quality of Russia's fledgling democracy.

Yeltsin's decisions constitute an enigma. It is noteworthy, however, that Yeltsin's handling of the legislature was consistent with a more general approach to risk that was evident throughout his tenure in office. As in many other areas, Yeltsin's behavior exhibited exquisite risk aversion when he was clearly doing well and wild risk acceptance in harder

[48] See Fish, *Democracy from Scratch*, pp. 201–210.

times. If McFaul is right to attribute Yeltsin's aversion to fresh elections in the fall of 1991 to a fear that his opponents would soundly defeat his supporters, one may characterize such a stance only as a bizarre underestimation of his own political authority and that of his allies when both were at their zenith. One might tend to dismiss McFaul's hypothesis as misguided, and Yeltsin's own claim in his memoirs as a defensive, post hoc rationalization, except that McFaul also presents evidence, based on in-depth investigation, that Yeltsin actually expected to *fail* to win the June 1991 presidential election in the first round. He expected the other four candidates, all in one way or another representing Communist Party interests, to deny him the fifty percent needed to win outright.[49] What is remarkable is how few people in Russia, other than perhaps members of Yeltsin's inner circle, shared Yeltsin's assessment. The author of this article resided in Russia in the spring of 1991 and cannot recall, in countless personal interviews and conversations with ordinary citizens and political leaders in a variety of cities, anyone ever sincerely expressing doubt that Yeltsin would triumph easily. In the event, Yeltsin captured nearly three-fifths of the vote, three times that garnered by Nikolai Ryzhkov, the second place finisher. A similar underestimation of his own authority and an accompanying aversion to risk precisely when he enjoyed greatest authority was again evident in the fall of 1991 and the spring of 1993, when Yeltsin forwent calling new parliamentary elections.

On the other hand, Yeltsin displayed a ferocious appetite for risk taking when he was in trouble. His abrupt move to dissolve the legislature in the fall of 1993 came at a time when his authority and popularity were in decline. His behavior in other realms reflected a similar affinity for bold, even reckless, action at times when he had good reason to regard himself as vulnerable. His decision to invade Chechnya in late 1994, as well as his sudden dismissal of his entire cabinet and appointment of Sergei Kirienko, an underqualified neophyte, as prime minister in the spring of 1998, both came in times of personal political trouble. Yeltsin's style seems to represent an extreme case, indeed almost a caricature, of the expectations of prospect theory. According to this psychological theory of decision making, individuals tend toward risk aversion in the realm of gains (or when they feel themselves to be doing well) and risk acceptance in the realm of losses (or when they feel themselves to be doing poorly).[50] In short, while self-interest motivated

---

[49] McFaul, Chapter 1, this volume.
[50] See Daniel Kahneman and Amos Tversky, "Choices, Values, Frames," *American Psychologist*, Vol. 39 (April 1984) and Rose McDermott, *Risk-Taking in International Politics: Prospect Theory in American Foreign Policy* (Ann Arbor: University of Michigan Press, 1998), Chapter 2.

Yeltsin's actions, the calculations on which his behavior was based were clearly shaped by bad information, misunderstandings, and systematic judgmental biases.

Yeltsin's fateful decision to forgo new legislative elections had enduring negative effects on democratization. Leaving the old Soviet-era Supreme Soviet in place robbed the new regime of a national legislature endowed with fresh, post-Soviet legitimacy. Furthermore, it virtually ensured the development of rancorous executive-legislative relations. It set the stage for the conflict of the fall of 1993 that would stain with blood what theretofore had been a largely peaceful change of regime. Subsequent elections for parliament changed its composition, but the virus of antagonism and mutual contempt introduced into executive-legislative relations during the early post-Soviet period continued to infect national political life through the end of the decade, culminating in impeachment proceedings against the president and intensified presidential efforts to discredit the legislature.[51]

The second major presidential decision that checked democratization was taken in the realm of economic reform. Many of Yeltsin's early economic policies, including rapid price liberalization and reduction of cheap state-issued credits to hopelessly unprofitable enterprises, represented intelligent and overdue measures. The centerpiece of Yeltsin's economic program, however, was privatization. Throughout the post-communist world, privatization has been crucial for establishing the rudiments of a functioning market economy. Market reforms, moreover, *pace* the faulty predictions and analyses of advocates of "gradualism" and statecentric approaches, have both spurred better economic performance and facilitated democratization.[52] But there are many ways

---

[51] See "Soglasie budet nedolgim," *Izvestiya*, March 16, 1999.

[52] See M. Steven Fish, "The Determinants of Economic Reform in the Post-Communist World," *East European Politics and Societies*, Vol. 12, No. 1 (1998), pp. 31–78 and M. Steven Fish, "Democratization's Requisites: The Postcommunist Experience," *Post-Soviet Affairs*, Vol. 14, No. 3 (1998), pp. 212–247. The point offered here is, of course, a matter of controversy, and represents a different view of economic reform than that presented by Yoshiko Herrera in her contribution to this volume. For arguments that there exists far more tension than compatibility between rapid economic reform and democratization, see, in addition to Herrera's chapter in this volume, Dmitri Glinski and Peter Reddaway, "The Ravages of 'Market Bolshevism'," *Journal of Democracy*, Vol. 10, No. 2 (1999), pp. 19–34; Mitchell Orenstein, "Lawlessness from Above and Below: Economic Radicalism and Political Institutions," *SAIS Review*, Vol. 18, No. 1 (1998), pp. 35–50; Adam Przeworski, *Democracy and the Market* (Cambridge: Cambridge University Press, 1991), pp. 183–187; Adam Przeworski, "The Neoliberal Fallacy," *Journal of Democracy*, Vol. 3, No. 3 (1992), pp. 45–59; and Luis Carlos Bresser Pereira, José María Maravall, and Adam Przeworski, *Economic Reforms in New Democracies: A Social-Democratic Approach* (Cambridge: Cambridge University Press, 1993).

to privatize. One particular aspect of the Russian program reshaped the economy in a manner that may have compromised democratization.

Privatization in Russia was carried out in two major stages. The first focused on the distribution of vouchers to the general population. Most citizens sold their vouchers to fledgling investors or to the managers of the enterprises in which they themselves worked. To a much greater extent than in the Czechoslovak voucher program, the Russian scheme privileged sitting enterprise administrators, many of whom secured controlling interests in the firms that they previously had managed but not owned. The program facilitated the continuation of the "*nomenklatura* privatization" that had already begun at the end of the Soviet period, but the voucher scheme in itself did not create the extraordinary, democracy-debilitating form of oligarchy that came to dominate the economy. That structure arose out of the second phase of the program, known as "loans-for-shares." During this phase, the government sold many of the country's largest and most valuable firms to a small group of private banks for a tiny fraction of the firms' real worth. Many of these banks had been established during the late Soviet and immediate post-Soviet periods as magnets for attracting cheap state credits and as currency speculation machines. The loans-for-shares scheme enabled them to seize the commanding heights of the economy. It contributed to the emergence of a private sector ruled by an oligarchy of financial-industrial groups (FIGs), most of which encompassed a large bank and an affiliated network of enterprises. By 1996, the FIGs in some ways resembled the prewar Japanese *zaibatsu* or the postwar Korean *chaebol*. Some officials actually characterized them in such terms and argued that they offered a viable system for reconstructing Russia's post-socialist economy.[53]

Explaining Yeltsin's decision to pursue the loans-for-shares program is difficult. Multiple factors may have been at work. Certainly some top government officials profited handsomely. Yeltsin may have regarded the scheme as a way to boost and solidify support for his reelection among well-endowed private actors. Still, explanations that focus exclusively on the pecuniary and political self-interest of policy makers may overlook a crucial source of the policy. For one thing, Yeltsin may well have believed that a Japanese- or Korean-style financial-industrial structure would provide the best basis for building a viable new Russian capitalism. Of greatest importance, however, may have been Yeltsin's desire, as well as that of the architect of his privatization program, Anatolii Chubais, quickly to render privatization irreversible. Given the

[53] "Oleg Soskovets: 'My ne otkazhemsia ot reform'," *Nezavisimaia gazeta*, March 12, 1996 and "Glava gosudarstva podderzhal FPG," *Segodnya*, April 2, 1996.

ideological zeal of Yeltsin and his subordinates and their concern that they could soon find themselves thrown out of power by forces hostile to economic destatization, *finding buyers fast* was what loans-for-shares was all about. Finding the "right" or "strategic" buyers, those whose purchases would maximize state revenues, those who would be the most likely to initiate enterprise restructuring, or even those who would most richly reward government officials, were secondary considerations, when they figured in at all. When the voucher program managed to create only the first delicate shoots of a privatized economy, another method had to be seized upon immediately in order to accelerate destatization. Given the supreme importance that Yeltsin and his team assigned to the "irreversibility" of destatization, dumping state assets – that is, selling them so cheaply that they could find buyers immediately, even under the highly uncertain conditions that prevailed at the time – became an imperative.[54]

The effects of loans-for-shares on democratization were more obvious than the motives underlying the policy. First, the scheme abruptly skewed wealth and income distribution. It concentrated wealth dramatically, creating a small and enormously wealthy upper class while swelling the ranks of those living in or near poverty. Russia thus squandered one of the few advantages for democratization that it inherited from the Soviet period: the absence of a Latin American–style social structure, with a numerically small but politically mighty upper class and a destitute popular sector. Loans-for-shares at least partially erased this advantage in Russia, while several neighboring countries that undertook rapid market reform, including Poland and Hungary, averted an explosive rise in the inequality of income distribution.[55]

As mentioned at the beginning of this section, a class-power and economic inequalities hypothesis cannot explain the low quality of Russian democracy, since Russia did not, in relative terms, start its post-Soviet life with gross inequalities in the distribution of wealth. But it is entirely possible that the economic transformations of the mid-1990s arising from the loans-for-shares program created new socioeconomic obstacles to democratization. Russia may now find its accountability deficit reinforced by problems of class power and socioeconomic inequalities in much that same way that these factors often confine democratization in Latin America, Africa, and Southeast Asia.

---

[54] "Glava gosudarstva podderzhal FPG," *Segodnya*, April 2, 1996 and "Ekonomike strany ne nuzhna politicheskaia likhoradka," *Kommersant*, April 27, 1996.

[55] *From Plan to Market: World Development Report 1996* (New York: World Bank and Oxford University Press, 1996), pp. 67–71.

The oligopolistic concentration of wealth not only skewed the socioeconomic structure, it also fostered the dependence of politicians on the support of one or several of a highly circumscribed number of sources of wealth and ensured that the private conglomerates themselves relied to a great extent on government favors. These conditions, particularly in the absence of any meaningful or enforceable laws regulating campaign finance or relationships between politicians and business in general, deeply corrupted the political class. In some instances, chiefs of leading FIGs assumed ministerial portfolios and places in the president's inner circle without even temporarily relinquishing their positions in business. Not only did the captains of finance and industry penetrate the state administration directly, but their ability easily to buy off politicians was a salient feature of Russian politics during the second half of the 1990s. The political power of the financial-industrial behemoths drove yet another wedge between officialdom and most of society and powerfully exacerbated the accountability deficit.[56]

The third crucial decision that undermined prospects for the emergence of democracy with accountability was taken in the realm of law enforcement. With only a bit of exaggeration, one may state that Yeltsin and his subordinates, at the time of the birth of the post-communist regime, virtually withdrew the state from law enforcement. Yeltsin and many of his liberal lieutenants, including and especially his first post-communist prime minister, Yegor Gaidar, overlooked completely the necessity for a hardy coercive apparatus.[57] Far from understanding that the immense transformations involving movement to a market economy would require refurbished and more sophisticated law enforcement agencies, Yeltsin naïvely regarded the market itself as an antidote to crime. Yoshiko Herrera rightly argues that Yeltsin and his team saw destatization as the essence of economic reform.[58] Tragically, destatization in practice extended even into the realm of law enforcement.

In hindsight, some of Russia's early post-Soviet leaders have argued that they acquired a state apparatus that was already in ruins, and that many post-Soviet pathologies must be blamed on inherited incapacity.[59] There is undoubtedly some truth in this claim; the apparatus that Yeltsin

[56] See "Vlasti gotovy prislushivat'sia k biznesmenam i bankiram," *Finansovye izvestiya*, June 4, 1998; "Prezidenta bol'she net, no kreslo ego ostaetsia," *Kommersant*, October 16, 1996; and "Finansovaia diktatura," *Nezavisimaya gazeta*, October 22, 1996.
[57] Gaidar, for example, on numerous occasions stated publicly that the new Russian capitalism was unjust and criminalized, but that such circumstances were completely inevitable and irresistible. See, for example, "Gaidar: Capitalist Revolution Has Been Won," *Monitor* (Jamestown Foundation), May 22, 1995.
[58] Herrera, Chapter 4, this volume.
[59] McFaul, "The 'Human Factor' in State Dissolution," pp. 15–16.

took over in the fall of 1991 was indeed decrepit. But the new custodi-
ans of the state, to understate the case, did nothing to strengthen the
agencies of law enforcement. That Russia's new liberal leaders would
associate the agencies of coercion with unfreedom was understandable,
given the Soviet experience. But Yeltsin and his subordinates did not distinguish between functions and agencies intended for political repression
and control and those designed to maintain public order and protect
persons, property, and contracts.[60]

The neglect of law enforcement and its agencies, which consequently
withered and moved from a state of partial corruption to one of total
corruption, spelled the retreat of the state from the maintenance of public
order. Legitimizing coercion – the matter that Immanuel Kant regarded
as the cardinal problem of political theory and that in practice represents
the foremost imperative of modern democracies, including and especially
young ones – was willfully ignored by Yeltsin and thus never even
addressed, at least not on the national level, during the early post-Soviet
period.[61] In practice, this decision spelled the swift, pathological privatization and pluralization of the forces of coercion.[62]

It is plausible to argue that at the outset of the post-Soviet period,
most major economic and political actors in Russia preferred that the
state maintain its monopoly, or at least dominance, in the realm of coercion. As in other societies, most private actors had an interest in the state
providing law enforcement. But as the state retreated in the early 1990s,
private security agencies become Russian's biggest growth industry.
Privatization of coercive functions created actors with an interest in
preventing the state from reentering law enforcement. The state's
withdrawal not only forced economic actors to provide for their own
security. It also meant that, using their own private security agencies and,
where necessary, buying the services or the noninterference of what
public offices of law enforcement remained functioning, they could place
themselves entirely beyond the reach of the law. The retreat of the state
therefore quickly created conditions under which portions of economic

---

[60] See Fish, "The Roots of and Remedies for Russia's Racket Economy," pp. 92–95,
108–112 and Fish, "The Predicament of Russian Liberalism," pp. 208–13.

[61] See Kant, *Political Writings*, pp. 136–143, 154–164, 256–257.

[62] See Olga Kryshtanovskaia, "Nelegal'nye struktury v Rossii," *Sotsiologicheskie issle-
dovaniia*, Vol. 8 (1995), p. 96; A. Maksimov, *Rossiiskaia prestupnost': kto est'
kto* (Moscow: Eksim-press, 1998), pp. 260–266; *Bezopasnost' lichnosti i biznesa:
Spravochnik '98* (St. Petersburg: Agenstvo AT, 1998), p. 4; and Vadim Volkov, "Organized Violence, Market Building, and State Formation in Post-Communist Russia,"
paper presented at the conference Beyond State Crisis? The Quest for the Efficacious
State in Africa and Eurasia, University of Wisconsin–Madison, March 11–13, 1999.

and political elites acquired an interest in keeping the state at arm's length. By the late 1990s, it was not at all clear that business and banking titans such as Boris Berezovskii, Mikhail Khodorkovskii, and Vladimir Potanin really had a strong interest in the establishment of vigorous, impartial agencies that were capable of universalizing the rule of law. Indeed, the same could be said for politicians such as Chubais, Zyuganov, Chernomyrdin, Luzhkov, and Zhirinovsky.[63] Each of these figures cultivated his own private security services, which protected his person as well as his organizational and business interests. During the late Soviet period, none of these figures had had a large personal security agency in place. All, or most, had had some interest in a state that executed normal law enforcement functions. It is far from clear that any of these figures or their many subordinates still had such an interest at the end of the 1990s. In short, the atrophy of law enforcement organs created conditions under which broad portions of the elite actually had an interest in thwarting the emergence of a state that monopolized coercion. Needless to say, prominent figures such as Berezovskii, Chernomyrdin, Chubais, and Luzhkov did not publicly announce that they opposed the rule of law; to do so would have been absurd and obviously contrary to their own interests. But by the late 1990s, each of these figures was benefiting handsomely from the absence of institutions capable of subordinating him and his economic activities to the law. This outcome was avoidable. It resulted from state officials' early policies of disdaining the tasks of reorganizing, reinvigorating, depoliticizing, and modernizing the agencies of coercion in favor of emasculating, underfunding, and neglecting them.

It does not require a stretch of the imagination to grasp how the state's retreat from law enforcement exacerbated the accountability deficit and degraded Russia's incipient democracy. The breakdown in elementary law enforcement and the subsequent rise of private mafias undermined popular confidence in the state and respect for the law. To borrow Durkheim's terminology, it delinked the life of society from that of the state and, for most individuals in society, maintained the state as an "exterior force" in their lives at precisely the time when the state's formal institutions were opening up to popular participation and influence. Ironically, at the very stage when the destruction of the hyper-authoritarian regime spawned a plethora of new rights of association, expression, and

---

[63] As of this writing, Gennady Zyuganov is the chief of the Communist Party of the Russian Federation; Viktor Chernomyrdin is the former prime minister and head of the Our Home is Russia party; Yuri Luzhkov is the mayor of Moscow; and Vladimir Zhirinovsky is leader of the Liberal Democratic Party of Russia.

political participation, the destatization of coercion left most citizens virtually defenseless and curtailed their ability to enjoy and exercise their newly won rights.

In sum, the choice of super-presidentialism, in addition to Yeltsin's decisions to forgo new elections, to implement a loans-for-shares plan in the privatization program, and to neglect the agencies of public order, undermined Russia's chances to achieve a full-blooded democracy during the 1990s. The seeds of the overweening presidency were planted during the struggle to bring down the Soviet regime, and they then germinated in the subsequent contest and showdown between Yeltsin and his opponents. Yeltsin's three fateful decisions were in every respect the products of personal will and calculation. They were unpredictable. No one, in fact, predicted them. The decisions were not even necessarily consonant with Yeltsin's own personal interests. Even if he intended to maximize his own power, authority, and popularity, his decisions certainly cannot be regarded as the best means to such ends. Like most policymakers, Yeltsin labored under information shortages and counterproductive habits of thinking.

This analysis implies that Russia's first post-Soviet decade could have turned out very differently than it did in fact. Russia could have followed the same road that Poland did – the path to full-blown democracy, to robust democracy with accountability. At the beginning of the 2000s, many observers are disposed to regard historical, cultural, geographical, economic, and international preconditions as having determined the destinies of democratic experiments before countries even embarked upon such experiments. The Poland-Russia comparison provides much grist for such deterministic thinking. Poland's Catholicism and Russia's orthodoxy, Poland's westward location, and Poland's relatively strong civil society at the time of regime change are often adduced to explain the disparity in patterns of democratization. Such factors may indeed have played important roles. On the other hand, had political outcomes been reversed, had Russia emerged from its first post-communist decade with a robust democracy and Poland with a broken-backed one, analysts would treat Russia's higher level of per capita income at the time of regime change, its large and vigorous intelligentsia, its privileged place as the unconquered imperial center in two successive empires, its cultural preeminence in the Slavic world, and its superabundance of precious natural resources as preconditions that clearly disposed the country to political success. Poland's relatively vigorous civil society, embodied in the Solidarity movement, would be seen not so much as an energizing asset as an obstreperous obstacle to painful economic and political reforms. Poland's lack of a democratic tradition would no doubt be adduced as a cause of the democratic deficit, just as Russia's is now.

Polish society's deep and widespread religiosity and its mighty Catholic Church would be seen as lamentable sources of hierarchy and nondemocratic, antisecular political-cultural impulses. Poland's crushing debt burden and extremely high repressed inflation at the time of regime change, as well as its immense and abysmally underproductive agricultural sector, would seal the case. What hope for democracy could there possibly have been for a polity so disfavored by initial conditions?

But Poland did achieve high-caliber democracy.[64] Its choice of a balanced constitutional system that divided power between the president and the legislature, its holding of new elections for both president and parliament early in the process of regime change, its eschewal of forms of privatization that greatly concentrated economic power, and its commitment to maintaining the state's monopoly, or at least predominance, in the realm of coercion, may have had something to do with its spectacular political – not to mention economic – success. While Russia concentrated political and economic power and dispersed coercive power, Poland dispersed political and economic power and concentrated coercive power. These were matters of choice and policy, not extrapolitical preconditions.

Russia could have been Poland – but it also could have been Belarus. Yeltsin could have abandoned entirely his commitment to open politics immediately after the August 1991 putsch and acted as Alexander Lukashenko did after winning the presidency in Belarus at mid-decade. In another scenario, Yeltsin could have been thrown out of office and replaced by his disloyal vice president, Alexander Rutskoi, whose ethical limitations and megalomaniacal delusions of playing Lenin seventy-five years after the Bolsheviks conquered Russia led him to incite violence in the streets of Moscow in October 1993.

RECTIFYING THE ACCOUNTABILITY DEFICIT

Russia may do well to avoid a Belarusian scenario over the next decade. But it can do better than just averting a nightmare. It can actually

[64] See Andrew A. Michta, "Democratic Consolidation in Poland after 1989," in Karen Dawisha and Bruce Parrott (eds.), *The Consolidation of Democracy in East-Central Europe* (Cambridge: Cambridge University Press, 1997), pp. 66–108. The disparity between Poland and Russia is reflected in cross-national surveys. At the onset of its regime change in 1989–90, Poland received a freedom score of 3.5 in the Freedom House survey. Its ratings improved throughout the decade, and in the 1999–2000 survey Poland received a score of 1.5, the same score that France received in the same year. Russia's score at the onset of its transformation in 1991–92 was 3, but its rating subsequently deteriorated, and in 1999–2000 stood at 4.5, the same score that Morocco and Peru obtained in the same year's survey. Freedom House, "Annual Survey of Freedom, Country Scores, 1972–73 to 1999–00."

improve the quality of its democracy. The following prescriptions ensue logically from the diagnosis of the problem offered here.

First, the constitution must be changed to reduce presidential prerogatives and invest more power in the national legislature. Following the onset of the economic crisis in the fall of 1998 and the appointment of Yevgeny Primakov as prime minister, some analysts argued that a great deal of power was already flowing to the prime minister and that the days of the super-presidency had already passed.[65] Such an interpretation of events, however, risked overlooking three important realities. The first is that the president still appointed the prime minister. The second is that the drift of power away from the president and toward the prime minister was the product of a temporary phenomenon: the incapacity of the president. The election of Vladimir Putin in March 2000 changed this situation completely. Third, a more powerful prime minister and a weaker president would not at any rate remedy the pathologies of super-executivism, of which super-presidentialism is one institutional manifestation. The problem in Russia is super-executivism, meaning a bloated, musclebound executive branch that is monitored and checked by neither the legislature nor the courts. Temporary – or even enduring – reallocation of power within the executive will not redress the problem. Russia needs a constitution that divides power between branches, be it a moderate presidential system such as is found in Georgia, Lithuania, and Moldova or a semi-presidential system such as is present in Poland, Romania, and Mongolia. From the standpoint of democratization, super-executivism has created nothing but disasters in the post-communist region. Were the price of super-executivism in terms of democratization offset by more extensive economic reform and superior economic performance, the trade-off might be "worth it." But there has been no trade-off between democratization and either economic reform or economic performance in the post-communist region. On the contrary, the evidence suggests that all good things have gone together, and all bad things have, too. Furthermore, "strong executive power," the attractive-sounding deception that has seduced so many Western social scientists, and especially economists, as well as so many citizens in the post-communist world and other regions, in actual practice has given rise to bloated but decaying state apparatuses, policy failure, and economic decline – not to mention democratic deficiency.

Even if super-presidentialism has failed in Russia, one could plausibly argue that a system that divided power at the national level would have led to an even worse set of outcomes. Such an argument rests on coun-

---

[65] For an interesting discussion, see "Lovushki: O paradoksakh rossiiskoi politicheskoi zhizni razmyshliaet politolog Lilia Shevtsova," *Trud*, March 18, 1999.

terfactual thinking about what *would have* happened had the national legislature been invested with more power and the president with less. Particularly given the dominance of the Duma by communist, nationalist, and various other antiliberal forces, one could maintain that a stronger legislature and a weaker president would have harmed democratization even more than the super-presidential regime has. Indeed, one could even assert that Russia has already experimented with semi-presidentialism during 1991–93, and that this regime produced only deadlock and bitter interbranch conflict, culminating in the violent confrontation between supporters of Yeltsin and those of the largely (but not exclusively) communist and nationalist backers of parliament in October 1993.[66]

Such an argument is prima facie compelling and widely held among liberals in both Russia and the West. It is fundamentally flawed, however, since it mischaracterizes the regime that Russia had in place in the early post-Soviet years. The Constitution that Russia lived under between August 1991 and October 1993 did not embody genuine semi-presidentialism, or for that matter moderate presidentialism, parliamentarism, or any other normal form of democratic regime. The Constitution in force at the time, a Soviet-era holdover, was a jumble of legal fictions and contradictory, ad hoc amendments attached during the Gorbachev era that reflected the liberalization of the end of the Soviet period. On paper, the then-parliament, the Supreme Soviet, held supreme power; in fact, Yeltsin enjoyed a host of decree powers that he secured at the onset of the post-Soviet period. The holdover Constitution's contestedness and utter lack of clarity were far more formidable barriers to the establishment of normal, nonviolent interbranch conflict and cooperation than was the fact that power was shared between the president and the parliament.[67] The regime in force in Russia during 1991–93 no more represented bona fide semi-presidentialism than the post-1989 Yugoslav Constitution, though parliamentary in form, established authentic parliamentarism in what de facto has been a personalist dictatorship.

In fact, the notion that divided power leads to "deadlock" and inefficiency, while concentrated power produces more efficient outcomes, enjoys no empirical support in the post-communist region. Some of the most remarkably successful cases of democratization, including Romania, Lithuania, and Mongolia, have occurred in systems that

---

[66] Such an argument is offered in, for example, Dmitry Mikheyev, *Russia Transformed* (Indianapolis: Hudson Institute, 1996), pp. 76–111.

[67] See Yitzhak M. Brudny, "Ruslan Khasbulatov, Aleksandr Rutskoi, and Intraelite Conflict in Postcommunist Russia, 1991–94," in Timothy J. Colton and Robert C. Tucker (eds.), *Patterns in Post-Soviet Leadership* (Boulder, Colo.: Westview, 1995), pp. 84–87.

separate powers. So too has the region's greatest success story in terms
of both economic reform and economic performance, Poland, unfolded
under a regime in which powers are divided between the president and
the legislature. In each of these countries, politics has sometimes been
hampered by the same kind of frustrating interbranch disputes that characterize American politics. Poland, where the legislature and the presidency have for much of the post-communist period been controlled by
politicians of rival political orientations, has often offered the appear-
ance of enervating interbranch conflict. Much the same might be said
about Mongolia, where interbranch squabbling left the country without
a confirmed prime minister for several months during 1999. But the costs
of separating powers have been paltry compared to the payoffs, which
have included more extensive democratization. Not a single case of either
impressive democratization or successful economic reform and performance has occurred under a super-presidential system.[68]

Unfortunately, as of this writing, the chance that constitutional change
will lead to a diminution of presidential power appears to be virtually
nonexistent. For some time during the late 1990s, the debilitating effects
Yeltsin's extreme infirmity on the polity and even the interests of some
crucial elites began to convince even many leaders who earlier had supported the super-presidency that a substantial change in the distribution
of power was needed. Indeed, something of an elite consensus began to
coalesce around the idea of the desirability of constitutional change.[69]
But Putin's coming to power has virtually ended any serious discussion
of curtailing executive power. Indeed, as of the first year of Putin's term
in office, public and elite discussion is focused on *augmenting* the president's powers, and Putin himself is of course seeking an expansion in
the scope of his own authority. After Putin's popularity and glamour
diminish, reforming the super-presidency may again appear on the public
agenda. At the present time, however, popular and elite relief with finally
having a healthy, vigorous president has eliminated serious discussion of
transferring great power to the legislature and the courts.

Doing away with or seriously modifying an entrenched institution
such as the super-presidency is difficult enough. Reversing the crucial
decisions that also helped consign Russian democracy to mediocrity and
decline is perhaps even more problematic. Clearly, the decision to forgo

---

[68] Fish, "The End of Meciarism"; Fish, "Democratization's Requisites"; M. Steven Fish,
"Moving Backwards: The Dynamics of Democratic Erosion and Reversal in the Post-
communist World" (Working Paper 2.67, Center for German and European Studies,
University of California, Berkeley, 1998); and M. Steven Fish, "Mongolia: Democracy
without Prerequisites," *Journal of Democracy*, Vol. 9, No. 3 (1998), pp. 127–141.
[69] Sharlet, "The Politics of Constitutional Amendment in Russia," pp. 197–227.

new legislative elections at the beginning of the post-Soviet period cannot be reversed, nor can its dire consequences be mitigated so long after the fact. The catastrophic effects of loans-for-shares privatization and of the withdrawal of the state from law enforcement, however, may be moderated by wise policies. Of course, preventing the pauperization of a large portion of the population and the takeover of the economy by a small clutch of conglomerates would have been far easier than reversing the trend after the fact. What is more, the infirmity of the economy is far too severe to hope for the early construction of a hardy social safety net that includes comprehensive unemployment insurance and other such desirable but expensive components. Still, some measures to reduce income and wealth inequalities may be taken. The provision of free transportation and subsidized food for pensioners, who make up a disproportionate share of Russia's very poor, has been adopted by several local and regional governments. Efforts to recover and invest the ill-gotten fortunes of many of the country's criminal oligarchs would represent another step forward. Any measures that ameliorate the growth of income and wealth inequalities without blatantly trampling on legitimate property rights may soften a barrier to the emergence of high-caliber democracy. The financial crash of the fall of 1998, which at first appeared to be an unmitigated disaster, actually had the felicitous consequence of diminishing the political power and corrupting influence of the oligarchs, some of whom subsequently fled the country.

Relatedly, if Russia is to have any chance of arresting the decline in the quality of its democracy, the state must reenter law enforcement. Vigorous reassertion of the state could have anti- as well as pro-democratic effects, particularly if coercive agencies are used for political repression and/or if they escape the control of elected officials completely. Given the character of the agencies of coercion during the Soviet period, as well as the persistence in or return to positions of authority of some personnel from that time, moreover, the hazards for democracy of strengthening the hands of those in charge of maintaining order may be considered particularly severe. Without resurrection of the state's coercive apparatus, however, Russian democracy, like Russian capitalism, is doomed to an early and ignominious demise. Even at the present stage, the criminalization of the economy and society has produced a brand of "freedom" that many citizens cannot enjoy and has powerfully checked ordinary citizens' ability to influence political outcomes and the direction of their own lives.

Yet, in order for the state to reassume its rightful place as guardian of public order, key elites must desire that the laws be applied and that the state be the agency that does so. As discussed earlier, by the mid-1990s it was not at all clear that there existed elite consensus on whether the state should enjoy sovereignty and monopoly in the realm of coercion. The government's neglect of law enforcement rapidly created powerful interests that stood to gain by protecting themselves and fighting their battles with their own private agencies, keeping the state's forces of coercion weak and subservient. Is the necessary elite consensus possible? Some forces will continue to oppose the reappearance of the state. But one may again detect a possible advantage in seemingly infelicitous trends. The financial crash of late 1998, by ruining some of the forces that opposed the revival of the state, may have cleared the way for its comeback. The Primakov government, during its tenure in office between the fall of 1998 and the spring of 1999, showed a penchant for moving against some of the forces that deprived the state of a monopoly on coercion.[70] The Primakov government scarcely rebuilt a sturdy law enforcement apparatus, but its actions did signal the possibility of a revival of official interest in reestablishing state control over law enforcement, a trend that one may argue continued to hold during the tenures of the governments that followed the dismissal of Primakov in the spring of 1999. Putin's ascension to the presidency may represent an auspicious development in this particular area. It is not yet at all clear that Putin will succeed in reasserting the state's primacy in the realm of law enforcement. But his desire to do so, along with his intention to reestablish the supremacy of the central government vis-à-vis regional governments, are the only matters that Putin has consistently and forcefully advocated from the time of his entry into national politics in the summer of 1999 through the early months of his presidency. Given that on all other matters Putin has preferred during this time to play coy and dissimulate, one may assume that at least in the realms of law enforcement and recentralization Putin actually does have both an opinion and a plan. Whether his aspirations are limited to resurrecting state supremacy in law enforcement or extend to deploying the agencies of coercion to subdue his critics and political opponents remains to be seen. If the former proves to be the case, Putin's law-and-order program will be entirely consistent with democratization and should not be attacked as antidemocratic by Western liberals, who so often neglect the importance of legitimate coercion for the protection of individual rights.[71] If the latter is true, Putin's actions will clash directly with building a nonarbitrary legal state, and

---

[70] "Reformatorstvo dolzhno vesti k ukrepleniiu gosudarstva," *Izvestiya*, November 20, 1998 and "Poslednii rezerv," *Itogi*, February 16, 1999.

[71] See Stephen Holmes, *Passions and Constraint: On the Theory of Liberal Democracy* (Chicago: University of Chicago Press, 1995), pp. 18–31, 262–65 and Stephen Holmes, "What Russia Teaches Us Now: How Weak States Threaten Freedom," *The American Prospect*, Vol. 30, No. 33 (1997), pp. 30–39.

will expose all of his rhetoric about establishing a "dictatorship of the law" as hypocritical and cynical drivel. With regard to the possibility of broader elite support for a state monopoly on coercion, it is noteworthy that elite perceptions of self-interest may change over time. Not only is the composition of the elite in flux following the economic meltdown of late 1998, but the calculations of important actors who remained in powerful places may shift. A comparative perspective furnishes some grounds for hope. Like Russia during much of the 1990s, early post-Soviet Georgia lacked consensus among elites over the desirability of state sovereignty in law enforcement and coercion. But the bitter experience of a breakdown in public order and the near-dissolution of the country into feuding fiefdoms convinced most elites, both within and outside of government, of their own interest in a state that controlled most of the guns and that enjoyed the power and authority to universalize the enforcement of the law over the country's territory. In the wake of this change, the mid- and late 1990s brought an upturn in the health of the Georgian state and an improvement in the quality of Georgian democracy.[72]

Russia's failure during its first post-Soviet decade to achieve democracy with accountability resulted from concrete choices and decisions. It was not foreordained by structural, cultural, or historical "givens" or preconditions, even though the Soviet regime undoubtedly left a consequential set of legacies. Russia's potential for escaping the trap of perpetual low-caliber democracy, and for avoiding even further degradation of the democratic gains made since the demise of the Soviet regime, now similarly depends on will, choice, and decision, not on impersonal forces.

[72] Between 1994–95 and 1999–2000, Georgia's freedom score in the Freedom House survey improved steadily, moving from a 5 (the same level as Azerbaijan in both years' surveys) to a 3.5 (the same level as Brazil in 1999–2000). Freedom House, "Annual Survey of Freedom, Country Scores, 1972–73 to 1999–00." See also Stephen F. Jones, "Democracy from Below? Interest Groups in Georgian Society," *Slavic Review*, Vol. 59, No. 1 (2000), pp. 42–73, and Ghia Nodia, "Putting the State Back Together in Post-Soviet Georgia," paper prepared for the conference Beyond State Crisis? The Quest for the Efficacious State in Africa and Eurasia, University of Wisconsin–Madison, March 11–13, 1999.

Index